THE LADY OF THE RINGS

OPTING FOR FREEDOM OF CHOICE

It is my wish to accompany you very often.
And to find together what we are both looking for.

To be one.

Wim Roskam
11-12-'01

To us... to We all

LADY

OF THE

RINGS

OPTING FOR FREEDOM OF CHOICE

Inspired by the true Lady of the Rings,
Linda de Redelijkheid

Written by
Wim Roskam

AKAIJA & ART

2ᵉ edition, by Akaija & Art, 2017
1ᵉ edition, 'Kiezen voor Vrije Keuze', ISBN 978 90 77247 96 9, was published
by publishing company *Uitgeverij Akasha*, the Netherlands in 2009.

Akaija & Art
Gijsbrechtgaarde 316
7329 CE Apeldoorn
Phone: 055 5335747
E-mail: atelier@akaija.com
Internet: www.akaija.com / www.akaijashop.com

Cover page design: **Sander Schaper**
Illustrations, photographs, paintings and lay-out: **Wim Roskam**
Translation: **Eliza White Buffalo**
Manufactured and published by: **BoD - Books on Demand, Norderstedt, Germany**

ISBN: 978-3-7460-1326-8

Preface

Before you begin to read this incredible book I have something I would like to say about it, not only because I have read it myself, but also because I have gotten to know Linda so well, her spirit that is, and from her and my spirit guide, Black Elk, I have learned that I share soul energy with Linda, allowing me to tune in with her experience and the many past experiences of her soul. Her story is a very special one of huge courage, tenacity, and integrity. It is understood by my soul and accepted therein as an offering of selfless love and revelation of spiritual truths. I do not wish to tell you anything of Linda personally because this book tells all that is needed to understand, of her loving heart and powerful spirit; but I will tell you that she has not ceased to exist in her unique beauty, but with her pure intentions and deeds in the afterlife she has continued to affect this world with divine devotion to Mother Earth and all her children.

I have never lost someone as close to me as Linda was to Wim, but throughout reading this book I could 'feel' that loss, or maybe what I felt is my interpretation of it. What I did feel was awesome to be sure; it was painful, and it was joyful; it made a lot fall into place, and it increased my faith and trust in the divine, and maybe that is why Linda asked Wim to share their story in this book.

Written with authenticity, the story is very real with real passion and acceptance, pain and understanding of pain. The message is clear: choice is a god given gift. You have free will to choose for yourself, and no matter what choices you make acceptance softens the road and allows you to trust others too. The flow of the Divine Will flows with the softness and strength of Love, through all walks of life. There is also a message of oneness: we are all connected and communication with those in the spirit world is available as well as communication to those in this world.

I believe Linda taught us to allow others to be who they are. She is still teaching us this, and also to trust in others' gifts, but not to the price of your own integrity because being you is the greatest gift you have; staying true to you, to your own unique path, will guide your choices no matter how intense they may seem. Ultimately, that will be your greatest success.

Eliza White Buffalo
Author of the Two Roads Trilogy

Omens

How can you describe the woman you love so deeply?
What do you say about her?
Do you say her name?
I can give you that right here and now: Linda.
What's in a name...

Would you show her photo?
But what does a photo tell you?
How beautiful she is? Only, she didn't like herself.
Can you judge someone based on a picture?
Can you look through a picture then... read between the lines, see through the pigments?
If so, are you psychic?

So, what *do* you write?
How she was... ? She isn't alive anymore, you see.
Now you know this too.
And how she was... she isn't now.
Then how can you describe her?
Do you describe how you lived together, how much you loved each other?
But does love end in death then?
Moreover, I now live with another woman.
Does this explain to you the relationship I had with her?
You're not biased, I hope? Do you jump to conclusions already?
Or does this speak for *this* woman... ? Marianne is her name.

And yes... I love her dearly too. If you understand how this can be... I'm still not quite sure you do.

So let me tell you my name too: Wim

Well then, maybe you now think you know enough, and so you can put this book away.

Linda was a woman who didn't like to speak in the past tense about someone who is deceased. And I must admit I didn't either.

But after what I've learned I dare to do so now. Certain characteristics disappear, making way for new ones. The old is gone. You grow, you change. That's why you're here, because the Earth is a school. If you don't want to change, then why are you still here? Are you're already perfect then... and happy, for sure? But anyway: she was, and remains, a very special soul.

Linda was born in Rotterdam, Netherlands, in 1954, but at 6 years of age she moved to Apeldoorn. I myself was born in 1960, and that same year I moved to Apeldoorn too, and came to live only two hundred yards from her home.

Still small, a few years later, I sat in the child's seat of my mother's bike, on the way to town. I don't remember much from this time, but one memory is very clear, and that was when we cycled past Linda's home. It was a white house with a low sloping roof and a very short little garden in front. Beside the front door sat a grown woman. Maybe she was knitting, or peeling potatoes. On the ground before her, a little dark haired girl was playing. What struck me was the pleasant, subdued atmosphere of that girl who was playing by herself. There was something that really attracted me to her, without understanding it, and I very seriously promised myself that I would soon escape from home, walk the short distance and knock on their door. I felt very sure I could make that happen one day. For a few moments then I wasn't a little boy anymore.

Picture yourself as the mother of a little girl, seeing a tiny little thing on your doorstep, asking with a matter of fact face, for the hand of your daughter...

Now, knowing Linda's mother, I know she wouldn't be that surprised. Apart from being amused she might even have taken the matter seriously in a way, knowing that when children behave in such ways they expose their older and wiser soul.

Shortly thereafter, Linda moved to Ulft, a tiny town near the German border, while I continued to live in Apeldoorn. I've never acted according to my plan, but I've often thought about it.

When Linda was older she and her mother read books, one after the other, about reincarnation, UFO's, dowsing, Atlantis, Egypt, ghostly apparitions, contacts with unseen beings, about anything that for centuries was unspoken of, except in back rooms behind closed curtains. Linda could talk with her mother for whole evenings about the things they were interested in together.

In addition, Linda was interested in dancing. She went to ballet classes and later also assigned for jazz ballet. She would have done extremely well if there had been a musical class, but in those days there was nothing like that in the Netherlands. She had the body for it: slim and agile. Ballet dancers must pay attention to their appearance. Slightly overweight is harmful and a strict diet is a must. To keep going one needs to be disciplined, and this she could do very well: stick to a strict diet, recording every calorie she ate. At times this looked a lot like anorexia, but not really, she knew that danger all too well.

Unfortunately she was rejected for the ballet academy because of a tiny irregularity in her back. The training she followed instead was to become a teacher in 'Childcare & Education' combined with 'Creative Arts'.

After graduating she went to Israel to work in a kibbutz. On the first day she arrived she fell in love with a Scottish boy of Italian descent. Other people warned her about him, but as it usually is in love matters, she didn't listen to them.

"Immediately, things went wrong on the first day," she said later. And everything kept going wrong; there was no end to it. Her boyfriend abused her. She earned some money in the kibbutz, but he spent it, even stole it from her if she didn't give it freely. He needed it to impress others, buy them presents, and he always needed more. But, she was in love, and because of this she was willing to condone his behaviour.

About half a year later she moved to a small apartment in Tel Aviv where she found work in a bar, mixing drinks and cocktails. Of course, her major hobby was dancing, and during her time off she spent many nights on the dance floor. These were the heydays of disco, and for many free evenings and nights she stood on the floor like a true disco queen! If someone else had the nerve to compete with her, showing off his or her own moves, then often a duel would follow to see who could get the most attention from the audience and who could dance so fast, so exciting that the other gives up? And this Linda could do, for hours if necessary.

Her boyfriend worked on a rig and stayed away for weeks in a row. She felt lonely, but then a stray dog that came to ask her for help because he was sick, joined her. She took care of the poor thing, but that meant she had to consult a vet regularly and the money she needed for this sometimes suddenly was gone.

Apparently she was not the only one her boyfriend stole money from, because at one point he was arrested and landed in an Israeli prison. Linda continued to support him, visited him in prison and after his release she took him back home, emaciated and scarred, which he refused to talk about.

After more than a year she needed to go home to the Netherlands, because her visa had run out. She wanted to take her dog with her, but the authorities had very high demands on the transportation of a dog on the plane. For this she had to buy a special dog transportation box. Then a quarantine period and several vaccinations were necessary, much paperwork and of course, money. She arranged everything, but just before leaving she was told that something was amiss. There was no time to meet the new demands, so she was forced to leave her dog behind. It wasn't her fault, but ever since she had a feeling she had left her dog in the lurch. 'I still remember how he looked at me when I left him there," she said sometimes, with tears in her eyes.

Pain... that never went away.

Back home in the Netherlands she soon found a job as a teacher at a school in Apeldoorn. Her boyfriend came a couple of months later and immediately wanted to marry her, because then he would have the Dutch nationality. But this didn't fool her because their relationship didn't go too well.

She couldn't decide to separate from him and defended him by saying that in his youth he had been badly damaged. One day he was gone for days in a row. By word of mouth she found out about his whereabouts and she looked him up in an apartment in Amsterdam where he was living together with a boyfriend in the homo scene. He let her in, and to please him she cleaned the house and did all the laundry. Then he told her dryly that his boyfriend was coming home soon and that she shouldn't be around.

At home her mother asked her: "Do you want to continue this for the rest of your life? Is this really your idea of a relationship?"

That was just the nudge she needed to finally put an end to it.

Together with her mother she consulted a psychic lady, who predicted she would soon be in a relationship with someone else: a boy with a beard and wild curly hair over his forehead.

But she wasn't at all ready for this, she said. She was far from recovered from the failure of her 'marriage', as she called it, which then had lasted about seven years.

Fatigue

In 1983 I met her during one of the folk dance evenings where we both participated. After one such lesson, I would go with her to her apartment, and in less than two months these incidental visits evolved into a permanent cohabitation. For me, an insecure young man, six years younger than she was, and not used to being on my own, it was a very bold step that said a lot about the attraction between us, which I had already felt as a toddler.

Many years later Linda asked me at one point: "What on Earth did you do? How did you do it? I wasn't ready for a new relationship! You just came in and stayed."

It must have been predestination. However, my looks didn't match the prediction of the clairvoyant woman's description of the new partner Linda was about to meet. But such can be arranged, and within two months I had a beard and with hair styling products it was no problem at all to provide me with curly hair above my forehead. Linda's smile was questionable when she remarked: "Well, this meets the forecast, and now I can take you home to meet my parents."

My own parents and my sister weren't as quite affected by my sudden departure and complete metamorphosis, but I felt that I was rapidly growing in harmony with myself. By the way... I've never since changed my hairstyle.

Linda and I got along together very well, but there was one feeling that I never completely could get rid of. I was always very afraid of losing her. "What does she really see in me?" I asked myself at times, because she was very self-aware where I was very uncertain, and also much younger. It was an inexplicable feeling that I never lost. She didn't cause it, because she did everything for me.

What struck me most were her eyes. Apart from me really being impressed by them, I saw a lot of hidden grief in them and I decided to never abandon her.

She did her job as a teacher very well and the students loved her. She could educate her kids in ways that is rarely seen. She was just, with a sharp memory and good hearing, not easily fooled, not by any of them. If a ringleader student really tried pushing the limits she would embarrass him or her. But the student would have asked for it, and afterwards, would silently admit that it had been quite right. Thus the worst students sometimes became her biggest fans. "Finally, a teacher who can handle me!" Classes that colleagues had the greatest difficulty with, she could handle just fine, and she did things that others never thought possible. A loose way of teaching was her speciality. For her it worked.

Lessons could turn into talking and sharing thoughts, but in her profession this was not a problem. Childcare & Education implies that issues such as drug use, smoking, sexuality, unwanted pregnancies, etc. are discussed, which are very sensitive issues for girls in the adolescent age. If such lessons are dealt with the wrong way these classes can turn into an outright failure and a major missed opportunity, but this never happened in Linda's classes. Sometimes students thought that they had only been talking about their problems, desires and friends, and about sex, condoms and the pill. But clever as she was, Linda led them exactly where she wanted them to go, and at the end of the lesson she gave them a stencil summarizing the topic of the day in great detail.

The students put her on a pedestal, and it was no surprise that at one point they proclaimed her as 'Teacher of the Year', and that was meaningful on a school with more than a hundred teachers!

"Finally, justice," she said at home, with that suspect grin on her face.

Her apartment was soon too small for the both of us, so we moved to a family house next to a park a small distance away. She let me know that she didn't want to marry and that she didn't want any children either. I had no problem with that at all, because I had the same view. We didn't need it. But what we also thought unnecessary was to give each other a ring. We loved each other, so what's the point in proving that with a metal ring?

Our love for each other was rooted very deep, but there was also a deep sadness in her that she couldn't talk about. Sometimes this sorrow surfaced during intimate moments, when she would suddenly begin to cry; tears she could express only during happy and safe moments. I felt that something was blocked up inside her, but I could never figure out what was bothering her so much that it hurt. It had to do with that sadness I had seen in her eyes the very first time we met. I would like to know her at every level and free her from this sadness, but it was so deep that even she herself couldn't fathom its origin.

I came to know her as an energetic person who could easily work on for half the night if she felt that something had to be finished; a real night owl. I too had no problem with this, but I had to get used to this kind of energy that I knew from no one else. She was practically able to do everything at once and still pay attention to the details of everything that she did.

But a few years later, this abruptly changed. In 1985 she drove home from school during a particularly violent thunderstorm. It rained so hard that she could see almost nothing, so she was forced to open her side window to see where she was. At that moment a giant bolt of lightning struck the road, or more likely her car. There was a pillar of fire, as she described it, deafening her ears. It was a rare, massive blow that startled the entire city, even me while I was miles away. A fire was started in the car dealership next to the road. Linda's car was blown sideways on the street. In large parts of Apeldoorn all electricity was cut down, and for weeks all television was offline. People told her that she had been completely safe because of the Faraday's Cage construction of her car, which electro-magnetic fields cannot penetrate. But they couldn't explain why for months after she felt a strange numbness in her entire left half of her body.

"That's the moment," she said later, "when my fatigue started." Before that time she was sprightly and active, but since then she had lost that zest for life and she's never been the same again, always feeling tired. When she came home from work, she increasingly needed to sleep on the couch while I cooked dinner. She managed to keep doing all homework for school, but that was it. Her fatigue became so serious that even during holidays she wasn't able to recharge her battery. But she never accepted that her work would suffer under the circumstances. Her students would receive the maximum quality education, and she demanded from herself that her work was done at all times. Luckily I could assist her with making and discussing stencils, papers and checking digits. No matter how much she suffered her chronic fatigue, she managed to continue doing her work.

It would take many years before we found out what had happened there and then that caused her to be so tired, and why there was absolutely no cure against it. Due to the extremely strong electromagnetic field of that lightning bolt, something had changed in her body, a situation that certain therapists nowadays call 'electron spin inversion', a change at the atomic level which causes the aura, which is the energy field of the body that filters or blocks all external stimuli, to be insufficiently energized. The aura becomes thin or tenuous and allows more stimuli to pass than is desirable. The long-term effects are mostly chronic fatigue and increased sensitivity. But this we weren't aware of back then. We only experienced the consequences.

Halfway through the nineties Linda's younger brother, Arjen got cancer. He went through the whole rigmarole: examinations, surgery, chemotherapy and all the misery that goes with it. Eventually, after a final operation, he was declared 'cancer free', but a few days later he got terrible headaches. He died about one week later. Linda had a very difficult time handling this, and felt confirmed in her already reluctant attitude towards mainstream healthcare and pharmaceutics. She didn't like doctors, pills and white coats. She only used 'the pill', which she found a very convenient invention for women, and in very rare cases she used Paracetamol, a mild painkiller, but that was it.

Arjen's illness marked the start of a period of serious difficulties in Linda's family. Her beloved grandmother and aunt passed away; her parents ended up in hospital several times and needed lots of help, help that Linda was willing to give. Despite her busy job and her eternal tiredness we visited them two, sometimes three times a week for help and support. Linda pushed things far beyond her limits, but she forced herself to go on. Her colleagues advised her to work less, but it took a long time before she gave in. After several discussions with the school's medical department she finally got the opportunity to work less. So she got one day a week off, but she used these spare days to visit and support her parents. They needed her help now more than ever, she thought.

In the late eighties, we had taken two cats into our home. First a Holy Birman, a beautiful, regal cat named Liselle Soraya des Quatres Montagnes who, with such a name, expected to be treated accordingly. And one year later, an ordinary black cat with white whiskers: Charonna Nefertete, with a less regal typical Dutch name: 'van Dike'. The two cats could get along very well and gave us lots of entertainment and distraction. They were our kids and were really spoiled, but cats, of course, have no problem at all with that.

One day when they were about five or six years of age Liselle walked to the back of the garden because she wanted to check out something in the bushes. Suddenly we heard a huge outcry and Liselle came running from under the bushes in a wild rush, but was confronted with Charonna accidentally standing in her way. Liselle was in a state of acting blindly on survival instinct, and seemingly for no reason at all; they were in a terrible fight with shrieking and yelling sounds.

Now cats can fight like maniacs, but Birmans, once engaged as temple guards in Burma, have it in their genes to go completely nuts in such cases, so this wasn't a normal fight, and it looked like Charonna was fighting for her life. We all yelled, trying to get them to back off. Where Linda got the nerves from I really didn't understand, but she did what I dared not; she jumped into the middle of the fight and desperately covered Liselle with her own body, trying to separate her from Charonna. Instantly her arms and legs were covered in bleeding scratches (those would play an important role in the future), but that didn't stop her.

Liselle escaped once again and the fight continued. So, I threw a sleeping bag over the fighting cats, and while Linda pinned down Charonna under it, I was able to force Liselle inside the house.

After that fight I leaned against the doorpost and I had this rare feeling of standing at a crossroads. "This will have far reaching consequences," was my thought. And that was because the trust between the cats was permanently damaged. We couldn't make the decision to get rid of one of the cats, an attitude cat lovers can well understand, because which of your equally loved ones should you put away? But that meant that we couldn't go on vacation any more, and in Linda's case a holiday abroad could have given her that extra boost of energy she needed so much.

Her fatigue continued. She would work, sleep, and eat, take care of parents, and for relaxation, one night we did Argentine tango dancing, or occasionally an afternoon shopping in a nearby city. Even in the long summer vacations she no longer managed to recover. Usually it took a couple of weeks and then she was more or less herself again and she got spunk to do something. But in recent years this was not enough, and what she really wanted, which was to be happy, never came about.

"With *you* I'm happy," she assured me, "and with our cats, though they can't get along together very well."

But something was wrong. Our love for each other should have been enough to overcome this, to make her really happy? But how?

The Lonely Road

In December 1999 she was invited for a Pap smear in the public Health Care screening program. "Nothing special," she said. "I'll just go to the doctor, do the smear and await the outcome." It was no reason to worry. She never responded to such calls, but because recently she had small amounts of excretion she thought this would be a good opportunity for getting it seen to.

Sometimes she would ask me, "Do I love you enough?" That was so sweet, because she actually told me that, in actual fact, she loved me very much, but that she had a notion she would fail in love. What could I have said to that? Frankly, I always had a fear that our relationship could come to an end, that maybe she would love me no longer; or was it that I found myself not good enough for her? It was an inexplicable feeling of losing, a feeling that I never really lost. I replied with something along the lines of: "I know you love me. Don't worry." I wanted to reassure her and let her know that it was fine, that she need not worry about this.

A few days after the examination, the doctor phoned to say that the outcome of the investigation was not good; they had found restless cells. But that message didn't seem to bother Linda in any way. She was even surprised that I was worried about this. It was as if she couldn't imagine that something serious could be wrong with her health. Of course a follow-up investigation was next on the agenda; to begin with, an appointment with the gynaecologist in the hospital. A couple of days later we went there.

And so, picture yourself in a big hospital, sitting on hard chairs in a protected area of the corridor on the first floor, waiting. People walk by, some quickly, some slowly, some talking, some retired into them selves. Some are doctors in white collars, some passing by in a wheelchair. You wait, you look around, staring at the clock, trying to read something, but you can't keep your attention on the text.

In the waiting area of the gynaecology department we waited amidst pregnant women. They had come for a routine check. One of the women said something to us, expecting that a very young-looking couple like us would be sitting there for a happy reason. I didn't want to worry her, so I gave an evasive answer and smiled vaguely. Linda said nothing.

At five o'clock it was our turn. The most difficult cases were saved for last. We were told what we already knew, troubled cells. There exists a table describing what stage the 'process', the clinical word they obviously preferred, is in ie. PAP1 to PAP5. PAP5 means cervical cancer without any doubt. Linda was diagnosed with PAP4. More numbers were presented to us, but at a time like that it's hard to remember much of the conversation.

The gynaecologist examined Linda using a viewing device and she wasn't very positive about what she saw. We could clearly see her distressed reaction. She pulled in another gynaecologist, a tall, very authoritarian man. They were talking about various types of cells, using technical names and scientific terms. But it was not quite that clear cut. It was obvious that more research was necessary. First of all, Linda had to give some blood, followed by a MRI scan, an ultrasound, a CT scan, a chest x-ray... "At least," he said, looking at Linda, "that's if you agree to that."

Well... it made sense, would you agree? There was reason enough to do those tests and the appropriate treatment plan can only be determined with sufficient data.

It was Christmas 1999, just before the Millennium. Such news is of course never convenient, but this was very bad timing indeed. Christmas Day was Linda's brother Rob's birthday, a very pleasant day, on which her family was almost always completely present. As always, we were looking forward to it, but now this overshadowed it. Linda had wanted to keep the news secret until after the birthday; however, her wishes came to nothing because she began to cry after a certain remark and eventually couldn't help but to tell everyone what was going on.

The tests began immediately after the Christmas holidays, and Linda went along with it all, seemingly taking it all in her stride, but after two weeks she stood on the scales and had lost fifteen pounds, purely from the stress. Her normal weight was one hundred and fifteen pounds, which left her then about one hundred. She had always hated hospitals, and even though it appeared she was not able to cope with it all, it didn't show; she presented herself as big, tough and strong.

On New Years Eve, on the millennium change, we were at home, and when the clock hit twelve we kissed and wished each other many happy years together, but it was with a deep undercurrent of despair. We were both very scared of what the New Year would bring. Dance music began to play on the television and Linda broke through our sadness, pulling me up to dance. Of course, she did a few of her spectacular dance steps, but then she cried, "This is the last time I can dance. After I have surgery, I can't anymore."

Even during the tests period, we went looking for alternative ways to support the regular treatment. We received several tips from friends and family, and so we came in contact with a number of alternative therapists that we expected to complement each other well, because relying on the hospital expertise alone was something we couldn't, and also didn't want to do.

So we learned about electro-acupuncture. Roberto, a naturopath in Arnhem, made use of this therapy among others. He was highly recommended because of his experience and expertise. The first thing he did was iridology, the study and mapping of the iris by a simple stereomicroscope. Using this, he could obtain a medical history within minutes, without the need for blood tests and x-rays. Obviously he had mastered this technique very well, because to our surprise, he listed one medical fact after another that perfectly matched Linda's case, even in terms of timing.

Next he started measuring using electro-acupuncture. Utilizing a sensor, he measured several meridian points of Linda's hands and feet. Because these meridian points are connected to corresponding organs, it can thus be deduced which parts of the body are well balanced and which are not. At the same time, it's possible to figure out what medication is needed to restore the balance. It seemed a very precise way of diagnosing, which surprised us and had us wondering why this technique wasn't used in the general medical practise. The results Roberto came up with gave an enormous deepening of knowledge into Linda's illness, and they were given in no time and with hardly any hassle. The measurements revealed that several of Linda's organs were totally out-of-balance and that her body was fighting very hard to regain health. She got various medications to help with this.

We also made arrangements with a therapeutic centre in Eindhoven in the south of the Netherlands, where a man, Jacob, had restructured his home into a practice. He worked with a wide range of electromagnetic resonance equipment, capable of destroying pathogenic factors such as bacteria and viruses by frequencies, while the immune system was strengthened at the same time. Most of his patients had serious illnesses, especially cancer.

We learned a lot in a short time about the latest developments in alternative health care, which had mostly to do with complex and harmonic frequencies with which the body can be diagnosed and treated. Given the complicated and very expensive equipment this wasn't 'just' an additional therapy outside the traditional system.

A man who impressed us very much was an English speaking Tibetan healer, Lobsang Tsultrim. This man had no equipment at all, but worked from his secular background and prescribed compressed mixtures of herbal medicines. His whole way of thinking about the human body was based on ancient insights that regarded every human as a whole of body and soul together. This man wasn't just one of many healers; his father had been the personal physician of the Dalai Lama. And speaking in terms of education and experience, he was in no way inferior to the highest trained regular specialists.

He looked at Linda, examined the urine she brought with her, stirred in it, smelled it, and then felt her wrists for a long time, using three fingers simultaneously, studying her heartbeat. An experienced practitioner of this technique can deduct a wealth of information from this.

He spoke little, asked a question every now and then and finally sat down, his thoughts focused, almost meditating. Then, still without speaking, he took Linda's patient card and began writing in a language that we could make nothing of. Finally he looked up at us and started to tell us about his findings. He said he had no X-ray vision and no expensive instruments he could use, but he noted that Linda had inflamed growths in her stomach. Whether these growths where tumours or not he didn't say and we got the impression that in *his* eyes this wasn't even important. It was not the term 'cancer' that was important, but what was going on with Linda as a whole.

He prescribed various herbs and advised her to meditate. He also found rest for her very important. Stress was no good. He looked at me as he said this, giving me a task to ensure she rested. He was friendly and we both liked him very much.

Then we wrote to a clairvoyant woman living in Colombia, South America. Twice a year she came to the Netherlands to treat hundreds of people. Her way of working was that she went into a trance and during this time an already deceased doctor took over her body to treat patients. This medium wasn't new to us. In recent years we had consulted this woman often. The consultation price was a monetary gift for an orphanage in Colombia. Everything was presided over by the Roman Catholic faith. We had heard good reports from various people. Also, Linda's and my parents had consulted her for years, so we thought that she was genuine, honest and trustworthy.

What we wondered was why the deceased physician, 'Dottore' as he was called, hadn't told Linda earlier that she had cervical cancer. After all, we had visited him months ago, in October, and Linda had mentioned to him about the abnormal secretion. We put it down to the language barrier, because the psychic spoke Spanish and her words had to be translated into Dutch by a translator. We wrote to the translator living in Curacao, and explained Linda's situation to her. She then contacted the psychic in Colombia with our query. The short answer came a few days later: 'Do what the doctors tell you and I will be there."

That was not very helpful, because which doctors did Dottore mean: the traditional ones or the alternative ones? We had contact with both. Later, when asked in person, he told us that he meant the alternative doctors. Anyway, we had to rely on our own gut instincts with that and hope that we would make the right decisions, but it wasn't as simple as it seemed.

At the start of the New Year the medical results came in. As expected, a tumour was detected, and although it was not very big, it was unfortunately in the wrong place. It sat just at the transition between the cervical and vaginal tissue. The oncologist proposed that Linda should receive radiation therapy. But to be thorough, he suggested that Linda should get a second opinion in another hospital in Amsterdam. That was... if we personally took the photographs and reports with us to that hospital.

The specialist in the AMC (Amsterdam Medical Centre) that we consulted accepted the folder of data, but without even opening it he remarked that he didn't need it. He was a surgeon, so he said, and his fingers could tell him exactly what he wanted to know. He would execute an internal investigation and would, just like the Tibetan healer, rely on his sensitive fingers to tell him what he needed to know. He quickly came to the same conclusion: a small tumour just at the edge of the cervix. He introduced a colleague who repeated the internal investigation and after a brief exchange of remarks they came to the conclusion that it needed surgery. Irradiation alone would be insufficient, they said.

The surgery they proposed was drastic. Therefore, after surgery there would be a 'small' risk of permanent disability and a high likelihood of impaired bladder control and bowel functions. The hospitalization would take about six weeks and the rehabilitation time was expected to be one year. Moreover, depending on what they would find, maybe radiation at a later stage might still be needed. And the consequence of that would be a 'belly that would feel like concrete'.

The specialists told us that right after the consultation we should go the appointment desk to plan in the surgery date.

At this point, we thought something strange was happening. This research was still a second opinion wasn't it? In other words, after this examination we would still go back to Apeldoorn and then hear from the gynaecologist there what would be the best option? After all, the diagnosis was exactly the same, only the suggested treatment was a different one. I said this to the consultants, but they told us that the treatment was their responsibility now and that it made no sense to discuss the results with Apeldoorn first. This took us by surprise and I asked if we could think about it first, but the response was: "Why would you think this over? Here the only option is surgery. It's a big operation and we don't do it by half."

It all seemed rather strange to us and we asked ourselves: surely, it can't be crazy to ask for time to think this over?

I tried again, but they weren't keen on that idea, not even for a week. It felt like we were committing an offence just suggesting it. Here was one of those important moments in your life where decisions are made that affect your whole life, and we were expected to agree with something so drastic. What difference would a couple of days make anyway? In such situations, it is normal that you first consider all options before making a decision, but here we were given no choice. We even were told that there *wasn't* any choice: the *only choice* is surgery.

But Linda and I were in tune with each other's thoughts and together we withstood the specialists. Eventually, with obvious reluctance, they allowed us a short break in the waiting room to talk it over after which we could go to the reception for planning in the surgery date.

Stunned, we left the room. It had just been thrust upon us "They make it seem as if it's nothing!" I said.

"We don't do things by half!" Linda echoed the doctor's words.

"Why don't they give us a week to think?" I asked loudly, "Does one week really matter that much?"

We were rebellious. Actually we were just angry. That's not the way to treat patients! Why didn't the opinion of Apeldoorn count anymore? They had done a mass of research and they had talked about radiation. In our ears this made a quite a difference. These men hadn't even looked at the scans and results, and on the basis of one minute feeling with their fingertips they concluded that a huge operation was needed for a tiny tumour of which only the location was unfortunate. It seemed like they knew beforehand what the next step would be and that this examination, the feeling with the fingertips, was nothing more than a formality.

What we didn't know at this point was that there was an internal miscommunication. I had opened the envelope that we had been given to pass on to the AMC, copied the data and thus had read the correspondence. In retrospect one *could* conclude that the specialist in Apeldoorn suggested transfer of treatment to the AMC. The words 'second-opinion' were not used at all. Not intentionally so we thought, but to us this was not communicated.

This 'minor' misunderstanding would have major consequences.

These doctors abided by the rules that were established by the hospital, the pharmacy or whoever it was who had written the rules or protocols. In their eyes, they acted in the interest of Linda's health, and so our response was incomprehensible to them. However, what they didn't take into account was that there are people who truly take responsibility for their own lives; people who you don't just force into something, who wish to make their own decisions based on the available data in combination with their inner voice. That's freedom of choice, isn't it?

Due to past experiences with her brother, Linda was already very disappointed in hospitals, and now it appeared, partly because of this, that she wasn't at all stress-resistant to hospitals, just as her rapid weight loss had indicated.

It was only years later while writing this book that I started to realize that this was a significant factor in deciding the road we were to go, as if it was meant to be.

We didn't talk for a long time. We decided to take matters into our own hands, and at the desk we said that we would go home and then decide what we would do. We said that we would inform them about our decision after one week.

What exactly caused us to make our decision I don't recall, but while talking about it we both felt: "We don't want this." That feeling grew in strength and by the time we entered the outskirts of Apeldoorn we were both convinced: "We won't do this." Not this devastating operation, the outcome of which was far from certain. What was the long term forecast by the way? Maybe we could talk to people who had undergone the same thing. We became increasingly combative.

In the days following that we did indeed contact a woman who had had the exact same surgery more than a year ago. She was still in a wheelchair. Meanwhile, we had found a number of therapists, who were, in our opinion, highly skilled, and we were convinced that now we had some very good cards in our hand, for Linda's healing. We decided to temporarily abandon the operation. We didn't even need to think about it for one week. We knew it already. Our sense of relief was very great. Instead of letting ourselves be pulled to the execution as convicts we chose to take the reigns in our hands and go our own way. At one point Linda emphasized her choice with these words: "At home I can fight. In the hospital I can't."

Unfortunately, we then made an important mistake; we didn't call back to the hospital in Amsterdam but kept quiet. "They ought to have treated us better," we justified to each other, but to be honest, the real reason was our hesitation to face another confrontation with these rigid doctors.

Stupid, stupid, stupid!

Of course, the gynaecologist in Apeldoorn wasn't fobbed of this way. He wanted to know why Linda refused the surgery and now even refused the radiation-therapy. He tried to convince Linda that in the alternative healthcare world we would find no salvation and that we had made a very bad choice. When that failed he tried to convince *me*, searching for openings in our defence. But during the last few days I had thought this over very well, and had come to the conclusion that if Linda wanted to go this way, I would be beside her on this road and would support her every step of the way!

Strange as it may sound, I had a strange feeling this was indeed the best choice. I couldn't discern that feeling, but I simply had the inner reassurance that this was the right path to go. But even if I had thought differently, I wanted to support her, to let her be free in her choices. Otherwise she would have to stand-alone. I was thinking, you love each other, don't you? Then you must be there for each other! Then you support each other! And you respect the choices and take whatever road is ahead together! That makes you strong because you are one!

But how do you explain this to an oncologist, a man of science? One who makes decisions based on rational arguments? Finally he realized that we weren't giving in and he let us go.

That's how we began our lonely road...

May It Be

May it be when darkness falls
Your heart will be true
You walk a lonely road
Oh! How far you are from home

by Roma Ryan
from the movie "Lord of the Rings"
sung by Enya

We wrote a new e-mail to Dottore in Colombia explaining what had come out from the tests, what decision we had taken, which alternative therapists we had turned to, and we asked him if those were the doctors he had meant. The answer came a few days later: "Linda may continue with the alternative doctor without surgery. That is the doctor Dottore was speaking of before." Which alternative doctor did he mean? We had several. But in any case, we felt strengthened in our decision. In recent years we had been told repeatedly that Dottore was a 'real' doctor. He didn't make use of primitive means. He knew his patients better than any earthly doctor would ever be able to. He cooperated with guardian angels and the angelic world and with their help he could even perform astral surgery if necessary.

In the New Year Linda wanted to start teaching like before, but I disagreed. She would need all her time and energy for herself now, but I found it hard to convince her. She couldn't abandon her students, she said. But finally she gave in, on one condition: she wished to see her students that would graduate this year a few times to prepare them for this year's upcoming exams.

So I printed all necessary papers for the rest of the semester and in January she went to school in her car. As usual I waved goodbye from the parking lot and I felt intensely sad. Was this the last time?

Somewhere in the communication with the specialists something had gone wrong, and because Linda didn't feel at ease with her GP there was barely any contact with her too. After the smear this particular GP had said almost condescendingly, with her hand under her chin, "My my... how terrible, child!" That was definitely not the way to approach Linda.

At the time we had no idea what the specialists and practitioner could do for us, because we had chosen an alternative way. I think that, if they had had more understanding for Linda's fears and had treated her in a more loving way, then we could have given them more trust. They didn't need to agree with our choices, but now we felt completely on our own, as it was clear they were thinking "If you don't do exactly as we tell you, than find it out for yourself." Were we so exceptional because we wanted freedom of choice? Did other patients in similar situations always give in to everything they were told? It certainly looked that way.

Linda kept record of a whole system of pills, capsules, homeopathic potions, Tibetan herbal pills, elixirs, etc. The cupboard was filled with them. We consoled ourselves with the thought that at least these medications were in harmony with nature. During the consultations all over our country I was always with her. So we came into contact with fellow patients, often with serious illnesses like cancer. Most of them had been told that the hospital couldn't help them anymore. They often had quite a long history of major surgery, radiation therapies, chemotherapies, but most of all... disappointments.

We met them regularly, because we made appointments on the same days. This proved very motivating, because we saw many of these people regenerating before our eyes. We also heard terrifying stories about what happened to them in hospitals, but... also in the hands of alternative practitioners.

One question that one of our therapists, Jacob, asked Linda after a couple of treatments was: "Have you cried yet?" At first we didn't understand this question, but we learned quickly that diseases like cancer never have a physical cause alone, but are always linked to an underlying hidden emotional trauma, some old pain or frustration of long ago that, after years of neglect and being put away, now surfaces physically, asking for recognition. With proper treatments such traumas are touched upon and re-activated, resulting in emotional reactions and sometimes intensive crying for days in a row. That's how blockages, that are the foundations under such disease processes, are cleared; a very important aspect of the healing process.

But crying... not Linda! She wasn't that emotional, walking through her home crying like some other women do... no way. Not her!

Other than consulting therapists, we too got to work at home. Over the years we had learned a lot in spiritual matters and knew that through meditation and visualisation one can support a healing process. It has to do with positive thinking, the powers of the mind. Now meditation was somewhat difficult for both of us, but what we discovered instead was to visualise.

Linda would then lie down on her bed and close her eyes. I would sit down beside her and next we started with a relaxation exercise for her body to rest. Then, to rest her mind as well, I would take her into a fanciful environment of peace such as a peaceful green sloping lawn, overgrown with flowers in all colours of the rainbow, and through which I would ask her to walk from the red flowers towards the violet flowers. Then she would enter a small white temple in which was a golden bowl with the purest water in it. She could drink the water, or wash herself with it, but what she did was of course to sprinkle her belly with it to cure the cancer.

The first few times we did this I used my own memory to come up with images of visualisations I had been in myself under guidance of experienced people, but I also felt an inner need to use my imagination and call up other images. Thus I became Linda's guide in an imaginary world of peace and light...

"Imagine you're in a beautiful garden... The garden is completely round and very beautiful, with many different parts, places where you can walk, screened with hedges full of flowers. Each part of the garden has its own atmosphere, its own flowers.

Everywhere there are flowers, some are in the ground, others hang from trees like waterfalls of colour, and from gates and fences. There are also birds that are not afraid of you and they sing beautifully. If you want it, they come and sit on your shoulders and eat from your hand.

Now go somewhere to which you feel attracted, a separate area in the garden where you feel fine. Go sit over there and enjoy the flowers, birds and all impressions.

If you've been here long enough, then say so and we will go on.
A twisted path leads to the middle of the garden. That's where we are going, for it is to a beautiful fountain, crystal white and the water is so clear that it emits light and is full of energy. Walk towards it and stop just before it. You look at the fountain, hear the water rushing while the light that surrounds the fountain now surrounds you too and makes you feel safe. In the middle, just above the fountain, a large floating crystal draws your attention. As you look at it the crystal seems to be widening. It is a very special crystal that has a lot of power inside. Stretch out your hands towards it, but don't touch it yet. Now close your eyes and close your hands around the crystal... and feel what happens...
The sounds of the sacred garden all around you fade away, and make way for the sound of the sea with sparkling waves of the surf. And the scents of the garden give way to the salty smell of the ocean... You feel the warm sun on your skin and you hear other birds calling for your attention. Your bare feet feel the warm sand of the beach.
Now open your imaginary eyes and look around you... "

This image of the garden was an ideal introduction to the place where I would take her afterwards. The crystal was a kind of star gate. I discovered that visualisations are only limited by the limits of your own imagination. But I was very careful here, because I was her guide and losing her along the way was not an option. I realised that it is not enough to simply say something like 'a beautiful fountain', expecting that she could fill in all the details herself. That may have been too difficult and if she didn't succeed it could have ended up in a failure as in: forget about it... I can't do it. And we couldn't afford to fail, certainly not in this, which I knew, deep down inside, would prove to be very important.

But after several visualisations being limited to the garden and the beach became a bit boring. Then I had a crazy idea... no limitations on the imagination... huh? Anything is possible... ?

So I told her, when evening fell and it got darker, in the distance there was a beam of light, originating from the stars that shone on a spot on the beach in the distance. I let her go there, and coming closer she could see where the beam of light was shining. "It is an old stone circle," I said, referring to the mythical ancient stone circles of which many are found all over the world, though Great Britain certainly is famous for them.

She could tell what the stones looked like and said that it had six huge stones. Old stones they were, weathered, standing like silent guards drafted around a seventh stone that laid horizontal. That was the stone that was lit by the beam of light. She could lie down on it and it felt very comfortable to lie on. It was just right for her.

As she lay there she was lit by the starlight, which she herself said came from the Pleiades. This light had all the colours of the rainbow in it, and she could direct this light with her thoughts. Thus she let the light shine in her belly, and then it turned green. In her mind she could make herself very small so she could take a look inside her belly. That made her an observer in her own body that now seemed very big, and so she could direct the light to precisely the right spots.

I let her describe what she saw in her womb. There a small team of men working in coloured suits was working, just like in a TV commercial in which a male club of Michelin men were cleaning the teeth with giant brushes. This team was working very hard to get rid of everything that didn't belong in her belly. The foreman told us that there was still much work to do and that we shouldn't disturb them, otherwise they wouldn't be ready in time. He turned and went back to work. Apparently he found us a nuisance.

One other time she told me that there was a whole bunch of green monsters inside her belly. They all had to be expelled from there one by one. That was something we could do together. She told me where one was hiding. I filled her in with "Yeah, wait... he's running like hell, but I can run faster and grab him. Yes! Got him! Here... take that!" And I dragged him outside and threw him into the salt water, which of course he couldn't stand and shrivelled until nothing was left of him.

"I find that sad... ," she said.

Okay, okay... I was too harsh this time. So the next one had to run for his life too, but it was his choice where he went to after that, but once outside the stone circle there was no coming back.

This stone circle was a sacred place, and a central point from which Linda undertook exploration. Because no matter how sensible it was to receive the healing light from the stars, it still was boring to just lay down in the stone circle and wait. So I told her one time, that from the skies above a big bird came flying toward her. After a few laps of circling above, the bird landed on the floor beside her where he looked much smaller than expected. It was a very friendly bird, with a very nice 'face'. He invited her to climb on his back and so she could fly with him.

And so they took off towards the sea. The stone circle got smaller and smaller; they had an overview of the increasing land and the sea. I asked the bird if he would take her to the ancient Atlantis beneath the sea. That was no problem for this bird and quickly he flew across the ocean and close to where Atlantis was, he dove beneath the waves with Linda. Once under the waves they arrived at a large pyramid, and the bird landed in front of it. Linda got off and walked up the stairs of the pyramid that looked somewhat like the Mayan pyramids of Chichén Itza, with stairs on the sides. Upstairs a high priest in an orange robe welcomed her. He asked Linda to lie down on some kind of altar and then gave her a special healing with an Egyptian Ankh.

I asked her if the priest gave her something. Indeed so… The priest gave her a special crystal. This crystal was not my idea. It was a small crystal she explained, very small, an agglomeration of jagged rock crystals. It would fit inside her pocket, but once she took it in her hands it would grow in size and float weightless. In this way it would hover above her belly and send extra healing energies. She was amazed about what she had received, so beautiful.

This is the way we were working together to fight her illness. Linda proved to be very easily guided by me in this fantasy world… but the word 'fantasy' was now no longer sufficient for the enlightening and liberating feeling that we both experienced while we were doing this. It was something that felt like a part of the two of us, something in which I could help and assist her in her difficult struggle. I felt this was important for her, very important.

I'm Ill

In April, five months after the initial examinations, Dottore came to the Netherlands again. We had looked out for that, considering him to be the leading figure in Linda's healing, because he was an astral doctor. The medium and her translator were dependent on volunteers in the Netherlands for shelter and practice space. As payment, people were asked to put an amount of money in an envelope, meant for an orphanage in Columbia.

During each of our visits Dottore assured us that Linda's health situation was improving. Linda had injections in her belly that had been personally customized for her by Dottore's astral helpers. One couldn't see a needle, but from experience I knew that these injections usually were very painful. During the consultation the translator wrote down the prescription. Dottore complimented Linda for all the work that we had done. He expected that she would be okay, and he clearly showed no worries about the future. Things looked good. To our question why, during his previous stay in the Netherlands, he hadn't mentioned the tumour, which he clearly must have known about, the translator's answer was "Rest assured Dottore knows his patients. He doesn't say everything he knows and he has his reasons. Patients could be troubled if they were told everything, and that could stand in the way of their healing process."

In fact all therapists told us that Linda was improving. However, Jacob was on the cautious side. I noticed that he wasn't convinced about this and wanted to see her as frequently as possible. It had to do with the fact that she still hadn't gone through an emotional process yet.

Linda didn't worry about that. "What's the point?" she asked. "What good will it do if I start crying all day long? It doesn't need to be this way for everyone, does it?" She thought it to be nonsense. Didn't we fight her illness with everything we had? Didn't we come at it from all sides at once, just not the traditional side? We had a small army of therapists working on it and spent quite some money on that. We saved the health insurance companies a small fortune. Only the pharmaceutical companies wouldn't be that happy, because they didn't get a penny from us.

Linda's weight showed no improvement having dropped to one hundred lbs., not even during the summer months, and that worried me, but all in all we thought we were doing a fine job considering it wasn't an easy road we had taken. It might seem easy doing it your own way, but it isn't as simple as that. It means that you must take full responsibility for all that you do, all choices that have to be made. A serious illness must be fought. What are your options? Which decisions do you make? Which people do you choose? Who can you trust?

We had deliberately chosen this way. Admittedly, our choice had also been influenced by fear, really, but it was a very conscious choice, because we took full responsibility for Linda's healing process. Otherwise this would be taken over by the hospital and then 'they' would decide what had to be done; we only would have had to agree with the treatment plan. But we weren't even given that option. We discovered that after you've been examined the next step is quite mandatory. If you agree to 'A', then you are also agreeing to B, C and D. Withdrawing halfway down the road is not appreciated. Perhaps that is understandable, considering the expense of the process, but who knows in advance what you are getting yourself into?

Even though Linda's weight stayed very low and she didn't cry in the way that was said to be good for her, I noticed her relaxing more and more. She started to let go of the stress of school, and occasionally we took nice trips. She even started to show interest again in creating things like knitting sweaters, a hobby that she hadn't had the energy for before. This made me happy.

After the summer, in October, Dottore came to Holland again and we managed to be able to see him the very first day he was in Apeldoorn. He confirmed our expectations; it had gone very well with Linda, there was much progress and he was very pleased. "Thanks to my hard work and her effort this was made possible," were his words. With his hands he made large gestures above her body, massaged her belly with a fatty substance and gave her a series of astral injections in her belly. We gave the envelope with money at the entrance and with a happy feeling we left, heading home.

A few days later something happened that finally unlocked her emotions. We had been helping her parents install a new big bedroom cabinet. That involved nothing less than a small relocation, and therefore Linda's eldest brother Rob and his wife were also present. It was a tough job and at the end of the day we were all very tired. Linda, who always kept her attitude of being tough and strong, had not spared herself. It was almost half past one in the night when we said goodbye at the front door. Linda kissed her parents who were happy that the job was done, but they thanked *me* for all the work. I kept my mouth shut, though I had this niggling feeling of having missed an opportunity, and besides, I wasn't sure if Linda would have appreciated me speaking up for her, so the moment passed. I should have known better.

Linda is someone who always compliments other people. She tries to see the positive side in what people do. If she sees that, though small it might seem, she mentions it. Among students this is very important, but mature people need such remarks just as much. It rarely happened that she herself was complimented.

"Now don't think I am fishing for compliments, you know!" I can almost hear her say now, even while writing this down. "Not at all, but occasionally I do need a bit of support too!"

While she drove the car towards home things suddenly came out. "My parents always thank you for everything you do! They seem to think that all I do is not worth mentioning. But I specially came for them all day long! While I'm sick! They never thank me! I have done this for them! And all the time I'm sick, you know!"

Of course we knew all too well how grateful they were, but sometimes you simply need someone to *say* this to you. This time she couldn't stand it anymore. She was rarely emotional and she hardly ever cried, not even last year, though there was enough reason to do so. And if it happened I could always find words to ease her pain. Usually my attention alone or the sound of my voice was enough, but this time nothing I did made any difference and the whole trip home she kept crying while steering the car along the dark canal to Apeldoorn.

Could this be what Jacob meant when he had asked, "Has she been crying?"

It was past two o'clock and it was very quiet on the streets. I still remember how we entered Apeldoorn still driving along the canal, then making a right turn on a very long straight road. Before us we saw the orange lights of lampposts disappearing into the distance. During the day this road was always busy with cars, but now we saw no one and while we drove no one came towards us. We only went by one lamppost after the other, standing beside the road as a row of light bearers.

Somehow this underlined her solitary grief, symbolising our way into the future: lonely... but lit.

When Darkness Falls

One of Linda's hobbies was knitting sweaters. This she did as long as I knew her, but in recent years she was so tired and yet so busy, that knitting sweaters was the last thing she could do. Now finally, after almost one year, she had calmed down so much she could show an interest in doing something for herself, like making a new sweater. It was a sign to me that she felt comfortable and at ease. It made me happy.

It was evening and the fatigue of the bedroom cabinet and the sorrow of the previous night had disappeared. Perhaps the shedding of grief had contributed to it so that she now was more relaxed. This also gave me peace. It was so nice. One of the cats was lying beside me on the couch.

Around eleven o'clock she had quite a strong urge and she said she was going to the toilet. Moments later I heard her crying loudly. I couldn't understand what she said, but she sounded very upset, so I ran towards her, opened the door and saw her sitting with a large piece of toilet paper in her hands, bright red with blood.

"What's this?" I asked. "Are you having your period?"

"The toilet is full of it," she replied. "And there are those big lumps too."

She seemed calmer than I would be in her position, without any sign of panic. "I had this a long time ago," she said. I knew what she was speaking of, because she had told me a few times. Around the time she was twenty years old she had lost a lot of blood during a period. She also told me that during every period she was always dying of the pain involved with it. "Like being pulled apart by four horses," she had said, "for days. I don't know how other women cope with this. Does everyone have so much pain?"

Of course she had told her practitioner about this, but he had shrugged his shoulders saying something like this simply belongs to being a woman.

Because of this excruciating pain every time she had her period, she eventually had decided to use the pill as a means to prevent menstruation. If you swallow the pill continuously, so not interrupting it for a week every four weeks, you prevent your period. This too she had mentioned to her practitioner, but according to him this could not hurt. "But I haven't told him that I do this all year long," she had told me. I knew this and had my doubts, but she was very resolute. This pain she never wanted again. The previous year she had experimented using less and less, but she hadn't dared to skip a whole week yet. Still, she would soon have been in menopause, and then she could start to completely get rid of the pill.

"Could it be that your body is finally throwing out the cancer?" I asked after I gathered my thoughts. She was still handling new pieces of toilet paper, which immediately became bright red

"How could I know?" she replied raising her voice. Now she was done. "There's no name tag on it!"

"Could this be Dottore's treatment?" I asked, in an attempt to explain something I didn't understand. I found myself eerily calm. "Maybe he did some spiritual surgery this morning, or had done so last night, and this is it all coming out at last." After all we had seen him just a few days ago.

She stood up, so I could take a look into the toilet. I had never seen so much blood in my whole life, even though most of it had been washed away. I was glad I didn't faint.

Now what indeed was this, an indication that her body was healing itself? But with so much blood? Or was this the inevitable result of our playing the doctors game with such a serious illness? The latter would undoubtedly be the reply of the traditional doctors.

That scary thought played in my head and forced me to yet again seriously reconsider our decisions. In fact this was my worst nightmare coming true. Were we being that stupid?

On the other hand I found our decision quite natural, for who could assure us that Linda was better off accepting the radical surgery followed by radiation therapy and who knows what else? These prospects were certainly not rosy either.

Decisive, I sought Linda's freedom of choice and my own inner feeling in this. After all, when I had come to know her about seventeen years ago, and had seen the sadness in her eyes, I had made up my mind then to never abandon her, to always support her, wherever our journey would take us. Who knows... could I have been unconsciously preparing myself for things to come?

Doesn't everyone have the right to make decisions in absolute freedom of choice, and while doing so one deserves to be supported?

Still the doubts remained. Perhaps we had made a very wrong decision. If you look at the options a hospital can provide... with highly trained specialists, with all the equipment... the enormous authority that shows off from the big buildings, and if you think of the underlying support of the multinational pharmaceuticals, the public health funds and the governments worldwide, then it's hardly possible not to be convinced of their case. Looking at it that way, we were acting utterly irresponsible.

But what also stayed in my mind was the question that Jacob from Eindhoven had asked on several occasions: "Has she been crying?" What hospital, which traditional medic, what medical university education, does ask such a crucial question, acknowledging that true healing is never about healing the physical body alone.

Yesterday, for the very first time, something was dislodged from the enormous grief that I knew was always present in her unconscious being. Was this connected somehow to this haemorrhaging? I felt the answer to this question was very important.

While listening and observing I slowly started to learn during the past months that people couldn't really recover from cancer unless they go through a process of transformation. Actually, that happens automatically - though not planned that way - when they are treated in hospitals and are confronted with the relativity of human existence, when they undergo chemotherapy or radiation therapy that makes them really sick. They lose all the hair on their bodies, dare not face other people anymore, can't keep any food inside, feel terrible all the time, lose weight, and live in constant stress awaiting the results of the last scans or blood tests.

Then, when it appears that the last chemotherapy did not do what was expected, and there are still high values of tumour markers in the blood, the oncologist usually suggests that 'they' have a new treatment, something that has not been tested fully yet, an experimental chemotherapy. Or additional radiation sessions are needed, involving weeks or months of hospital visits and feeling insecure. Other people undergo extensive surgeries and sometimes body parts are amputated in a final attempt to save the body.

And *if* all goes well, then one must learn to live with the consequences of surgery, radiation and chemo. Life is rarely as it was before. And always there remains that tension in the background: will the tumour stay away? What can I do with my life now? What's the point of my life?

It's inevitable that people in this situation experience intense emotional processes, and somehow they will come to rock bottom. Everything then is topsy-turvy: soul and body. Then tears will come out one day, and the true feelings, the pain, the frustration, the sorrow is shown to the world. There's no escaping it.

After such a period in life, people often will have changed; they will see things in life differently. Finally they can be happy with what life has to offer them, with the extra years they have been given. Their life has changed, because *they* have changed. They start another job; deal with things that caused so much pain in the past and now focus on their happiness. And when looking at all those 'healthy' but stressed people everywhere around them, they might wonder what on earth they are making such a fuss about, because *they* have experienced the relativity of earthly life and realize there is much more to live for.

That is quite some transformation! One might almost wonder if the side effects of chemotherapy *do* make some sense after all.

And Linda? All in all I didn't see her going through such a transformation process. Until yesterday that was, in the car. Then something had come loose that was nagging her for a long time. One small piece; was that the beginning of her healing? But did that have to be accompanied by such a bleeding?

The next morning I started working early as usual in my study. Linda was no early bird, so I let her sleep quietly. Around half past eight that morning I heard an alarming cry coming from upstairs and I ran up the steps to be confronted with a scene that would be forever burned onto my retina.

She was standing straight up on the bed, holding her nightgown slightly up with one hand so I could see red streaks over her legs. She was panic-stricken.

"Look here!" she cried. I didn't see what she meant, but she stepped to one side and then I saw something red between the blankets. I pulled the blankets away and I was shocked when I saw a huge red lumpy mass in the middle of the bed. It wasn't watery so I assumed that the mattress had already soaked up a lot of moisture. We pulled the sheet away and I lifted one of the mattresses. Only then the magnitude of this dawned on me, because I saw a huge dark stain on the lower side.

"I woke up in the blood," she said after I asked about it.

Whether or not this haemorrhage had occurred just before she woke up, or that it had been going on all night, we didn't know, but I suspected the latter.

"How much blood can one lose before you lose consciousness?" I asked, but of course she couldn't know that either. We tried taking stock of the total amount of blood she had lost, but that wasn't easy. How much had she lost the previous night? Hard to tell. In any case, she was still conscious. "Can you make it to the bathroom?" I asked.

"Of course," she said. But I didn't think she was very eager to go, afraid of what more she might discover. But she had to, and when she did, even more blood came out.

I asked if I had to call an ambulance, but clearly she didn't want to. "And then what?" she said in a sharp tone. "What can they do? And what do we tell them?"

Because she was over-reacting I didn't argue with her. That was something I had learned over time, and just saying that she *had* to go to the hospital was certainly the wrong approach, I knew. In fact I couldn't totally disagree with her.

We decided to contact Dottore as soon as possible and let him explain what was going on here. The week before, when we had consulted him for the first time in half a year, he had praised Linda saying how well she was doing.

Dottore always started treatments at ten o'clock and we expected to be able to reach Bianca, the translator, just before that. It was only a short while away, so we could sit it out. One more hour wouldn't make much of a difference now.

It was hard to catch Bianca, because things were hectic there when the first patients entered the house, but I got her on the line and told her what had happened, asking if Linda had to go to the hospital now. Firstly she said that Linda didn't need to worry, because Dottore kept close record of all his patients and as soon as something was going on he would be aware of it and would take whatever measures were needed. If Linda had experienced a significant blood loss he would know and he would help.

She advised Linda to lie down and to lift her legs to stop the bleeding. After some urging she also consented on asking Dottore a special question as soon as there was an opportunity.

During the morning she called back with Dottore's reply: "Whatever comes out is good. I caused these haemorrhages. There were still malignant cells in the bladder, bowel and uterus. I've cleaned everything. Everything is clean. Lie down with your legs up. A blood transfusion is unnecessary. Have faith."

That more or less made us feel comfortable, but we were very surprised to hear that apparently there was tumour growth in the bladder and bowel. He had never said anything about that before. There were tumours in her belly? Why hadn't he told us so? It went so well he had said. She even received a compliment that there was so much progress! This we didn't comprehend, but we were glad to hear that she didn't need to go to hospital. Dottore had everything under control and had even deliberately caused the bleeding in Linda's best interest. If he was that sure of this case, then we trusted him.

Still, the haemorrhages weren't over yet, because the next day she lost more blood. I tried to estimate the total quantity of blood she had lost and realized that conservatively estimated she had lost at least three litres. She was still conscious, but because I didn't trust in that entirely I made another phone call to Bianca that same week. Her answer was short: "Whatever comes out is good. Let it come. A blood transfusion is unnecessary.

By the end of the week the haemorrhages stopped. Linda could hear her heart beating very rapidly in her ears and she had trouble even getting up the staircase. She had been lying with her legs up nearly all the time and began to get pains in her legs. She tried to lay back in normal position so she could relieve her buttocks, but she was so afraid now by seeing all this blood coming out of her own body, that she hardly dared sit up.

Two weeks later we went back to Dottore because the haemorrhages eventually didn't occur anymore. We had a lot of questions that we were eager to hear answers to, and while he gave Linda the usual astral injections, we asked these questions; questions like why he had not told us last time that he had seen malignant cells in the bladder, bowel and uterus. We were sceptical. Out of the corner of my eye I saw Bianca standing with an understandable smile.

His answer was that if he were to say everything he would be so busy with that most of the time, that he wouldn't be able to help so many people in one day. I knew from my father who kept record of all patients in his excel database (that I had set up for him) that on busy days Dottore sometimes treated around one hundred people. Another question we had was, are the haemorrhages now over?

"A little more," was his answer.

'More!' cried Linda. "I have almost nothing left."

And those lumps? What were *they*? He repeated what Bianca had told us already. "Everything that comes out is good. Let it come. It would have been very dangerous if that had been left in place," he said. "It's good that it comes out. I have cleaned the whole uterus and took out everything. The haemorrhages are a sign that everything goes well."

He emphasized that Linda had to have patience and trust above all. It seemed like he was blaming her for not having enough faith. All in all Linda was reassured somewhat and in the weeks after that she gradually recovered and the heart beating in her ears disappeared.

The path narrows

We had recently been looking for a new family doctor, but this was far from easy because it's unusual for people to change doctors. We were always confronted with the question *why* was she looking for another family doctor. They all knew each other and when somebody isn't happy with a colleague, it leads to questions. Linda was searching for someone that would make her feel safe, but how do you tell this to somebody tactfully? And what doctor is waiting for a cancer patient that doesn't want to follow the usual protocols, let alone hospital advice?

In November new haemorrhages started, nothing extreme but certainly suspicious. This left us feeling captive of our lonely position as Dottore was far away in Columbia. Linda didn't want to go to her regular family doctor, and communication with the specialists at the hospital had been terminated.

Through the grapevine we found a former family doctor who was now practicing non-regular healing methods. He was prepared to treat Linda but not as a family doctor, and that was just the whole point. He emphasized that she had to look for a family doctor, but who would that be? In fact, Linda had no official person to fall back on during this phase of her life where she desperately needed someone in the traditional medical world she could trust.

Because of this isolated and difficult position he was prepared, as a former family doctor, to make an exception and to prescribe a medicine to stop the haemorrhages: Cyclokapron, a relatively new medication that influences clotting of the blood.

So, for the first time in years I went to the pharmacy. While waiting for other customers of the pharmacy, I had this strange feeling of swimming and going forward but somehow winding up backwards. Going to the pharmacy does not feel right, as if you are really sick and that's that. So I felt very relieved when I got outside again, going back quickly to the mutual trust and intimacy of my *vriendinnetje[1]* who was trying her very best to get better.

When at the end of November she had another big haemorrhage, she took the new medication, and we were relieved to discover that indeed it appeared to work. An hour later there was only a slight discoloration in her urine. Knowing that now we had something to stop the haemorrhages made us feel very at ease and safe. For weeks we had lived in fear not knowing if she had internal haemorrhages or not. So, you feel more at ease knowing that it can be managed with medication.

Now however we had another problem to deal with: cramps or pain deep within the muscles of her buttocks possibly caused by the unnatural position of keeping her legs up. I massaged the area trying to find the muscle that caused this cramp. At first, it was helpful but the muscle cramps always returned. I had a hard time finding the right spot because every time she would say "Yes, that's it", and a little later it appeared not to be so. What I didn't understand was why the spot deep under her buttocks muscles seemed to be close to her pelvis; not the most logical place to have muscle aches.

We still owned an ultrasound massage device and when I tried that out on her it appeared to work at first. However, a couple of days later she said it didn't work anymore. It seemed like the painful area was getting bigger. Next, I bought a special massage gel that should also help with muscle aches. At first, that also worked quite well and from then on I applied the gel a couple of times a day until my hands were very sticky from the gel.

In spite of everything, the pain was keeping her awake more and more. For that reason, she was prepared to take half a Paracetamol[2] to see if that worked. She never took any pain medication, as she almost never had headaches; a blessing I thought, as I always kept a couple of those pills close

---

[1] *The word 'vriendinnetje' is a Dutch word. 'Vriendin' means 'girlfriend', whereas 'vriendinnetje' means 'small girlfriend', like 'vriendje' means 'small boyfriend', usually referring to children's playmates. But among lovers those words sometimes are used to express more intimacy and innocence. As there seems no suitable English equivalent, it was decided upon to leave this word as is.*

[2] *In the Netherlands Paracetamol is mostly used against headaches. Paracetamol is an ingredient of Vicodin.*

by just in case. Half a tablet worked just fine, but after about six hours the pain slowly returned.

If you never take anything like Paracetamol, it works great at first, but your body gets accustomed to it and then you have to take a higher dosage to get the same results. After two days she had to increase the dosage by a quarter of a tablet. Another couple of days later she felt it necessary to take the Paracetamol twice daily instead of once.

This didn't feel right, although I wasn't too worried about it at the time. She was trying to get better, but yet again I had that feeling of swimming upstream... You feel that you're moving forward through the water but how come you're ending up backwards?

We were soon out of Paracetamol and I bought her a new box; this times a larger one of fifty tablets. In the meantime, it was the end of November and we had been dealing with all this misery for a month now. Linda didn't want to risk new haemorrhages and that caused her not to leave the house. I cancelled all her appointments, also my own, so I didn't have to leave her alone. She protested, but she was also happy about my decision, as she wasn't happy to be alone anymore.

When she ran out of the Cyclokapron prescription, we called the former family doctor again. He wasn't very willing to renew the prescription. We could understand that he was facing a difficult situation: Linda being diagnosed with cancer of the uterus; a patient that refused go to her own family doctor, who had refused treatment at a hospital and now came to him for a prescription to stop serious haemorrhages. What do you do in a case like that as a former family doctor?

Of course, it's an absurd situation and I can imagine that people reading these words are thinking, or that *you* think: "they are absolutely crazy."

I think that as a result of your upbringing, your education, your life experiences, and even more importantly, what you hear in the media... in a situation like this you form an opinion. It wouldn't surprise me if many of you would call us 'irresponsible', to say the least.

I called my own family doctor - I had one for myself, although I almost never went there - and I told him our story. His reaction was to be expected just like that: 'irresponsible'. He insisted on persuading Linda to get treatment from a doctor. He asked what medication she was on and when he learned of the Cyclokapron, he compared it to a cannon ball. He didn't say what he would prescribe instead though. He asked if Linda wanted to see him for treatment, but I knew Linda would not want that. She wanted a family doctor that would *listen* to her; really listen and one open to alternative treatments, a family doctor who would be open to homeopathy, electro-acupuncture, biofeedback therapy, Tibetan herbs and natural healing. If such a doctor would also be able to connect to Linda, that would be wonderful. A doctor who accepts that there is more out there than meets the eye, would be her absolute preference.

Try and make that happen! This was our most important dilemma. Linda had emphasized more than once, that she had nothing against regular doctors, but they are always so convinced they are right. "They won't even listen to me!" she said. If there is one thing that goes for almost all alternative doctors whom we've met in the past, and they are many, is that they take their time to listen. Also that most of them see the human body as a whole rather than looking at the illness separately or only looking at the affected part of the body. Naturally, you don't have to look any further if you have a broken arm or a splinter in your eye, although you could, as even such accidents have story to tell, but we are not talking about that right now.

All doctors and specialists, who we'd met so far, totally turned down everything that wasn't according to their belief system. During the short conversations we had with them, it turned out that most of them were not even aware about any of such therapies, devices and treating methods. Unknown makes unloved, so the saying goes. But even if they had some knowledge about it, they were bound not to talk about it.

Professionally there is a big taboo: a doctor with an open mind to alternative treatments will not be very willing to admit it. 'Alternative' *suggests* 'not scientifically researched and tested treatments', with a high danger of being treated by 'quacks'. When a doctor gets involved openly, he will be on thin ice, and with his income depending on the regular health care system he might even be risking his career.

Would it be a coincidence that the popular Dutch actress Sylvia Millecam with breast cancer was sick at the same time as Linda? When Linda learned about Sylvia's struggle, she felt very connected with her and as no other she understood her dilemma. Sylvia too wanted to go her own way, but after she had died the pharmaceutical industry and a group of government officials used her case to try to limit the free choice of cancer patients, while the naturopathic doctors, who had treated her were prosecuted.

Ultimately, Linda got a prescription for ninety more tablets from the former family doctor. Maybe he overstepped his boundaries and if he did, it was really grand of him. With this prescription we could go on maybe until the end of December, which seemed far off under these circumstances. It would allow us the time to find a suitable family doctor, although at the time we didn't have the slightest idea what these pills had in store for us.

Oh Holy Night

During the month of December we were very much on our own. I hardly left the house, only to quickly get some groceries. Linda's parents, my parents and my sister Mieke were the only ones who came to visit and offered us their help. However, since I was in good shape, I was perfectly capable of managing on my own, and I declined all help.

Fortunately, there were few new haemorrhages and so she started to feel a little better. Only the pain in her buttocks muscles remained which made it difficult for her to sit or lie properly. To make her feel more comfortable, I bought an imitation sheepskin. This seemed to work, however now she could not do without Paracetamol. The pain was too prominent and would not subside.

At one point, she uttered "Do you realize it has been seven weeks now! Seven weeks! How much longer! Another week? Two weeks? Another month? Do you have any idea? Tell me!"

There was another matter we had discussed before, but somehow never had gotten around to because it didn't matter enough to us. We had been living together for seventeen years but had never felt the need to get married; neither one of us felt it was necessary. On top of that, we did not want any children, if that would even constitute a reason to get married these days.

Legally, it seems to make sense to get a piece of paper. If you want to draw up a will you need at least a domestic partnership contract. I had never insisted as she was the one with the steady income and nearly all the stuff in the house was hers. So what did I have to offer? Only for the last couple of years did I make enough money as a freelancer to make a reasonable contribution.

Because of the severe haemorrhages we were no longer so sure of the future and so the sensible thing to do was to register as a domestic partnership and get a will drawn up. We discussed this with a lawyer and December 14th was the big day. Linda had inquired whether she could sign at home if necessary, but she felt secure enough to join me.

The lawyer's office was a bit sterile, but to this day it still made us feel special, almost as if we were getting married. Getting married is in essence nothing more than the signing of a piece of paper. It's the whole fuss surrounding it that causes butterflies.

I had arranged for some cake and we treated ourselves afterwards; that was the least I could do. She seemed happy, but I could sense her unspoken thoughts for not showing this. Our mutual love was big enough to be each other's sole heir, although for a moment there it looked like I would be the only one who would gain from that. I wished I could make her really happy for once, after all the years of fatigue.

We still had to draw up a list of each other's possessions, which neither one of us enjoyed doing. Linda expressed our feelings strikingly one day saying, "I hate to write this all down. It almost seems as we are having a divorce!"

Those words expressed exactly how much she loved me.

What she really wanted, as she did each year, was to visit her eldest brother Rob for his birthday, which is on Christmas Day. She especially wanted to go this time, although we would have to plan it very carefully. It meant sitting upright in the car for at least an hour. She wanted to go through with it; she had been planning way in advance which presents to get. I was tasked with getting them, although we weren't sure whether we would be able to go or not. Everything had to be just right.

A few days before Christmas, as she was knitting her purple sweater again, a new haemorrhage started, serious enough to increase her dose of Cyclokapron. She had been experimenting with the dose to make it last as long as possible. It was supposed to last her until just after Christmas, but with this new haemorrhage she went back to the recommended higher dose. I was getting anxious... would this mean not being able to go to her brother's birthday?

She didn't say anything, but I knew how fed up she was with it. She was tense and tried to hide it, although it was showing more and more. She did her best to be upbeat and look at her best for others. Despite this new haemorrhage she wanted me to continue with the preparations. She decided not to get new clothes, as she usually did other Christmases. We spent vast amounts of time in front of the closet to find something suitable. She had plenty of nice clothes to choose from, however, this one had been worn earlier that year... this one was out of fashion... this one did not match anything else and that one needed new accessories! I had to sit there and judge, but I enjoyed seeing her busy like this, while doing my best to come up with arguments that made sense for or against a certain choice, but most of all I tried to prevent saying anything dumb. I'm sure all married men are familiar with this feeling.

On Christmas Eve we had everything ready for the next day - clothes, presents etc. Linda had decided to take a shower and wash her hair the night before to avoid having to do this on Christmas morning, as she felt unsafe in the shower. These days I was always there to keep an eye out. While I was seated on the toilet cover, I watched her rinse her hair. At some point I noticed a red drop falling on her right foot, a few seconds later followed by another one. At first I thought I had imagined it as the water washed it away quickly. I waited. Then I noticed new drops as they fell on her foot. I wondered how serious it was. The water prevented me from making a good assessment, but it seemed to indicate the beginning of a haemorrhage. I mentioned what I witnessed. She stopped immediately and watched her feet. There it was again... a red drop of blood that was washed away instantly.

"Oh please no!" she cried. "Oh please no!" She cursed silently and sat down on the toilet. It looked serious and she asked me if there was any Cyclokapron left. But we both knew the answer to that. We were all out as we had not been able to find another doctor. We could not impose again on the former family doctor, especially not tonight. Murphy's law...

This was a bad time to start haemorrhaging. It was 10 pm on Christmas Eve and there were only skeleton crews on duty. All we could do was hope for the best.

"Whom can we call?" she asked. We could not think of anyone that might have been of help right then. We called some people nevertheless, but most didn't even answer the phone. I called my parents and they were ready to come over, but what would they be able to accomplish? Hold her hand? They proposed we call an emergency doctor. That thought had crossed our minds of course, but before doing anything drastic, we decided to wait and see if things would get worse.

An hour later the haemorrhaging started again. This was clearly a big one, so I decided to start making phone calls to find out who was on duty, no simple matter I discovered. I had to call several numbers to find the right phone number to call. I stayed close to Linda, sometimes next to her on the bed. Every time she went to the bathroom I joined her and made my calls sitting on the edge of the bathtub or on the bathroom floor. She had to go to the bathroom a number of times and every time the toilet bowl was red with blood.

"What do you want me to do?" I asked her.

"If you call they will send an ambulance to pick me up," she said. "I will have to go straight to the hospital then."

I agreed with her. Not something to look forward to.

I tried to gauge the loss of blood to estimate how much time we had left before taking drastic measures. A nasty gamble, as her life would be in jeopardy if I would make a mistake.

After a while another big haemorrhage occurred, and then another one soon followed. The intervals were too short and the amount of blood way too much. Linda started panicking and suddenly declared that I should get a doctor. She even considered an ambulance taking her to the hospital. "Let them admit me! Get that ambulance to come and pick me up! Then they can make X-rays! Then they can remove everything! GO ON, GET ON WITH IT!!!" She was getting to the end of her tether. She had never expressed anything like this before.

With a very ambiguous feeling I picked up the phone. On the one hand, I knew how serious the situation was. On the other hand, I also knew that she was not being comprehensive right now. Somebody else would have taken advantage of this moment of weakness and would have called a doctor immediately... I didn't want to take away... how do say it... her independence, her dignity, by taking over the situation just to give in to the do-what-everybody-else-would-do-in-a-situation-like-this principle.

I called the number I had gotten from the doctor on duty, but nobody answered, again another number to call. Clearly, family doctors worked together and had set up rules for who would be on duty when, but apparently the chain was broken. I called the next number and even before answering I got this uneasy feeling. From the corner of my eye I could see it was just a few more minutes to midnight, and from the answering messages I gathered that the doctor on duty would transfer to the next one at the stroke of midnight. It was Christmas Eve and every twelve hours another doctor on duty; this must be the worst moment of year to call with an emergency.

That indeed became apparent quickly. I'm not sure anymore who it was that I got on the phone and that probably is for the better. The first question hurled at me was why I was calling at this hour. He sounded unfriendly; I clearly had disturbed him during his cosy Christmas Eve with wife and kids. I tried to explain our very good reason to disturb him and that I had not picked this moment on purpose. We couldn't help that we needed his aid right now.

I don't exactly recall the conversation word for word. I tried to explain what had happened, but the conversation remained very difficult and I got the feeling that I would rather not mention everything that had happened, although I'm sure he was not paying any attention at all to what I was saying. At the end, he felt it was not necessary to take any action at this point. No ambulance would be required, he did not prescribe Cyclokapron and we should wait until the next morning to see if we still needed help. We didn't need to worry about Linda bleeding to death. He was upset; upset that we had called him at exactly this moment.

Distraught I put down the phone and told Linda what had transpired. She already had some idea based on my reactions on the phone. Usually she would criticize the way I conducted a conversation like this, pointing out things I should say or that I should not say. Not so this time.

I really had no clue what to do next. Call 911? Wasn't this something of an emergency? Should I drive her myself and take her to the emergency? For some reason, we did not feel like it anymore. We might get a similar reaction from the doctors over there for calling them away from their cosy Christmas Eves with their families and kids.

Linda shrugged her shoulders. She also had no idea. The moment had passed for the hospital and traditional medicine to take over her treatment. "I'll just go on and die then," she said. "Then so be it."

She took the phone from me and called her parents to let them know we were not able to make it the next day. The next time they came over and if she were still alive, they could take the presents and give them to Rob.

That night she lost a lot of blood, but around 4 am it stopped. She didn't die, but we were back to square one. She decided to put up her feet again, put cold packs on her belly and keep very still. The pain in her back was worse than ever, but she decided against Paracetamol, which would thin her blood. She was in a constant state of fear.

Holy Holy Night!

Wandering through the Night

Immediately after Christmas, I called one of the volunteers for Dottore's practice located in the South-Holland region. She suggested she contact the translator for Dottore in South-America. This started an intercontinental exchange of faxes and e-mails resulting in a call from a woman called Maria who lived close by in Apeldoorn. She was a therapist and knew Dottore very well. She claimed that Dottore had instructed her how to treat Linda.

She sounded like she didn't really want to do this and even before seeing Linda in person; she put forward a condition that she apparently had discussed with Dottore earlier. I suggested she should talk this over with Linda directly, but she held off for now. She wanted to discuss this with me first. She shared that Linda's illness was very complicated and her treatment would take a lot of time. For that reason it was imperative that Linda would be committed to the treatment all the way and that she should trust her and Dottore one hundred per cent. Only then Maria would be able to take over Linda's treatment with Dottore's guidance.

At first, it wasn't clear why she underscored the "one hundred per cent" issue so much, but later it became evident that she would not allow any other therapists interfering; they would undermine the treatment and Maria apparently believed that Linda's life would then be in danger. That was her condition and having said that, she would now talk directly to Linda. She would have to ask for Maria's help explicitly and personally. I told Linda what I had heard and handed her the phone. Linda had no problem with it, although I could clearly see the surprise on her face.

Maria mentioned there was one more hurdle to be taken and that was for Dottore to get permission for the treatment from his... spirit superiors so to say. We would be told when we would visit Maria in a couple of days.

During the month of December the pain had increased to the extent where even high doses of Paracetamol were unable to offer relief. Linda could hardly sleep because the painful area was extending. She said it felt like a big egg was protruding from her body somewhere close to her tailbone. She did not want to be touched there anymore, even looking at it made her cringe with pain. I had to change my tactics continuously when treating her, as she could bear less and less physical contact. Because she would not allow me to massage the painful area anymore, I had to come up with something else. I was astonished to find that when I put my hands on the painful area very carefully or kept them a little above it, the pain would subside, remarkable. It appeared I was discovering and exploring my own magnetic healing powers in the process.

Because she was unable to sleep, Linda started pacing up and down the living room at night. At first I didn't notice it because I was asleep. I did not yet wake up every time she got out of bed, but my guess was that she had done this only a few times so far. Slowly, however, my "mother instinct" started to kick in and one night I suddenly really awoke to what was going on.

I noticed she was no longer next to me in bed, but evidently had gone downstairs. I wondered why she didn't come back to bed. Still half asleep I looked for her and found her in the darkened living room, in her nightgown, pacing up and down between the kitchen and the sofa, sometimes with one hand on her back, then with both hands on her back. I sat down on the sofa and watched her for a while as she was dragging herself towards the kitchen. She turned around and walked towards me, gazing into the void. If I could detect anything in that look, it must have been despair.

It was the middle of winter, the heat was turned off, and so the room was bitter cold around this time of night, and after only a few minutes I was already trembling with cold. She told me she was unable to lie down, but walking seemed fine.

"You better go back to bed," she said. "I'll join you later".

"How long have you been down here?" I asked, ignoring her previous remark.

"A couple of hours," she replied toneless as she made another turn.

"And all this time you have been pacing up and down?"

"I have carved up the carpet." Her voice sounded flat.

It appeared she had been doing this for a couple of nights because she was unable to sleep. The way she carried herself looked painfully tiresome; just looking at her made me tired. My heart sank to my stomach watching this happen while my rational mind seemed unfettered. This was not happening, not really.

She didn't mind that the room was cold. "Heat increases the pain," she told me. When she approached again I sank to my knees and felt her legs - they were cold as ice. She was cold to the bone. I got up, pulled her against me and embraced my forlorn *vriendinnetje*. Cold to the touch, and more so on the inside. She seemed at her wit's end.

"Don't you want to come upstairs for a while?" I asked. "You are cold as ice. This can't be good for you". Maybe my warmth made her realize how cold and tired she really was, but she felt so miserable that she withdrew completely and hid behind a great big wall. In fact this was a big cry for help, but she didn't let on and said the opposite.

A touch and a few words were enough to make her come upstairs with me. I wanted to get her a hot water bottle, but she told me no. She took a Paracetamol and in bed let me warm her up with my body heat. No touching as everything was aching and was too much for her to handle.

In the meantime it had become morning, but our day-to-day routine was messed up anyway these days. I had gotten used to springing into action at the strangest times of day or night. This past night had worn her out and together with the Paracetamol made it possible for her to get a little sleep. This was another crucial moment that made me aware... well... I'm not sure what I was aware of actually. It seemed like one big horror.

Her pain was so intense, especially at night. During the day there was enough distraction; she could call people on the phone or she would be called. Sometimes she had something to do, but more importantly... it was daylight. Daylight had always been important to her, but now it seemed of the utmost importance. Why would that be?

I had suggested before that she hold a hot water bottle against the painful area, but she had dismissed the idea every time. Just the thought of something hot against that painful area! I kept insisting though and finally she was willing to try. At first I got it all wrong: too much water, too hot, she needed it wrapped in a towel etc. After a number of tries we got closer and the hot water bottle seemed to make a difference. We tried different water temperatures and she tried different positions. Then finally rejection was exchanged for approval.

That first time it almost seemed like a wonder drug, that's how well it worked. For a couple of hours she was able to get some decent sleep. The second night we tried it again, but this time it failed: put more water in. Or not... Less then? Hotter water maybe? A thinner towel? After ninety minutes of trying all sorts of things, the wonder drug had been reduced to no more than a Band-Aid.

"Maybe if I take a Paracetamol first," she said, "and then put the water bottle against my back... then the Paracetamol can kick in and I can get some sleep." That's what we tried and when she had found the perfect position I joined her, and she finally fell asleep. We were exhausted as it was way past midnight again.

Less than an hour later I was abruptly awakened by her angry cry: "That damn water bottle!" she screamed and threw it in the corner. She had fallen asleep on top of the bottle and the hard edge had caused her to wake up from the pain. Normally, the pain would have been reduced, now it made her cringe.

"Do you want me to get you another Paracetamol?" I suggested, but she didn't want one. "That won't work now!" she replied. "I took the other one less than two hours ago. Otherwise it won't work at all! And then what do I have left?" I had no answer to that.

A deep sigh came from her. "I'm going downstairs."

"What are you going to do?" I wanted to know.

"Dun no" was the answer.

She went down the stairs to a room we called 'the computer room'. Our townhouse had three floors: the top floor was our bedroom and the second floor consisted of three rooms with the biggest one being the second sitting room. We kept some of our older furniture in there making it a comfortable room just to sit and relax. Cats enjoy comfort and ours were no different. Our cats had claimed this as their room and so we renamed it 'the Cat room'. The second room on this floor was my studio, or the 'Airbrush room', which was littered with drawings, frames, paint stuff etc. So the third room was 'the Computer room', which next to a computer also contained a big closet with all of Linda's school stuff.

It was this room where she planted herself on the chair behind the desk and started to look around. I watched her standing in the doorway. After a little bit she took a stack of folders and papers from the big closet and started going through them. Silently, she browsed through the papers and studied some more in-depth. Some papers she pulled from the stack and tossed them aside. I went into the Airbrush room and started to putter around. This way I was close to her in case she needed anything. It was two thirty am, but what did it matter?

I heard her rifling through her stuff and occasionally tearing up some paper. At least she kept herself busy and that made me feel more at ease. Every now and then she called out to me and I joined her for a bit. We would talk about what she had found. Her frustration from earlier seemed dissipated.

This was how we managed to get through another couple of hours that night. Close to six am she was tired enough to try sleeping again with the help of a Paracetamol. By the time she would wake up it would be daylight again and it would be a brand new day.

What does the Future hold?

On New Year's Eve we had the first appointment with Maria. She let us in and asked Linda to sit beside her desk. I sat diagonally behind her and waited expectantly.

Maria explained again what she was about to do and insisted again that she needed one hundred per cent trust from Linda. "There can only be one captain on a ship," she said. We didn't understand why she made such a big deal out of this. We had never really met and we hadn't told her anything about the other therapists we had consulted and all the things we did. What had she heard about us? Had Dottore told her, or had she been talking to other people and drawn conclusions from that?

Whatever... Dottore had been granted permission from his superiors, she said, so she was allowed to treat Linda. She had received a lot of data from Dottore and in this first session she would use most of the time to check these data and put together an overall picture of Linda's illness. On that information she and Dottore would make a treatment plan as a base for later sessions.

Then she started asking Linda a series of questions while she held Linda's wrist. She used some kind of kinesiology, a method to check the tension in a group of muscles responding to the patient's answers, much like a lie detector works. Linda said afterwards that she was unable to enforce a 'yes' or a 'no', which she obviously had tried doing. That's like her.

Maria went through a long questionnaire and was given a comprehensive picture of the past and current state of Linda's disease. At one point she went rapidly through Linda's life from birth to see if her findings were correct so far. She finally came to the present day, and then continued, in the future. She called out several months and when she arrived at January 2002 she stopped.

"That's odd," she remarked.

She did it again and at January she again stopped.

We asked what had stopped her and she said that from January 2002 she couldn't test.

"Does that mean that Linda has been cured then?"

She shrugged. "I don't know," she said. "It could mean anything."

At the end of the consultation she told us her findings thus far. She told us that the cause of Linda's cancer was located in three previous lives. In the next session she would start working on this.

There was also something about Linda's blood making it difficult to solidify naturally. A lack of, or maybe the presence of a particular element had to do with this. Also various situations in her present life and the resulting frustrations caused by them played a role. But before she went to work on that she would exchange information by fax with Dottore.

Of course we expected to hear that Linda's cancer was much more than 'just' a tumour in her abdomen. Maria's findings confirmed this, but the complexity of this disease surprised us. Linda was happy to hear that Maria could get her new prescriptions for Cyclokapron through a friendly contact. But what really gave us both much comfort was that experienced people were treating Linda on a much more fundamental level than ever before.

I found it incomprehensible that in the traditional medical world these aspects were completely denied. The technical possibilities of modern medicine are extraordinary, but why are all the physicians, family doctors or specialists totally ignoring the fact that diseases are meaningful signals from the body that something is wrong at the soul level? To really cure a disease the least one can do is try to understand those signals to get a picture on that level.

Happy New Year went smoothly. Because this was a special night we watched television. I had bought some delicacies and of course a few Dutch 'oil balls' that are most appreciated on New Years Eve, but only in Holland as no other country seems to have them. My parents and my sister came by for a short while and at midnight we saw the fireworks from behind the windows. We hugged and kissed and wished each other a year full of health and many more years together. We said it with pain and uncertainty in our hearts, but at such moments the joy that is everywhere reflects on you making you forget for a while the miserable situation you're in. But shortly after midnight, when the biggest fireworks display was over, Linda said she would like to go to bed and so we were back in our reality of lack of sleep and pain... lots of pain.

Sometime early in January 2001 we finally found a doctor that seemed suitable. His name was Storms. Initially we chose him because according to what we'd heard he wasn't totally opposed to alternative options. Strange coincidence was that, of all family physicians he was the one closest to our home; nearly at walking distance. Apparently one shouldn't search for solutions to problems too far away.

He listened attentively to us and thankfully took plenty of time. We put all the cards on the table, and I think he was greatly astonished, but he hid it well. I felt that he couldn't cope with Linda, but obviously he didn't wish to abandon her. Perhaps he thought that she was the typical example of what might happen when you engage in alternative therapies.

He confirmed what we already had heard about him, that he had studied the teachings of Rudolf Steiner. Sometimes, in addition to the usual regular treatment, he made use of this therapy. But he was very clear that he was scientifically educated and that his methods were traditional. Before he could do anything he wanted to know exactly where he was with Linda. To begin with he wished to know what it was that Linda wanted from him. "First we must talk about the *process*," he said as a real doctor, not calling a serious illness by its true name, just like in Harry Potters books, referring to 'You-Know-Who' instead of using the name Voldemort.

Linda came straight to the point and answered the unspoken question; she said that she thought that the cancer was gone. "That's why we did all those therapies," she said. "Everyone tells me that I don't have cancer anymore. Only inflammations are left. That's what causing the bleedings." With what she said she had generalized all therapists, because not everybody had told her that, but I saw no use in correcting her now.

Doctor Storms emphasized that, according to his background and in his eyes, we had done nothing. In traditional terms, he meant, we had done nothing. Although he didn't say it aloud, we noticed that he was convinced that it was a cancerous tumour that caused the bleedings. But he didn't want to engage in a yes-no discussion and searched for the right tactic with which to approach Linda.

He asked if she was willing to undergo more examinations. But, he added, we would then have to agree to whatever treatment plan came out of that. No mid turn.

Again we walked into the brick wall of western medical science. No thanks. That was against Linda's wishes.

Then he turned to me and tried to figure out how much I agreed with her choice. I wondered whether he wanted to see if he could persuade me to choose his side, or that he just wanted to know where I stood. I chose Linda's position, but in my answer I made it clear that we understood him and were aware of the consequences.

It may sound bizarre to read that Linda was so convinced that she no longer had cancer, because of the bleedings, pain and all the clues that were there. One would think that you have to be totally blind not to accept the obvious, but please don't forget that we were in the middle of a situation here. You have no good perspective like that.

Now, in retrospect, while writing this book, things fall into place. Now I can figure things out, now can I see the signs, unravel connections and now do I start to see a bigger picture that slowly expands over the years. It's like ascending in a balloon from your home. First you see only the living room. Then you see the whole house, next you see the neighbourhood, the whole town, the roads and fields surrounding it, and then you start seeing the rivers, lakes, seas and continents and finally you start to see the cosmic connections involved, connections usually neglected by almost all people.

This much bigger picture was not about Linda's cancer itself, but about *the reason why* she had cancer, the *real* 'process' that she was in, and about the unique options she now was presented with to choose from. Nothing in life comes without a good reason.

I'm now convinced that Linda, on a soul level, knew perfectly well what really was going on inside her body. And because I allowed her total freedom to make her own decisions, her soul was able to direct her moves, making decisions from this inner wisdom, not derived by my personal wishes. I considered it my task to guard her soul's freedom, allowing her total freedom to choose her personal road, and to try to accept where that road would bring us, no matter how strange it might seem. From the earthly perspective neither Linda nor I then understood the backgrounds or her soul's choices. But we both 'knew'... somehow we knew.

Strange as it may sound, maybe it was for the better that we didn't have this perspective at that time. Otherwise we might have had second thoughts.

But even if we had been convinced that cancer was still present, and maybe still growing or even spreading out, I don't think we would have chosen the traditional way. Hospital, radiation, chemotherapy... weren't doing any real *healing*, but merely fighting symptoms. No matter what way you look at our situation, the outlook was uncertain in *all* respects. That thought too played a role in rejection to the option that the doctor showed us here.

What also played a role was that we then were very convinced of the expertise and knowledge of Dottore and Maria. After all, he was called an astral doctor who, fifty years ago when he lived in Colombia, so we were told, had helped thousands of people. The medium was said to channel a doctor of the poor, a legendary doctor, even to this day: dr. José Gregorio Hernández. Apparently after his death he had continued the good work, and now in the other dimension he had much more perspective and a knowledge that every earthly doctor would envy.

To return to dr. Storms... once he was sure what we wanted, that we still refused to enter the traditional circuit he knew where he stood with Linda. He agreed with her request to use Cyclokapron and from that moment that part was taken of our shoulders.

She could get prescriptions whenever needed. Also, there were many painkillers that could be tried, which hopefully would work better than the Paracetamol Linda used so much now. But Linda was very reluctant to ask for any painkiller, fearing its side effects.

Amà

What we hadn't done anymore for quite some time because of the bleedings and the stress, were the visualisations. It wasn't easy for Linda to lie down quietly and concentrate, but after she woke up she felt at her best, so that was a good time for it. And one of the very first times we did it something very strange happened...

We started the visualisation like always, through the beautiful garden and the sacred fountain with the crystal to the beach and into Linda's personal stone circle, where the light of the stars above illuminated her.

While she was lying down with her eyes closed we could talk to each other. No deep discussions of course, else she would lose her concentration, so usually I would keep my mouth shut to let the starlight from the Pleiades do its work.

At one point she suddenly remarked, "There's something next to me."

That was strange. Apparently she saw something that was wrong. I had not said anything so there was no reason to use her imagination now. She tried to look at it, but had trouble with it, so I asked her a few indirect questions to focus her attention and clear her vision. A question like 'what do you see' wouldn't work here, but questions instead like 'is it big or it is small?' might just trigger her to open her inner eyes further and fill in whatever was presented to her. She could not give an exact description, but she got the impression that it was not a 'something' but a 'someone'.

That was even stranger. I asked her if she felt at ease with it, because we certainly didn't need any more trouble, but she said that it felt good. This person, or this energy, whatever it was, stayed with her for the rest of the time, so we let it be for now.

The next time we did the visualization Linda could describe the energy form better, and now she could even make contact. Indeed it was a person, a woman. Linda described the woman to be very beautiful, very serene, with a most beautiful face, but Linda didn't recognise her. She was seated beside Linda, wearing a light dress and was barefoot, and she played in the water with her feet.

Apparently the stone circle was situated halfway in the sea. That was a fact I hadn't known until now, but I hadn't asked, assuming it was situated well above the shoreline high on the beach. But no, I had only provided a rough outline of the scenery and Linda's imagination filled in the rest, and certain details had slipped our attention.

It now turned out that another dimension had been added to our doings, and not even Linda was in control here. This we discovered during the next visualisation, because the woman had not shown herself to Linda yet, and so at one moment I said to Linda that she was now standing in front of her. But that did not work. Linda said she could notice the shape of a woman, but that it seemed like a doll. There was no life in it.

This woman came when *she* decided to come; it was not up to us.

But we were very sceptical and asked ourselves if what was now happening was okay. We knew there was a danger involved in summoning spirits and we didn't need any more problems. We had enough as it was.

But after a couple of visualisations Linda remarked, "She's a friend! I always wanted a friend with whom I can have fun, can laugh together and do crazy things. And this is a friend!"

What was remarkable was that not only Linda, but I too was very happy when this woman was there. I could even feel joy! And I didn't have to do anything for it... it simply was there. We had contact with someone from the Spirit World.

Now, that may sound heavy and I don't expect you to accept this right away, but the loving feeling of intense joy, happiness... they were very real and very present, especially in Linda, but also in me. She made us happy! So from that moment on we tried to be in contact with the woman as much as possible, but when she didn't show up we went on with what we usually did and didn't worry. And sometimes she was only there for a short while and then left, but never without cheering us up first. Her presence was a light for us in this lonely battle. We had help!

After one or two more sessions we also got her name. First Linda thought of names like Martha, Mary or Amelia, but suddenly she knew: Amà. At that time we had never heard that name before, but to my knowledge it has nothing to do with the now globally beloved 'Mother Ama', apart from the Latin name that is, The Beloved.

Linda could ask her questions, but receiving Amà's responses wasn't that easy. And there were a lot of questions that Linda wanted answers to, about her illness, the bleedings, the therapies, if she would get better, how long it would take before she was totally cured, and why all this misery. Those are heavy questions and I could tell Linda in advance that if Amà really were a being from the Spirit World, she wouldn't answer every question like Linda wanted. Of course Linda realized that too, but she wouldn't be Linda if at least she wouldn't give it a try.

To begin with we were just very happy with her. Linda and Amà had a lot of fun together. Amà always brought a little white dog with her called Taksi. Linda was surprised and asked if they were allowed to keep animals in the Spirit World. "Of course!" Amà said. "Why not?"

Taksi was naughty and always tried to get in the stone circle, but that was not good for him. Amà then took a ball or stick and threw it far away. Then he ran hard after it and came back in no time for the next throw. Later he started digging a hole in the sand, looking for a bone or whatever. Of course that was not just a hole, but a very deep one, so soon he was completely out of sight. It was very amusing to see only sand flowing over the edge.

At one time Linda and I were trying to catch little green monsters in her belly and send them away, but there were two monsters that escaped all our efforts to catch them. Whatever we did they outsmarted us all the time. Halfway Amà entered the stage, sat down and watched us amused. We had already found out that Amà was always very cheerful and that she couldn't be caught out, so we asked her if she could help us with the monsters. She had a playful and unexpected solution. She told the little monsters that a little further on the beach there was an ice-cream store where they sold very tasty sorbets and... today they were for free!

Well that didn't fall on deaf ears and they left straight away for the ice-cream store. Once outside the stone circle there was no possibility of return for those wretches, but that wasn't our concern. We were laughing loudly. "The fools," laughed Linda and Amà together.

Another time we were at work to clean Linda's insides from negative energies. While she was inside the stone circle I put my hands on her belly, closed my eyes and visualised that I could get deep inside her belly to clear away everything that didn't belong there. That needed a lot of concentration and creativity from me, but over the previous months I had gotten an almost full-time training in how to heal, whether is was with my hands, my voice, or through my imagination, to find ways to help her. And always we discovered new ways, unexpected opportunities, or we were given something that helped us further, even if it worked only once or twice. In fact Amà was one of these, a friendship from the Spirit World that was a very special gift to us.

This time I wasn't able to remove a big ball of negative energy from her belly. Linda tried from inside to push the ball out while I tried pulling it out with my hands, but for some reason I had trouble 'grabbing' it. We were right in the middle of this struggle when Amà arrived at the scene. Linda always kept me informed as soon as she got down there. I asked Linda immediately if Amà knew any way to get rid of this ball of negative energy.

Her answer was both unexpected and humorous...

"What ball?" she said. And Linda described how Amà simply picked the ball out of her belly and kicked it with such force that it went way over the horizon and straight into deep space.

"Wow!" was Linda's humble reaction after a few seconds. "She must be a formidable football player. How she can kick balls!" And we all began to laugh.

Because we couldn't predict when Linda felt good enough to be able to concentrate and lie down for another session we did it whenever it was possible. Sometimes there had just been another bleeding, or some incident that made her sad or depressed, and especially at such times Linda needed to be there between the stones. At such times Amà was always there, waiting for us to arrive. She was always very aware of our situations, and Linda didn't need to say anything.

What she then did to start with was to grab both Linda's wrists. Linda did the same to Amà, and then Linda got a tremendous amount of energy. "That feels so good," Linda said. "I get completely recharged." She wished that she herself had so much energy.

Any time we were in a hurry Amà didn't waste any time by calmly walking to the stones but they both ran together hand in hand along the shore to the stones; Amà in her white dress and flowing hair, and Linda in her short frayed jeans and red T-shirt. This is an image that really impressed me, because Linda had told how magnificent that was... running hand in hand along the beach, splashing through the water, laughing aloud. They loved it and I could see it so clearly.

By the way, Amà said that Linda should dress better in the house. Linda had always been very devoted to paying attention to her appearance and had closets filled with beautiful, carefully selected clothes, and now she didn't care the least bit about it. "When you put on more attractive clothes you feel less sick," Amà told her.

"Yeah, that's easy for you to say," replied Linda. "You always wear the same white dress." That made them both laugh heartily again.

Sometimes I felt a little left out, because they had so much fun and I couldn't join them. Linda knew this and told me as much as possible what was going on, involving me where she could. She repeated to me what Amà had told her and if it wasn't during the visualisation, then shortly afterwards. She asked Amà when she had passed because we felt that that couldn't have happened very long ago. Amà then said that she had been in a car accident a couple of years ago and she and her dog were both killed instantly.

Then Linda asked if Amà had to reincarnate again soon and Amà said that indeed she would go back again one day. In that life she would die very young, which would be very sad for her parents, but it would also be an important lesson for them.

"But not for a long while, don't you worry," she quickly reassured Linda.

I asked, thinking about this, if she was Linda's guardian angel. I knew that everyone on Earth has a guide, or guardian angel, a very conscious astral soul in the Spirit accompanying us on Earth, taking care that no unnecessary deviations from the life's plan are made, all out of pure Love and with respect to a soul's freedom of choice who has willingly chosen to learn certain lessons on Earth to grow in Love.

"I'm not her guardian angel," said Amà through Linda to me. "But I am a good friend of hers."

Besides Taksi and Amà there was another soul who visited us on the beach. That was Zebra, a funny zebra that wasn't just any zebra. He was obviously a very conscious being and though it wasn't said, I thought that he was perhaps a human soul who presented himself as a zebra to Linda; that worked better for her, was not so confronting, and while playing this role he could easily cheer her.

A couple of years ago I had designed a greeting card for a publishing company. Linda sometimes had put forward ideas that I then had developed and airbrushed. One such painting was a funny one, a zebra on a tropical beach before a colourful sunset, standing next to a small table and consuming a sorbet! It was one of Linda's favourite paintings and since then it has hung on our wall in the living room.

Once, Linda had just arrived at the beach when Zebra greeted her. He had a big straw hat on and stood before a table just like on the painting. He even had a straw in his mouth! That made us all laugh happily and since then Zebra often had that same hat. Sometimes he allowed Linda to sit on his back, but that wobbled of course and wasn't wise in relation to the risk of bleedings. I didn't understand, because this was still 'only' a visualisation? How could that hurt? But I didn't argue.

These visualisations were extremely important for Linda, for both of us by the way. Apart from the healing powers that visualisations are known to have, I'm convinced that we now had been given a contact with a Light Being from the Spirit World. Linda felt happy during the contacts with Amà. Happiness that even I could clearly feel, and for hours after a visualisation that strong feeling of joy stayed with me, no matter the intense difficult situation, helping me through much of the day. Wow... I really needed that!

The Curse

The first months of 2001 we were really on our own. Linda tried to spare friends and family and didn't want anyone to notice that she was ill. She only accepted visits when she felt good, because that was what we wanted. Because of this we were entirely dependent on each other, with only an occasional visit from someone who wouldn't take no for an answer. Mieke, my sister was one of those who managed to get through our blockade.

Another reason was that Linda couldn't stand crowds. A visit took a lot out of her, so she allowed that only occasionally. In fact, all was too much; flowers that someone had brought made the room fidgety with their bright colours and whimsical shapes. She loved flowers, no doubt about that, but no matter how beautiful they were, now she couldn't handle seeing them. Cooking smells, music, and television, all was too busy. It was only much later that I learned what this was all about, namely her very weakened energy field. This aspect of her illness was about to play a very important role in the future.

At some point in the middle of the night, after the failed water jar experiment, I suggested I keep a warm damp cloth to the sore spot low in her back. She allowed me to do so. So I kept a washcloth in warm water, squeezed it and put it to the aching spot. She was not impressed, nevertheless she asked for a warmer piece. That worked better, but an even hotter piece did much better. So much so, that from that moment on I was shuttling back and forth with 'red-hot' pieces for over an hour. I burned my fingers and my hands were hurting from squeezing, but this was exactly the right temperature.

Now we had a very convenient way to ease the pain locally for a short time and so this became part of our sleeping ritual we now applied several times a day, for during the nights she couldn't sleep at all. It even worked for more than a few days, unlike all else that I could think of.

There was one big problem, super sensitive as she was: she woke at every sound. Just a faint cracking of the wooden stairs, of something else anywhere in the house, caused by temperature changes, could wake her up, let alone a phone that was ringing, or a doorbell.

This then needed further measures to be taken. Of course the cats weren't allowed to disturb Linda so I made a barricade to the bedroom at the bottom of the stairs. That was something the cats thoroughly disagreed with. Like every cat they hate closed doors and blocked passageways. If a door is open they don't go through, but don't you dare close it! It's no coincidence that Saint Peter, guarding Heaven's Gate, asks every cat "Now what shall it be? In or out?"

So it came that one night my carefully constructed barricade came crashing down the lower stairs because of a powerful cat's actions: in itself quite amusing, but a disaster for Linda.

Unfortunately, despite all rituals and managed care it was impossible for Linda to sleep more than two or in rare cases three hours a day. And for that we had to work hard for the entire rest of the day.

During the first month of the New Year 2001 we had many appointments with Maria. During the second session one of Linda's past incarnations came up. Maria explained that an illness, just like an onion, has to be peeled layer by layer to get to the core. These layers can be minor illness-processes, but also emotional processes or even unfinished business from past incarnations.

For this Linda would lie down in an easy chair, and Maria would ask her to close her eyes and relax. Maria then took Linda's wrist to feel what was happening and also to check if Linda was honest in her answers. Because we had done many visualisations and so Linda could be easily led.

She ended up in a life as a woman somewhere, in a small fishing village. It was about one thousand years ago. The fishing community was poor and all the men spent long times together at sea. They left in small boats and came back many days later with the fish. The women of the village were then left alone. They were responsible for the upbringing of their children and were very dependent on each other. Fishing determined the revenues of the whole village and when the men returned there was joy everywhere. But life was hard and the people seemed to be very religious, because there was a church in the village with a priest who led the community.

As in her present life, the woman Linda had been in this past life 'saw' more than most people around her. Linda was not a clear clairvoyant, but she had a sharp vision and alertness. At school she did her job as good as possible, but legal measures, which were said to improve education, often resulted in more work and frustration, because they apparently were made from behind desks and not developed in real life. If the board wanted to implement some changes, Linda often foresaw if it was going to work out or not. But usually she was the only one and thus the only one who opened her mouth. Such was not always appreciated, because how could she possibly know if it was not even tested? Then it was hard to swallow for her that often it turned out she had been right, but without anyone of the board admitting it.

Something like this also featured in the fishing village. She had learned that the priest was not as honest as he seemed to be. He managed the community's money, but used it more for the church and for himself than for the community. "He buys nice trinkets with the money for the church," said Linda. She had discovered it and told the women about it. They heard her, but they were not easy to convince, because Linda could not prove it. She did her best to convince the women, because she thought it to be unfair that their husbands were away long times at sea under harsh and dangerous conditions; they were the ones who had to work so hard for that money. And then a priest who didn't spend any time at sea used that money for his own good. She found it unfair and so she incited the women to undertake something against the priest.

Finally she had them all together to talk to the priest about his behaviour. But he succeeded in bringing the women into doubt and isolated Linda. One by one they left her, afraid as they were before the priest or the power he represented, and Linda came to be on her own with it.

So far Maria seemed to agree with the story Linda told. I too felt, looking critically and cautiously, that Linda gave this information spontaneously. And then came a part that was remarkable.

Linda had had several discussions with the priest in the church and had accused him of violating her on one of these occasions. There was a single certain event that was clear in her mind. She also remembered another moment when she chased the priest with his own cross trying to hit him with the cross. Later, at home she had to laugh when she told it to me in more detail. She had been running after the priest, hitting him wherever she could with the long cross.

Maria, or Dottore, clearly disagreed with this and asked Linda to take a better look. What Linda reported wasn't right, she said, but she did not say what, because Linda had to tell it herself. She protested, but eventually it came out that it wasn't the priest who had violated Linda, but that she had provoked the priest and later accused him of sexual abuse in front of the entire community. The conclusion was: it was her own doing.

I myself have undergone a fair number of such regression sessions and they all follow a similar pattern. It is a very good method of bringing into consciousness old and forgotten traumas that frustrate people in the present, and to raise awareness of certain obstacles in the present that are linked to events in the past. Unprocessed traumas, even those from past lives, can eventually weaken a person's health and make them sick. Yet such a therapy only works if it is done without bias. In addition the information from a patient must come out voluntarily, without pressure. The one who guides the session must therefore ask the right questions. This is an intuitive technique that asks for creativity and experience. However, if properly applied, it can be very enlightening, because it raises consciousness of the link between present problems and forgotten causes in the past. Thus it can happen that suddenly people start crying during the session. Deep traumas are then worked out when the pressure is released, resulting in more clarity, making life much easier afterwards.

But in this case, something wasn't adding up, because Maria kept asking Linda questions until she admitted that she was the one seducing the priest instead. Later that day when we talked about it again, Linda repeated to me that the priest had raped her and not the other way, but because she was afraid that Maria wouldn't treat her anymore if she had stuck to her original story, she had admitted the other way.

It is not normal for a regression therapist at this stage to know where the regression is leading. This is usually only evident when the patient tells it himself. However, it could be that Linda refused to accept her own role in the story. Anyway, to me she insisted that the priest was the culprit.

Now that she had put the blame on herself Maria asked Linda what exactly were the priest's words to her in the church? Because Linda couldn't tell at that moment, she was allowed to think it over at home and tell this during the next session. Together at home we devised a plausible answer that hopefully would satisfy Maria, "For this thou shall bleed".

The next session was a few days later and Maria was content with this answer, and then it became clear what had happened next. Because Linda had seduced the priest and later had tried to blame him in front of the community, the priest cursed her. A curse in itself isn't that evil, Maria explained, but a curse with the power of the entire church behind it, is extremely powerful and can be at work even in later incarnations. Apparently the core of this curse was indeed, "For this thou shall bleed".

The way this information had come out was wrong. Even now I can't tell what is true and what's not true, but my impression is that the questions Maria asked were leading the witness. In a court such questioning would be forbidden immediately. As a result, not all of Linda's responses came from her unconsciousness, but from her mind, resulting in a mixture of truth and fantasy. Then what's the therapeutic value?

All in all... apparently there was a curse, which haunted Linda even after a thousand years, making her sick. Dottore had given Maria the knowledge and resources to neutralize this curse, because Maria had done so before in a few previous likewise situations. Instructed by Dottore, she had crafted a wooden cross, and he had also given her citations that she had to use during a ritual that she would perform during the next session with Linda. This ritual was to be repeated three times and only then the ancient curse would be lifted and the actual treatment could be started.

You Walk A Lonely Road

By no means was anything going fast enough for us, because Linda was desperate to get rid of the pain and the incidental bleedings. This placed a tremendous strain on our lives that was almost unsustainable. The endless nights were long and dark, but now even the days were hard to survive.

The problem was caused by the medication Linda had been prescribed. For the bleedings she used Cyclokapron, an agent that works by narrowing the blood vessels. Paracetamol however has a vasoligating effect. Linda discovered that the effects of Paracetamol were undone within minutes after she took Cyclokapron. It was an impossible combination.

In order to still take both drugs our days had to be split up in four segments of six hours. Such mini days followed a set pattern. Once she woke up Linda would try to remain in bed as long as possible, because the pain was still manageable. Then she would wake me and I would cook some food, or do whatever needed to be done. We set an alarm to warn us when she had to take another Cyclokapron. Immediately thereafter the pain increased considerably, but before Linda could take Paracetamol to ease the pain she had to wait at least two hours, or it would have no effect at all. Then was my time of helping Linda to heal one way or another, to ease the pain as much as possible, because the less pain she had the better she would sleep.

Such a schedule is extremely exhausting and meant that we went to bed and got up and ate at the oddest times of the day and the night.

Linda's biggest problem, in addition to pain and lack of sleep, was that she had nothing to do. She didn't dare leave the house except for the visits to Maria. She was unable to read a book, the television was much too vibrant, and all that needed concentration was out of the question. What she could do was to call people who could advise her, help her, or just wanted to listen to her. Some sent or gave her energy and some even could provide physical help. But most of all she talked to her worried parents, who never put the phone down, were always available, and always had something to talk about.

During that period I was barely able to complete my freelance work as a calligrapher, let alone do the household chores. The kitchen was a battlefield. When shopping I behaved like a prize winner having won five minutes of free shopping, on the run at lightning speed grabbing all sorts of things from the shelves that maybe would be needed. In rare cases I used the vacuum cleaner and threw a few things in corners, as long as it was out of the way. But taking care of the cats was the only thing I never skipped.

Gradually I began to experience a very heavy tight feeling in my chest, a feeling that comes with not getting enough sleep over a long period. It was like I was gasping for breath just to get enough. In retrospect I now find it hard to comprehend how we kept it up. I think it was mainly possible because there were many people supporting us, thought of us in silence, prayed for us, sent us energy, lit a candle, and who knows what else. Likely there were more people aware of our situation than we knew of. Not only people on earth but, as you now understand, we also got a lot of help from the Spirit World, the Other Side, though we were only aware of Amà and Zebra.

During the month of February my mother and my sister announced that they would come to help us at home. Protesting was not an option, they were coming and that was that. On the phone I always said things were okay, or something vague, but obviously that wasn't true, Linda just couldn't stand the energy of busy people in the house. Of course there were organizations like Home Care, but because we had never been in need of them I didn't think of that as an option. Apart from that, I was unable to predict in advance when we would be awake to open the door and let people in. Linda's sleep periods were more important than anything else, so even if we were already eligible for home care, the question remains if we were ready for that kind of support.

I was very concerned about Linda's weight. After the first tests at the end of 1999, her weight had dropped from fifty two to forty five kilograms. She had never been able to regain these seven kilograms, but at least the first year there was no further drop in weight. However, when the bleedings started her weight began to drop, because her body lost huge amounts of essential nutrients. In January she weighed only forty-two or forty three kilograms.

Several weeks before that Linda had been prescribed a potent analgesic, Tramadol. It was said that this was a very effective, long lasting and safe painkiller, but because Linda was so hypersensitive she was very reluctant to use it. One evening however, she said she would try this instead of the usual Paracetamol. She took a tablet and we spent a couple of hours working through the usual ritual before sleeping. But nothing happened and she didn't feel sleepy at all. The pain was unchanged.

"Now what!" she said disappointed. "This doesn't work at all and I can't use different painkillers at the same time. Now I have to wait a long time before I can take anything else!"

I looked again at the box and read that it said 'one to two tablets at a time'. Perhaps the dosage was too low. After some protest she agreed to it and again we worked through the sleeping ritual, again without success.

Then she felt sick, nauseous. She began to gag and vomit. All the food from that evening came out again. If there was something I was afraid of, then this was it. So much effort into getting her something to eat, and because of such a stupid synthetic pill all these efforts were in vain. I felt really bad about pushing her into taking a second pill. And if it wasn't enough, she kept vomiting the whole night, until only green bile came out.

Needless to say that her final weight the next day had dropped several ounces. Indeed the pain afterwards had eased for a few hours, but now she felt so bad that sleeping was impossible. What a price for a few hours of pain relief!

Since then, we were very careful with other pain relievers, perhaps too cautious. However, during the course we tested several types. If you have so much pain, then you are likely to be influenced by the wonderful stories about the latest pain medications that work so very well, are absolutely harmless, etc. etc. We discussed this with our family doctor and tried various painkillers, but always without the desired result. Linda simply was too sensitive.

This adverse reaction to medication, so I learned much later, was also to be related to the loss of her protective energy field, her aura. Only at that time we didn't know that. Finally we did the only sensible thing and we stuck to what worked, if only for a little while, Paracetamol.

Maria performed the ritual to lift the curse three times. She muttered softly the Latin quotations dictated by Dottore while she moved the wooden cross back and forth over Linda's body. It looked very mystic but we hoped that this curse was finally reversed. Then she proceeded with another incarnation of Linda's. That life appeared to be very similar to the first, because Linda's role was again that of a single rebel fighting against a representative of the Roman Catholic Church, in a struggle for justice. The circumstances were different, but essentially she did the same thing, though it didn't result in being cursed.

The third incarnation was a curious one. That one must have been only a few hundred years ago. Linda had been educated in what could be compared to the 'modern scientific healthcare system', being the village physician for the local population. He, because she was a man in that life, was very convinced of himself, and rejected the special knowledge and methods of those who had been raised from birth to become a local herbs specialist, usually a herb woman. From what I learned from Linda after we got home from this session, she believed that this could very well be true. But she had learned from that incarnation she said, and saw things with very different eyes now.

The impact of those two incarnations was not even close to that of the first one. An interesting detail was the medium, and thus Dottore, was working under the umbrella of the same church. When the medium went into trance, all the volunteers and present clients sang the Roman version of 'Our Father'. In the practice there was even a picture of the medium in conversation with the Holy Pope in Rome, who apparently knew about her work.

Now that all this had been said and done Maria gave Linda a few tiny grains of a homeopathic remedy, the purpose of which was to cure a certain aspect of her illness; one of the shells around the inner core of her disease problem, so to speak.

Besides Linda's past lives, her present life was a point of discussion, as was to be expected. The point was to discover what event had contributed to the onset of her illness, how she had reacted to those events and whether they still unconsciously gnawed at her in some way. At one point I too became involved in the conversation, because I might be able to add something to Linda's story. I called it Linda's hard work. She was so into her work, was such a perfectionist that all of her time and energy went in it. This was true, but then I made a remark that I would come to regret very much... I continued to say that I sometimes felt wronged and felt sorry that she had so little time. She was always working, always tired so that we hardly had time for each other. While I said this I realized that this could be misinterpreted, but as Maria led the conversation, there was no opportunity for me to elaborate on this. Unintentionally my words may have sounded a little accusing, but once spoken, words can't be erased and have to be dealt with.

In the car on the way home I already felt my comment was wrong. Linda asked again for the comment and I tried to explain, but couldn't find the right words and even reinforced what I had said. She kept silent after that. Back home we did the things we normally did. I gave her the Cyclokapron and later the Paracetamol. She ate her food, but all the time I felt an atmosphere of accusation. Or was it disappointment? I saw it in the way she looked at me. I saw it in her posture, even as I watched her from behind. She didn't speak to me and wouldn't tell me exactly what was troubling her. I felt something had gone wrong, but didn't understand what had made this impact on her, and I couldn't figure it out on my own.

Her fighting spirit was gone. I felt miserable and tiptoed around her because she gave me no chance to discuss and rectify whatever it was had gone wrong. I felt I was losing my *vriendinnetje* and asked God to help us. *Something* had gone wrong. Now how could we move on from here?

The next day, without speaking she took a few blank sheets with crayons and started drawing. I sat there, but she didn't respond to me in any way, as if I didn't exist. Her movements were brusque and angular, and I didn't know what else to do than to wait and see what was coming on paper. Linda sketched a hole from above. It was a pit, black as the night, and from it there was a raised hand with fingers spread wide open.

I started talking, because I thought I understood what was going on, and that was that she was seeking help; that she had now reached rock bottom, totally left on her own. I was thinking that she had always been so strong and tough, that she had never been dependent on others and therefore never had to ask for help, and that she was finally able to do so.

I said all this, but it was a monologue because she didn't respond. I said that I was always with her; that I would help her to climb out of the pit, help her to find the steps.

I bet it wasn't all psychologically justified what I said, but eventually she began talking again. I felt I still hadn't touched the core of what it was really about. I was guessing and feeling uncomfortable, feeling that tension and that horrible uncertainty that I had done something completely wrong, without understanding what it was.

Then I came to what I had said yesterday. I felt perfectly well that something went wrong there, but it didn't dawn on me what exactly. I told her I didn't blame her for the fact that there was so little time for us both to give to each other; the situation was simply like that. I felt I was starting to touch the core of the problem. I was getting warmer.

"But you did say it!" she said, breaking the silence. "And not even directly to me."

She had done so much for me. After all, I didn't have a steady job, didn't earn the money to pay for our living. I could always stay at home, do freelance work and write certificates, while she was working every day at school and every night, even during most weekends, struggling to complete the work. She was always tired and never had time or energy for her to have some fun, to express her creativity. And she was so very creative!

She was the breadwinner really, and it was only for the last few years that I had some income that contributed a share worthy of being seen. Never had she complained about that. That is a gift, truly remarkable.

I thought I had always realized this, but in fact I have to admit that the true depth of this gift first struck me there and then, and even now that I write it down, I again feel that I never had really realised how big this gift was.

So why did I make such a comment to Maria? That was what really hurt her, much more than I had realized. I had hit her in her soul... words from the mouth of her only *vriendje*, for whom she worked so hard. She just didn't understand that and she felt terribly disappointed.

Of course we had discussed this more than once, and I've often wondered if I should have done more to secure a permanent job. I was trained as a teacher, but felt most uncomfortable before a class of kids. Linda knew that and would never ask me to do the same work that was draining her energy. I had followed other training courses, but had failed to find a permanent job as a calligrapher. Now that my freelance work had started to pay off quite well I didn't bother to search for such a job anymore.

It took a long time and I needed many words to make it clear that I was sorry I had said what I had, that it wasn't justified. "I love you!" I told her. "I would like nothing more than you to get healthy again. That's what we fight for! That's what you are struggling for to achieve, for me, for your parents, and for our pussycats."

She didn't respond immediately to all that I had said, but I felt that the tension slowly disappeared, and that she started behaving normally with me again. She had forgiven me.

And as for me... I had learned a very important lesson!

We still had an appointment for the end of February with Roberto the naturopath, made well before the first bleedings had started. But Maria had clearly stated that there can only be one captain on a ship and so we didn't know what to do with this appointment. Linda needed something to show her that things were improving and Roberto's measurements could show that. We were working with Maria two months now and saw no progress. Although the bleedings occurred less, they were not gone. Linda couldn't reduce the Cyclokapron, and all that Maria had given her so far was a few grains of a homeopathic remedy.

There was no real trust between Maria and Linda. Maria could demand that Linda believe in her but this type of faith is a matter of the heart and can't be demanded. The only reason we hadn't seen Roberto was the bleedings, because as a result of them Linda didn't dare travel so far. Eventually we decided to go to Roberto, but then openly discuss all

Roberto would say with Maria. Linda wouldn't take anything without Maria's permission. All Roberto was allowed to do was the testing and to show the results.

The meeting with Roberto proved to be like seeing an old friend. He was really happy to see us, as were we. His measurements corresponded with Maria's findings, which assured Linda that Maria did a good job.

We had planned to be completely open with Maria, and so I phoned her to say that we had seen Roberto and that he came to the same conclusions as she did. We didn't want to hide things from her, I added, but it would have been better had I not phoned her at all. She reacted as if she had been slapped up the face. She had demanded one hundred per cent trust and faith in her, and this demonstrated that we didn't have that. So she withdrew and cancelled all the remaining appointments.

We hardly could believe what we were hearing. We discussed everything with her and now this! So then Linda phoned Maria herself, and finally she agreed to discuss things with Dottore. Surely he would understand?

Apparently so, because a few days later Maria called us and acted friendly again. However, she agreed to one more appointment to test a few things, and that was it. The treatments were not continued.

Maria's attitude was typical of too many people who felt that Linda went way too far in her way of drawing attention to herself. I think that attitude was caused by the fact that Linda absolutely didn't look like she had a serious disease. She had undergone neither chemotherapy nor radiation. So she still had all her long hair intact and when other people saw her she looked at her best, beautiful. She dressed well then and knew how to use make-up. A cancer patient? Nothing revealed that. And yet she demanded so much attention from Dottore. After all, there were many more very ill patients. It simply didn't fit.

There was something else that I didn't realize then. Linda and I were very closely connected to each other. Her illness demanded everything from us. All our energy, time, and even every minute of our sleep were sacrificed to this cause. Unlike Linda, who used make-up to hide the marks, this was obvious when looking at my face. I looked grey and drawn out because of the lack of sleep. People sometimes asked me how I could go on like this, thereby implying that Linda demanded far too much from me, and I found myself defending Linda at such times.

Our choices implied that Linda, in her fight to survive, demanded a huge toll on me, but this came from the misunderstanding that seriously ill people go to a hospital. Instead our battleground was at home, so how can she be that ill? You see, Linda's choices were my choices; she wasn't on her own. We were connected, and together you're strong! That way you fight together for what you're worth! That's oneness!

We noticed that none of our other therapists had any problem that we consulted other therapists. After all, in a hospital several specialists work together to treat patients.

Faith... one hundred percent faith doesn't come by flicking a switch and saying "From now on I have one hundred percent faith in you." This is a matter of Love. You give your trust to each other by saying that you believe in each other totally. Such faith is built over years, or it comes from deep within, out of love, like Amà effortlessly had gotten our total trust.

Can you... may you then *demand* total trust? And isn't that something completely different, something that comes with a totally different name, *surrender*?

But hospitals were no different. They too demanded total surrender. Alternatives were not accepted and their position was exceptionally strong. Most people find that very normal, like the way things are. Or they don't know any better, and so that system works for them.

But Linda wasn't a normal patient.

You walk a lonely road.
O how far you are from home...

A Victory?

There were many people aware of our struggle committed to us, far more than we realized at that moment. I screened Linda from all contacts I knew she couldn't handle or didn't have the energy for, but some people managed to get through for their kindness and non-judgemental attitude.

Kevin was such a man, a wonderfully friendly man who could get along with Linda and also had certain magnetic gifts, which he offered free of charge. At first we didn't think highly of him, but he was very quiet and when he started working with Linda our opinion changed. While Linda sat on a chair, he made strange gestures around her, quite different than I was used to seeing a magnetizer doing, but after only a few minutes Linda's pain subsided! We were impressed. How could this be?

According to Linda he was welcome to come every day then, but he didn't have so much time and besides that he said that it wouldn't be good either. Every four or five days he came, and after a couple of visits Linda asked him how far she had come in her healing process. He kept silent for a few minutes and suddenly he measured a good distance at the edge of the table, saying "This is how far you have to go." Then he measured a very small distance within that stretch and said, "This is how far you are now."

"Such a short distance!" Linda said. But she didn't sound very disappointed. Kevin seemed to get his knowledge from somewhere deep inside and he could handle her very well. His honest answer felt good in a strange way.

Sorting out her school cabinets, an activity Linda had taken on during long nights to distract her focus from the pain had long since finished. She had sorted out a few other things, but that too was finished and now she couldn't think of anything to do.

"Now what!" she said to me more than once. Neither of us had an answer. Almost everything required concentration, and sorting things out had been a physical activity most of the time. Reading a book was out of the question. Watching TV was too loud and she certainly couldn't handle the busy movements and bright colours on the screen. We tried playing a simple card game but she could only do that for fifteen minutes. Lying in bed also caused her pain, and so she went walking again back and forth in the living room for hours. Sometimes she walked like a crooked old woman with two hands on her aching back, moaning in pain. She preferred doing this in the dark, without heat. I kept around so she wasn't alone. Usually I had something warm at hand, like socks and a soft sweater, but she refused them most of the time, saying that when she got too warm the pain would increase. She sometimes insisted that I would go to bed. What was I going to do with a crooked, ugly monster that could only talk about pain walking back and forth the room?

I wouldn't leave her like this, trying to comfort her by talking to her, looking for conversation. I knew how important it was that she didn't feel like she was facing her illness on her own. But one night I discovered another reason that I was glad I hadn't gone to bed to sleep.

Sometimes the pain was so bad...

On a freezing cold night, while it was snowing outside, she took the house keys and went to the door to the garden. She turned the key and opened the door. I asked what she was up to but she shrugged and said nothing. She wanted to step outside but the only thing she was wearing was her nightgown!

"Out?" I asked. "You're crazy! It's snowing! You'll freeze in the cold and you'll get pneumonia. How are you going to get better then?"

I walked up to her and grabbed her softly by the shoulders. I sensed that she was about to burst into tears. "I can't," she sobbed, "I can't do this anymore! I want to fight so much... for you and for the kitties, but how am I supposed to do this? Don't they understand this up there? Things can sometimes be too much, you know!"

I really tried everything to persuade her to cheer up. But I could only think of so few things to say. What do you say in a situation like that? "Be quiet now little one... all is good? Do not worry? Trust me? Dry your tears? It will pass?

In a movie this always works. The heroine with tears running down her cheeks, who is comforted by her lover, only looks more beautiful with the glossy tears. How romantic! A true love story!

This movie was so different. This was the real thing, as hard as it gets, nothing to romance. A few comforting words won't help here. I couldn't think of anything to say that would even remotely comfort her. There was nothing I could do against the pain. Nothing and no one could do that. "Tears let it all out," they say. But they didn't now. It was awful!

After standing in the open door for some time she allowed me to turn her around and hold her in my arms for a short while. I held her head, tears streaming down her face. She had become ice cold. I talked and said many silly things to her. I don't remember the words anymore. All that mattered was that I was with her, talking to her, so she could hear my voice and didn't feel alone.

I was glad that I could stop her walking out of the door in the middle of the night while it was snowing and freezing. What if I had been sleeping while she went into the garden? Then I probably would have found her under a bush somewhere? I would never forgive myself. What if it happened again? I even wondered if I *should* restrain her, but I pushed those questions away quickly. I didn't want to think about them.

A few nights later a similar incident occurred. The Cyclokapron had just neutralized the working of the painkiller and the pain quickly became unbearable. Linda felt terrible in the small bedroom and said that she was going downstairs. I asked what she was going to do, but of course I knew the answer, walking. She accepted the warm socks I held up and even put on a pair of jogging pants and a sweater! She told me that I could stay upstairs. Semiconscious, a low alarm went off in my mind, because my heart began to beat.

"Oh dear," I thought.

She went downstairs and I followed her closely. She first went to the bathroom and started combing her hair in front of the mirror. It felt very strange to see her busying herself like this as if she was going to work like in better days without the illness. But this time she acted aloof, did not speak to me, and her body language told me she didn't want me to help her with anything.

When you live together, love each other; you become sensitive to each other. Only a faint indication is enough to know something is out of the ordinary, be it positive or negative. I now felt distance between us. My heart felt squeezed in my chest; tension, and I felt like I had to be so careful, like walking on broken glass. All because of just a few words, but maybe more so by what she didn't say.

She was ready in the bathroom and walked down the stairs. I didn't understand, because we hadn't quarrelled. Why did I still feel so bad then? What was going on here? What was she up to?

Then suddenly I ran upstairs, grabbed my pants and my sweater and hastily ran down the stairs again, paused a few seconds on the first floor wondering whether I should follow, but then ran down the second stairway. She was sitting beside the table, busy pulling on her boots.

"Where are we going?" I asked in an ordinary tone, while I damn well knew she was going to do something without my company. She didn't react, as if she didn't hear me. I felt out of breath, my heart was beating strangely. It was like we were fighting, without anything being said like that.

She had her boots on and looked in her school bag for the house keys, a gesture that belonged to the morning ritual of going to school. I decided not to pretend I didn't know what she was looking for, but brazenly put on my shoes a little further in the room. Whatever she was up to, there was no time to waste if I had to follow her. Meanwhile she grabbed her coat and looked for something on the shelf in the kitchen. She couldn't find it, was impatient, and finally had to break the silence, saying, "Where are the car keys?"

She wanted to go by car? What were her plans? Driving? To where? To her parents? Where else? Where can you go in the middle of the night?

"They aren't there," I said. "They're in my pocket."

I felt empowered because I could now decide whether she should have the keys or not. But I went to get my coat and grabbed the keys from a pocket. I wanted to say that she could only go together with me but I knew it would be counterproductive if I forced her into a corner. So I gave her the keys and asked, "Shall I drive?"

Without saying anything she took the keys, opened the door and pulled it immediately behind her.

Semi panicking, I looked on the shelf. I knew there was a second set of car keys and I threw everything aside, but luckily I found them quick, grabbed my coat and ran out of the door. She was already in the car seat, trying to adjust it, so I unlocked and opened the passenger door and sat beside her.

"What are you doing?" she said. "Don't you get it?"

I shrugged my shoulders. "I don't know where you're going, but I'll go with you."

This was so double sided... actually I loved it sitting beside her like that on the passenger seat, like nothing was wrong. She always drove because she got nauseous otherwise. The last time was many months ago and now I realized how much I missed that feeling, but now there was something terrible wrong that alarmed me.

"I have to go alone," she said. "You must stay here with our kitties."

"Then where are you going?" I asked. "To your parents?"

She didn't answer.

I tried to think of something but it did not dawn on me, because I didn't dare think of that one option. What could she be doing now at this hour with a car? She had no bag of clothes with her. But then... she had brought nothing at all.

Wait... I had a very nasty suspicion.

"So do you want to drive into a tree or something?"

She paused for a while...

"Something like that." She muttered it more than she said it. She stared into space. Something had snapped inside her. It was out.

I searched for words... couldn't find them.

What do you say to something who's going to commit suicide?

I had no idea.

Finally I asked, "And so you had to comb your hair?"

Slowly I got from her what she was going to do. She wanted to drive the car into the canal. That was what seemed easiest. No one would be injured that way, no accidents. I would be fine; I could take care of the cats very well, she had seen that. Her parents, brothers and I would grieve but we would get over it. It was better this way.

I said I would be worrying intensely if she were going to do that because I wouldn't know where she had gone. I wouldn't know where to look. I would blame myself that I had done wrong. I would have failed. The cats would miss her. Her parents had already lost a son and now a daughter too?

I knew I had to be careful of what I was saying otherwise I would push her away from me, making it easier to continue her plans. Her life was at stake. I think I tried talking to her conscience, making her feeling guilty should she see it through.

Eventually she went inside with me. But it didn't feel like a victory for I had not convinced her. For now she was back in the house. I knew that tonight nothing would happen again, but tomorrow, and after tomorrow? How many nights like this would there be?

I thought of something to prevent it. I hid the keys. But tired as I was I didn't memorize the spot and so it happened a few days later that we were going to see Roberto and I couldn't find the car keys. There I was, with Linda impatiently standing behind me. I felt pretty stupid when I retrieved the keys from under the carpet. An absurd place!

"You did not really think I would drive the car into the canal?" she asked quietly, almost apologetically. "I could never do such a thing."

She really surprised me there. It was just as if she was someone completely different and had no suicidal thoughts at all. Could she do something like that? No way. What was I thinking?

I kept silent for a few moments. "Then you really played the part well," I said.

I felt relieved, but also realized the seriousness of the situation, the danger always lurking... and the dilemma...

Can you stop someone who wants to commit suicide? *Should* you stop someone? Is it an obligation? And what about people who are in so much pain? They have good reasons, do they not?

What would I do in the same situation?

Acceptance

In April Dottore would be in Holland again, but April didn't come fast. A winter never lasted as long as this time. Every day was a struggle and all the time Linda's life hung by a thread. April... oh if it would only be April already! Then Linda would probably have regained some of her health and with the help of Dottore she could get completely better.

Without the guidance of Maria we were cautiously trying to decrease the amounts of Cyclokapron that Linda took. This went well, because for many weeks now she hardly suffered from bleedings.

A few times per week Linda called a friend of mine, Sattia, who had knowledge of Eastern meditation, Buddhism, and of the related art of healing. He suggested that Linda would say the mantra 'Om Nama Shivaya'. Not once, but, as is usual with mantras, thousands of times, or that she would write down the name 'Hanuman' eight thousand times at least.

The power of materialization, the power of thought creation, calling for help, placing yourself in the Light, we understood the importance of all this, and started implementing the singing of mantras into our daily rituals, usually at bedtime. Often when Linda was walking up and down the room at night, crippled by pain, she would repeat those words: Om Nama Shivaya. For hours, monotonous, sometimes without any power left in her voice to barely hear the words.

Praying was something we never did, apart from Linda in school with the students. The few times I prayed I didn't feel at ease so to start praying now was something I considered hypocritical like 'never pray unless the going gets so tough you're thinking if it doesn't work then there's no harm done'. That kind of praying I considered rubbish. When you pray then you should try to be sincere, but when are you? Was I honest when I now started praying or was it just an opportunistic cry for help?

"Almighty Father... .
It's not my habit to pray.
That I'm doing so now is in fact only because my vriendinnetje,

Linda, is so very ill.
I ask you to help her.
But I know it might not be the highest intention that she will heal.
That's not what I want to ask.
As a matter of fact I don't even want to ask your help.
I know we already get it from you and your helpers.
Thank you for all the help that is around us.
I feel it not, but I do know.
It has to be, otherwise we would never have made it this far.
Thank you for everything.
Amen."

For me that was a long prayer. I have never prayed often, and even now I rarely do. It is still not in my nature to do so as a standard practice, no matter how sensible it may be. Faith as 'prescribed' by the church wasn't our thing. We didn't need a religion to know that there is a higher realm, that there is a one God. We even had contact with this world and it felt so good. And it was in this contact we really felt this... Love.

But I really meant what I was praying then. Well... basically everything in me shouted one word, HELP!!!" But I had this idea that the Great Spirit or the Almighty One - I don't like the word 'god' so much - was very well aware of our situation and would never abandon us. If the Almighty One really was Love then it would hurt him to see his, or her, children suffer like this. He would, in his infinite Love, never abandon one single creature. If he allowed something like this to happen then there certainly had to be a very important reason. But... then it had to be a reason that was totally beyond our comprehension. The words Linda cried out so often still reverberate in my head: "Why then? Why? This doesn't make any sense. Should I learn something from this? Well, now I know! Enough is enough! Why is this? Why! Why!! Tell me!"

Then she looked at me with intrusive eyes, asking, demanding even, for help. Angry, desperate, abandoned. Or she would cry it out, upwards, to whoever was listening up there, if someone listened at all, because she couldn't see it. The pain didn't decrease, only got worse, so surely nobody could be listening. Did they? Wasn't she left in the lurch then?

I couldn't answer. It was very strange, but actually I knew the answer, or at least part of it, without being able to say or describe it in words. At least not in words she would accept, because that was what it was really all about.

I knew my *vriendinnetje* now for almost eighteen years and was full of admiration for her. In my eyes she always looked very self-assured, full of self-confidence, conviction. With her my existence got more meaning. She would never do anything without a good reason. If there was some injustice in her eyes or something wasn't right, she would take action to set things right. She would think of solutions, she might defend me with passion, or she would push her colleagues to stand their ground and make a point, just like she had done in those previous incarnations. At school there were plenty such situations. If she failed or if something simply wouldn't work for whatever reason, she would have a hard time. She couldn't stand that. This resistance, this not being able to resign, not being able to let go of what can't be changed was something she had trouble with. At school, in her family, with the cats... there were many such situations. If she didn't succeed, or something couldn't be solved for whatever reason, she would wreck her head thinking about it. She then looked for solutions, for something that could be done about it. If that meant she had to spend a lot of her own time and energy to make it work, then so be it. If one of her parents or her grandmother was very ill... then we would go there, for an hour, the afternoon, all night if necessary; we would stay there, doing errands, going to hospital, whatever, and after midnight we would go back home. And if needed, we would do this for months, sometimes three times a week.

Of course... then all work for school still had to be done. If the situation required it according to her, then she could efface herself completely. She did this for me, for her family, for the school, and, as she had proven last year, she also would do this for herself, fighting her own disease. If you put your mind to it, pump enough energy into it, have sufficient options, if you have enough cards in your hand to play so to speak... then any problem is solvable? Is it not?

However... what if the situation goes over your head, and despite all your tremendous efforts you cannot prevent all from going its own way, or even going totally out of control? What if you are getting sicker and start to have more and more pain, what if you start to lose the battle? What then? How do you cope with that?

Of course we talked a lot to each other about what was wrong with her, looking for reasons, looking for answers, looking for solutions, things we could do about it, or if things made sense in some way. Why was she in so much pain? Why all these bleedings? Why didn't the painkillers work? Why couldn't she sleep?

"Maybe you need to learn to accept," I said at one point, finally feeling brave enough to withstand the coming storm, expecting her reaction.

"WHAT do I have to accept?" she cried out.

That was the reaction I meant to point out. Withstand the storm...

"Do I have to accept that they are messing around with the notes I've given my students after working with them all year long? Let's give this one an extra point because that looks better? And so we climb in ranks in the Daily Magazine's contest 'Best School of the Year'? Must I accept that the cats are fighting with each other? Should I accept stray dogs murdering our ducks in the park, because all bushes are cut away and some locals refuse to leash their dogs? Should I just accept that? And then this pain! How can I accept this pain then? How should I accept this disease? How can I? How can they ask this of me?"

In moments like that one... me looking for answers just like she was, in the middle of a situation like that, a situation you have a very hard time with, I had the greatest trouble in giving her any sort of answer at all. What do you say in this situation? Should I have told her that she simply had to accept it? That she couldn't do anything about it? That it was predestination? That she shouldn't care a bit? That she just had to turn away from it? "Be quiet girl, things will be fine... it will pass?"

In moments like that one... I had no answer.

"I don't know," I said with a faint shaking of my head and shrugging my shoulders. "I really don't know."

Maybe it is a good reason to look for help from above, ask God, or Allah, or Shiva for answers that would give meaning to all of it, to make sense of it. Or should I say 'make sense of the nonsense'? Because that's how it felt.

Partly because of this we started doing what we had never done before... mantra chanting. Well, Linda did that already with the words 'Om Nama Shivaya', but she did that without understanding it fully. Mantras are similar to prayers, singing sacred texts. The ways the words are sung are as important as the words themselves. At first it was our intention to just do *something*, anything at all.

In those days we thought that with the singing of sacred mantras you ask the help of certain higher forces in the universe. From then to now I began to think it is a little different. You don't ask the universe to come to you, but it's the other way; when you raise your vibration by singing mantras *you* are more connected to the universe.

Whatever the effect of all these mantras was, in retrospect I know that we really did connect to the cosmos, to a divine power. A force we were yet to need very much soon.

A long Road

From the cat's room we could see that the cherry tree in front of the window had begun to flourish. Each year the tree grew more beautiful and bigger. We had seen it planted as a small tree, and now it was a mature tree. The first thing the tree did in early spring was to bloom exuberantly. Notwithstanding its beauty, Linda wasn't just happy with it. "I need space," she said. "I get short of breath when I cannot see the sky. It suffocates me. Soon the petals fall off, but then big green leaves take their space and I won't see any sky then."

I now know that this too had to do with her failing energy field. People who are seriously ill and weak suffer from this, in this case the extra sensitivity for narrow spaces. Alas, I then didn't know how to do anything about it.

The reduction of the Cyclokapron didn't ease her pain and sleeplessness as much as we had hoped for. In mid-March she only took three-quarters instead of two or three pills, but this hardly made a difference. As soon as she took any dosage the pain got worse within minutes. Still we were very careful to taper off, because we were convinced that these pills were for her bleeding, and we wouldn't take any chances, certainly not when the previous month showed virtually no blood loss at all.

We had worked it out so that when Dottore was in Holland again, Linda would be ready with the toxoplasmosis treatment and would have the reduced the Cyclokapron dosage to zero. We believed that which was started by Maria, would be completed by Dottore. He was a doctor in the Spirit World. He could even perform surgery from there. He had access to past lives of patients, as we had already experienced. He assisted earthly surgeons by guiding their hands. He accompanied therapists like Maria who could communicate with him. In short, no earthly physician or therapist could compete with him. His skills were practically unlimited. And most importantly, he worked from the God Source, from unconditional Love.

Only in the last few weeks in April, when the dosage was less than a quarter of a pill, did Linda feel a difference, with the pain staying at lower levels. No one could advise us in this. I once had done some research about Cyclokapron, asking what was known about side effects, dosages, etc. I then was redirected from hospital to hospital and reconnected from specialist to specialist. Suddenly I found myself in the protected internal telephone circuit between specialists, where outsiders have no business at all. I got questions regarding my background that I tried avoiding at first. Why did I need to know this? Was I doing research for a study? What patient did I have? With such complaints and such drug usage, treatment should be done in hospital, why isn't this the case? Are you a specialist or a GP? Oooh... .. You're not a doctor! And suddenly it felt like doors slamming in my face and the conversation became very hostile.

I didn't give up and finally the best method was to be as open and honest as possible, saying that I was a non-initiate, which of course I was, but I didn't feel like that anymore. I made it clear how I got their number, and sometimes even said that we had consciously chosen an alternative route to treat Linda. Gradually I found the right approach and then it appeared that friendly specialists did exist.

However, I got contradicting answers. One said that this medication could be used without any problem. No harm done. Side effects like Linda experienced were unheard of, because there were patients, mostly women, with severe menstrual bleeding, using it for years without any problems. Someone else however told me that this medication made no sense in Linda's situation, it didn't work. Next I got a scientific story about clotting factors, deficits or abnormalities in the blood in some patients, for whom this medication was developed. In cases such like Linda's it would have no effect. Weaning off the dosage was not necessary because there was no physical dependence.

Aha... was that so?

In that case Linda had used these awful pills for nothing all this time? Had we gone through this misery 24/7 for nothing? Did that mean she would have had much less pain, could have slept better, her total condition would be much better and I wouldn't be totally exhausted? Could that really have been the case?

We didn't worry about that too much, it simply was as it was. Still, it gnawed and added more weight to our sense of loneliness. Anyway, she was on very low dosage now and it was such a relief! Instead of six hours per mini-day we now were able to lengthen these days to seven hours and longer. The only downside was that we now woke up at different times every day, so our bodies couldn't get used to any rhythm at all. But it happened a few times that we forgot to set the alarm clock and Linda would sleep all night. "That is so nice" she would say. And so it was, because a good sleep reduced the pain a lot afterwards.

Still the tiny amounts of Cyclokapron she took caused a tremendous increase in her pain. This surprised me and made me wonder if it was wrong. It seemed there was some kind of counterproductive placebo effect, like an allergic reaction to the pills. I couldn't know then, but this reaction was also to be related to her seriously weakened energy field, her aura, which had made her hypersensitive.

Late April had finally come and Dottore was back in the Netherlands. Unfortunately he didn't start in our town, but that didn't stop us from going to him. Only problem was that it was a two-hour drive. How could she endure it? Luckily we still had Kevin. Maybe he could treat Linda just before the trip. His short-term treatments with special techniques worked very well and had positive effects on her pain, never causing side effects.

We had experienced opposite reactions too. Several people remotely treated Linda, sending her energy. Crazy as it sounds; Linda often couldn't handle these energies. Of course it's very kind and thoughtful that people do help each other, but sometimes Linda got lots of extra pain. Asking about the moment the energy was sent it proved that it exactly matched the moment Linda's pain suddenly increased. Again, it was something I didn't understand, but it didn't happen with everyone. Sattia's remote healing sessions as part of his meditations never had this effect. So how could it be that other people unintentionally caused her extra pain?

This too I learned was related to her extremely low energy. Thus she had lost her protection and had become super-sensitive. When someone then sent her lots of energy it was overkill. Carefully we tried explaining this to those people, but in response we were told that we were ungrateful, because superfluous energy automatically flows away, they said.

Maybe that's true, what did I know? But I saw Linda's responses to such energy healings. We had done the same for sick people too, so I could understand their reactions, but I think it all comes down to the manner with which you send energy. Thoughts have power and whatever you send, there's always a receiver somewhere in the cosmos.

Do you simply send lots of energy to a sick person because you think you should? Perhaps you're trying to help someone because that boosts your ego as in "Look at me." In that way you determine what is good and what is bad for someone who's ill, but do you really know what's good? Maybe you are doing something, which is precisely the wrong thing at the wrong time.

When you don't know this it's better to light a candle as an act of love. Nobody needs to know that you do this and you leave the disease, the transformation process, to the cosmic powers to decide when and where and how things should be done. The Almighty, the angels, our guardian angels know exactly what you're doing and will appreciate your help and use your energy, your love, in the best possible way.

Kevin was very friendly and very quiet. He felt that Linda's health situation was tricky, although slowly improving, but still went ahead. He also knew Dottore and talked positively about him. On the day we were going to Zeeland, to Dottore, he came just before we set off, and gave Linda another treatment. Dottore would ensure that she would be able to handle the trip back home, so we all expected.

We would arrive just after noon and hopefully would be allowed to be the first for the afternoon consultations. We had plenty of time allocated for driving the one hundred and thirty mile distance. After the first miles in Apeldoorn I stopped the car on the side of the road, covered the driver's seat with the soft sheepskin, and we changed places. If possible, Linda really wanted to drive herself to prevent getting nauseous. "You need to be vigilant!" she said. "You cannot sleep nor do anything else while I drive."

After only a few miles it turned out that she could handle things just fine. She drove well and again I experienced one of those rare moments I fully enjoyed. This felt like before... before when everything was normal. I was used to sitting beside her while she drove to the stores, to her family, the dance, to shop in Germany. Talking together while I took the landscape in and she drove, meanwhile discovering birds of prey sitting on poles all along the route. Everything went well and we arrived way too early in Zeeland. Because we had forgotten to bring something with us we stopped at a small local mall to purchase the required item, and I asked her if she wanted to stay in the car or come with me. To my surprise she came too, and so I found us walking between stores. It was nice to see her enjoying being outdoors and window shopping. For months she had locked herself up at home, with only a few visits to therapists. And now she was here, outside, with the sun was shining on her face. Shouldn't we have done a lot more of that?

We indeed had timed it perfectly, because within minutes after we arrived, Bianca, the translator, announced that we would begin. So we would be witnessing the opening prayer and subsequent 'Our Father' to help Fiona to get into the trance state needed to channel Dottore. Even during the prayer we were admitted to Bianca and Fiona, who now was in a trance and thus the personality of Dottore was present in her. Soft music played in the background and there was a slight smell of incense and medications. He, or rather Fiona, had his eyes closed as usual and stood quietly behind the couch, waiting to start treatment. Bianca was there for him as an assistant to reach things and to act as a translator for Dottore, who only spoke Spanish. She would translate the questions we had printed out at home and probably would provide some extra information. Meanwhile Linda had stepped up onto the treatment couch. Dottore and Bianca must have been well attuned to one another because no words were needed; she handed him a bowl with cotton wool. He placed his hands on Linda's body and made gestures as I had seen before, indicating he was magnetizing. Sometimes it seemed he pressed energy in her aura. Meanwhile, he explained what he saw and answered our questions.

"It's going very well," translated Bianca. "Much progress has been made due to his work and your commitment."

He said he had always guided her and would do so in the future. "Without my help she would have bled to death long ago," he said. That sounded eloquent.

From aside I watched everything, taking it all in and pondering about every detail. I found it mighty interesting to observe an astral physician at work through Fiona. Now he started massaging Linda's belly. Again he used the fatty substance and rubbed it firmly on her belly. Afterwards Linda would say that he had rubbed very harshly and we hoped it wouldn't affect the bleedings. Then I saw that he gave her a series of injections in the entire abdomen. I saw no needle, only the cotton wool used to dab the pricks. From my own experience I know that those injections were very painful, mostly because he kept the invisible needle or whatever it was for a long time in the skin, moving it back and forth. Everyone we spoke to had received these injections, but why did they hurt so much?

We were lucky, because suddenly Bianca said, "Behold the light." She referred to a lit area around the heart of Fiona. Fiona had a white coat and indeed we saw an orange yellow spot around the heart area. We had already seen this once before. Frankly we didn't need this, because it looked kind of fake, but that was an irreverent idea, of course.

Linda asked if he could do something to her back and she showed him the places where she was always in pain. Especially the pelvic bones on either side of her lower back, she meant. She had to turn around and then I saw that Dottore gave her multiple injections right on those spots. That looked very painful to me, but I was happy that Dottore spent a lot of time on Linda. He was by now busy with her for over ten minutes, and that was unusually long. Most people were finished within five. Dottore emphasised that we should have faith.

Again! Faith! As if we hadn't been largely going on faith! But we forgave him and Bianca that comment. He added that even after his return to Colombia he would keep on treating her in Spirit. I too was allowed to take a turn on the bench, but I only received one injection, because I had no complaints.

In the waiting room was a picture of Fiona photographed together with Pope John. Apparently she was so well known that even the Vatican made use of her services. There was also a folder with testimonies of people who were miraculously healed by Dottore. We had ourselves talked with people saying that because of Dottore they had made much progress in their healing from their illnesses or complaints. We hoped that his treatment would be just as much effective for Linda.

Near the entrance we bought the herbal remedies that Dottore had prescribed and we handed over the envelope with money. As usual we had put fifty guilders inside. Quite a great amount for a few minutes, but it was for the children's home in Colombia.

Once in the car Linda said that those injections had hurt terribly! And precisely on the sensitive bones that always caused so much pain. I looked at the place on my arm where I still could see the prick of only one injection. It still hurt a little. So I could imagine what kind of pain she was then in, the injections were not something to relieve pain! Apparently this was a necessary part of the treatment, but I was amazed that she had not uttered one single sound while Dottore gave her all these awful injections on the sore spot.

We ate the sandwiches and cakes and drank fruit juice. Then I gave her the usual Paracetamol and drove the first kilometres back home. As soon as we were on the highway we changed places and she drove the rest of the way, but the ride back was horrible. Everything hurt so badly and it took so long before we got home! For the last few kilometres she was constantly moving and turning in her seat without effect. What we, and Kevin, had expected from Dottore didn't happen. The pain was worse, much worse rather than less.

The following week, Dottore was in Belgium, just over the border near Limburg. We decided to go there too and the same ritual repeated itself. The consultation was shorter this time, but again Linda got many injections in her belly and her back. And so the trip home was as bad as the other one.

The Defeat

The day after our visit to Dottore in Belgium, just after Linda's parents had gone home, there was another bleeding. It seemed a small one, but of course this wasn't a good sign.

"Want a Cyclokapron?" I asked, but she shook her head.

"No! I will not go back to using those horrible pills," she said. "Maybe it will stop in a while, just by itself."

She quickly got onto the bed to calm down.

Tensed, we waited. This couldn't happen, could it? All those weeks she hardly took any Cyclokapron, and all the time things went well. Everyone led us to believe things were going for the better. And yesterday Dottore had said how well things were going. So how could this be?

Half an hour later it appeared that this bleeding was a very bad one.

"This is not good," I hissed between my teeth. "This isn't good."

"Quickly, give me Cyclokapron," Linda said, changing her mind.

We decided that I should phone Dottore in Belgium, hoping not to interfere too much, but Bianca said she didn't mind, she was used to such occasions. I wanted to hand the phone to Linda, but Bianca said no, because she could talk better to me.

"You shouldn't worry so much," she started. "Dottore takes care of all his patients. He already knows about this bleeding and has taken action." Next I heard her discussing with Dottore in the background and then she continued, "Blood transfusions are not necessary. Dottore has everything under control."

Then she added a few last words, "She should trust Dottore!" she repeated to me. "Linda easily panics and this does her no good. This undermines Dottore's treatments. Keep her calm."

I apologized once again for interrupting and thanked her and Dottore for this conversation. Then I told Linda what Bianca told me in private, about her panicking too easily. Linda protested of course and it made her pretty angry. "We are trusting them, aren't we? How can I trust even more? What more does he want from me?"

I didn't know either. But it was good to have been in touch like that and to know that obviously Dottore was in control. He would help her.

However, the bleeding didn't stop. As she lay on the bed it started again and she could barely make it to the bathroom, otherwise the whole bed would have been flooded. A huge wave of blood came out and moments later she held a big dark red liver-like object in her hand, so big that she could hardly prevent it from falling. She looked at it for a moment and then put it aside on a tissue and on the ground, to have her hands free for new paper and towels. What was it? Was it part of the tumour?

What I didn't know at that time is that blood outside the blood vessels in the uterus begins to clot, causing fluids and cells to be separated, which results in clot formation. When the uterus is totally filled then suddenly it empties in a wave. So the actual bleeding didn't take place at the toilet, but all the time.

"Shall I call an ambulance?" I asked, because this was way too much blood. We hadn't discussed it, but I now had to ask this question that burned on my tongue. We had to consider this option, no matter what Dottore had said. The quantities were impossible to estimate because so much immediately flushed away.

She hesitated. She didn't know what to do, but looked pretty calm. She wanted to call her parents she said, and so I dialled their number and gave the phone to Linda. Of course they couldn't actually help her, but as always her mother had a few supporting words to say and Linda could release a bit of the pressure while talking.

After a few minutes Linda gave me the phone indicating that I should talk to her mother. I listened to her mother who tried to calm me, saying that she had suffered from bad bleedings herself in the past, and *her* mother too. Apparently this was some kind of family 'thing'. She also said that blood transfusions aren't that bad because the people who donated their blood gave it out of love, and that is a good energy, isn't it?

Her father wanted to speak to me too. He said he understood our way of thinking, but suggested we better call an ambulance straight away because there's a limit to the amount of blood in her body. So with the four of us we concluded that we should call the ambulance now. Even while talking a new wave of blood came out. That was just the push Linda needed. This really had to stop. The loss was way too much in a short time and there was no way to tell when and if it would stop.

For the first time in my life I called an ambulance. As I expected I was able to talk quietly, almost too quiet. I assumed they were used to talking to panicking people unable to think clearly. Fortunately, I had no problem with that. I knew that in such situations keeping a calm head is a must, or at least keeping up appearances. I had to repeat what I had seen a couple of times because the woman on the other side told me that a bleeding always looks worse than it actually is. So I described the dimension of the big clot that had come out and that convinced her. They already had our address and I said I would leave the door open.

After that conversation, I looked at Linda. This was a defeat. All this time we had tried to prevent ending up in a hospital. No foreign blood in her body. No surgery. No other people deciding about her life without asking, while she was under anaesthesia. But what choice did we have then? That was the only sensible option left, wasn't it?

"May they just give you a blood transfusion," I said.

Come to think of it... what does it really mean when you are being transported to the hospital by ambulance? That you automatically give up all control? Would I lose her now forever? Would she even come home, would she still go through the whole rigmarole we had been able to avoid all this time?

We would find out soon enough. On the other hand, I also felt a bit of relief, for now she might be treated by people who knew what they were doing, and decision-making would be the responsibility of others. That dilemma again!

We questioned whether the specialists really knew what they were doing. They worked according to set rules and had the law backing up their actions, but were they really committed to their patients? Did they know everything as well as might be expected? We had heard many stories to the contrary. Many mistakes were made in hospital. Hospital bacteria, antibiotics that no longer work, medications that contain nothing natural anymore, patients being reduced to a disease or an ailment rather than a human being, surgeons knowing their patient solely by dossier, specialists being seduced by luxurious holiday trips to prescribe expensive medications, chemotherapy with devastating side effects... we were scared. Was this what we worked so hard for?

Linda ordered me to grab her travel bag and to pack it with the most important stuff, and then I called my parents so they were aware of what was happening. They said they would come to us and clean up the house. That's great, I thought. This help we could use indeed.

Then I heard the siren in the distance. That's a sound that, once having been heard in such a situation, never again sounds the same. An ambulance on the estate... the neighbourhood wouldn't overlook that. I think that not one of the neighbours knew what was happening in our home all along. That would now change drastically. I opened the door for the paramedics, and behind them I saw the ambulance being surrounded by neighbourhood boys. The news of the day...

The paramedics were very friendly and forthcoming and I told them about our situation while going up the stairs. They talked to me about the stretcher and the difficulty of the winding stairs, but Linda heard and said that she could walk down herself. She sat on the toilet again. Blood spatters could be seen everywhere and the big lump with red tissue beneath it, was still on the floor; it seemed pretty convincing should they have had doubts about the necessity for the call out.

They started trying to get an IV needle into Linda's vein, but that didn't go very well, not the way Linda was used to. She was giggly and making nervous comments, seemingly unfazed, but I knew better.

I watched the scene from aside. Two women in green and yellow suits, a large box of medical supplies and two-way radios that occasionally squeaked. Linda was on the toilet. Red toilet paper was everywhere. One woman sat down in her stiff scratchy clothing in order to get the IV needle in. A few tubes lay on the ground, a thrown away needle cap... that was too thick. There were torn plastic bags in which sterile needles had been. Our phone was on the ground. It went off.

I picked it up and without waiting to see who it was, I said into the mouth piece that they were now busy with her and cut off the connection. I'd have to call back at a more suitable time.

The needle was in. They attached a bottle of saline to it to restore Linda's blood volume. Linda insisted that she would walk down the stairs. She had no sweater on, just her nightdress, and she walked with her bare legs gently down the stairs. There a stretcher was put in place. We looked at each other briefly.

"I will come back again, my love," she said. "I will come back."

"I love you," I replied. Who knows, I might never have been able to say that again.

And she replied, "I love you."

She got onto the stretcher and was tucked in by the nurses. Belts were connected and then they wheeled her outside while I came behind them. They asked if I wanted to come too, but I refused. I had to pick up some stuff and it would be much more convenient to have a car with me. As I watched, my love was pushed into the ambulance. She looked at me and pressed her fingertips against the glass. I did the same.

I watched as the ambulance, lights flashing, but without siren, sped out of the estate. There went my *vriendinnetje* without me. I stood on the same spot as I used to stand when Linda went to school. But I didn't like waving goodbye.

I hardly noticed the neighbourhood boys who were watching at arm's length

I turned around. What should I do? Oh yes... I grabbed some stuff together. I looked in the bathroom. Those blood spatters again... The toilet's inside and outside was covered with them. There were more new clots too, and red toilet paper, and kitchen paper. On the ground were more of the same, bright red towels, needles, caps, phones, red underwear and more blood. I wondered what my parents would say after they had cleaned all this. The bed was a mess. I went to look after each cat and talked to them to reassure them. Cats have little facial expression and can't talk, but I saw that Charonna, the black cat, looked frightened. She had heard everything and didn't like this kind of stuff, panicky talk and strange voices, heavy footsteps, doors and crowds.

The other cat, Liselle, the Birman, seemed laconic, more able to stand the situation... seemingly. Pets pick up emotions from their owners, but don't usually show it. I hoped they were able to cope with it. I provided them with food and water and clean litterbins.

My parents could be here soon. Within minutes I was ready. I grabbed the bag, car keys... oh yes, don't forget the house key, took a coat, closed the door behind me, turned the key, walked to the car, opened the door, stepped in and... then I didn't know.

What's the shortest route to the hospital? Something so simple! Which hospital is it? Where is that again?

I couldn't imagine the way there, didn't even know if I should turn left or right after leaving the estate. But I couldn't stay here, so I left at random and hit the road to the right. I had to drive a long way as a result. I simply couldn't think of a better way. I only worried about the gasoline supply. The warning light had been blinking for many miles yesterday and I had forgotten to refuel. Gasoline... it looked like blood.

Linda had just arrived in the emergency department of the hospital, which consisted of a dozen beds separated by curtains. Two people from the nursing staff were there. They took Linda's blood pressure and also some blood tests. Then the questions came.

Linda answered all the questions, but I saw her hesitate to give full disclosure. I felt it would be wise to put all the cards on the table now. Yet what had this brought us so far except irritation with the doctors, because they didn't understand us and ended up more or less saying, "Well, look at it this way. It's you who's ill. Not us."

So how would we go about getting them to open up to *us*? Because what we always had noticed was the undisguised disgust of everything alternative. When we told them too much we would be facing the same reaction; irritation and misunderstanding. Was no one able to put himself or herself in the place of a frightened and stubborn patient like Linda?

The nurse asking the questions didn't know anything about Linda of course, so she asked if the bleedings could have anything to do with a pregnancy or menstruation. I felt Linda's tension when she had to answer this question and wondered what she was going to say next. This nurse was clever, because her next question was a smart one, and crucial at the same time, "What do *you* think is the cause of the bleeding?"

"If I tell you, you will be biased," Linda immediately replied defensively.

The nurse looked at her quizzically. "Why should we be biased?" she asked. "We just want the fullest possible picture. That's in your best interest. I understand from this situation that there must be a history already? Then we can retrieve your patient record."

Linda hesitated and then said more vehemently, "I would like you to be unprejudiced, but if you look into my case your opinion no doubt will be fixed. Cancer... doesn't cooperate with surgery!"

Luckily, this nurse was very friendly and did her best to understand Linda's situation. Maybe it was because she was a woman herself and related to Linda on that level. She asked the right questions and Linda told her story.

We wanted them to investigate how the actual situation was right now, because Linda was convinced that the bleedings were not related to the cervical cancer, but maybe by the consequences from it, like inflammations. This may seem absurd to read, especially from a mainstream point of view. But given the enormous efforts we had put in to combat the tumour, and given the progress she had made according to Dottore, this wasn't such a strange way of thinking... from Linda's point of view.

Now that this conversation and the first tests were finished the temporal conclusion was that indeed she needed blood, but not so fast that she couldn't wait for blood with her specific blood type, because the bleeding had stopped for the moment. Blood was to come from another town. In the meantime we were taken to a separate department and transferred to a gynaecologist who had been called from home and was dressed in evening clothes. Fortunately this was not the same obstetrician who had referred Linda for a second opinion to Amsterdam.

The gynaecologist took Linda's dossier, looked through it and started a conversation about the findings so far and the current situation. He wanted to hear from us what it was we wanted from *them*.

Well... actually we expected that *they* would determine that. After all, Linda was brought here by ambulance. Naturally we expected a blood transfusion. But I got the impression that this was not that clear cut and that treatment might not be automatically given. The file of course, revealed that Linda was an uncooperative patient who hadn't listened to prior treatment proposals. Taking this into account this doctor didn't want to impose Linda with certain treatments. He gave us a choice. Either she was now registered, investigated and treated according to the means and methods the hospital would find fit, or she went home now. She would receive a blood transfusion first, but that was it.

I tried a few times to ask for at least an ultrasound, so we would know exactly what we were up against, but the gynaecologist wouldn't consent. Bang! Another door slammed shut.

This doctor worked by the book. In my eyes he acted rightly... from his background. But why did we feel so misunderstood and alone?

I wondered should I put Linda under pressure now to co-operate? She would probably listen to me now. Having fought so long and so hard, only to still end up in a hospital? But what were the prospects now? What were we facing? We didn't know. Before, she had been examined first.

The option the doctor suggested was the most obvious one and definitely the easiest. But was it also the right one? For saying 'yes' now, would mean saying 'yes' to everything that would follow.

If the hospital concluded surgery, then surgery it would be. If they would think chemotherapy or radiation, then that was what she would have to accept. If necessary they would do it all one after the other. And if it turned out that nothing had the desired effect, then she would have gone through this misery all for nothing, at best as a case study for the doctors.

One advantage perhaps was the pain medication. But since she reacted so strangely to almost any painkiller, I found even that dubious. They of course could prescribe morphine, but our own doctor could prescribe that. And he once had made a remark about morphine I hadn't forgotten, "As soon as we start that then it's end of story."

If Linda would say 'yes' now, then the doctors would decide when she would get morphine, and given Linda's extreme pain, they would start it right away. In other words... then the specialists would decide about her life! They could even decide how long they considered her life to be worth living. They could sentence her to death just by a medication.

Again we faced an all-or-nothing choice.

For me it was especially important to support Linda, backing her up, even if her choices were different from mine. But that was not the case. I wanted her to feel free to choose whatever she wanted to, by listening to her heart. I would be with her. Her choice would be my choice. We were one. We thought the same... and again we decided to go our own way, the tough way... the lonely way.

Shortly after the blood arrived, three bags. Ultimately, it was well after midnight by the time Linda received the blood transfusion in a separate room. Mieke, my sister, came to visit us and asked if she could help us with anything, but her visit alone was just the thing we needed, so we didn't feel entirely alone in this very quiet and uncomfortable hospital at night.

To my most dearest love

Early the next morning we were back home, a home that unfortunately provided no security against this misery. We had been through so much pain here that it gave no relief to be home now. So... what next? At the hospital we had been advised to take the Cyclokapron only twice a day. That was better than every six hours.

My parents and Mieke had clearly been busy that night, as the tower of dishes in the kitchen had been removed and cleaned, many other things were cleaned up, and the bathroom was completely clean. That must have been quite some job for them all. I called my parents to thank them but was not prepared for their reaction. I heard in my mother's voice that she was terrified of all the blood that they had cleaned up. That was quite something indeed. I had warned them beforehand, but I think they absolutely had no idea of what they would find. In fact, this was the first time they saw themselves confronted with the naked truth of Linda's illness. Until last night they had never seen her sick, only heard my stories. Linda had managed very well to hide the awful reality of it from them, but this was the reality.

The following week Dottore was in Apeldoorn, our town, and both my parents, Linda's parents, ourselves, and several other people we knew went to him. We only dared to go because it was only five minutes driving. Given recent developments we were full of questions and we wanted very much to talk things over.

That Monday morning we were among the first to arrive in the waiting room. The consultations were soon to begin. We were tense, insecure and very afraid of what we would be told. Actually, we expected that Dottore would recommend that Linda go to the hospital, that he wasn't able to adequately treat her with this condition and its extreme pain. That was not what we wanted to hear, but we were prepared for this.

We were the first to be invited in his consultation room. Bianca said Dottore already knew about Linda and that he had given her astral blood injections. She added that such an injection is a very special substance, which is six times as concentrated as blood.

Meanwhile Dottore came and stood beside the treatment table and Bianca translated his words with a smile, "Well, say what you have on your mind. I will answer all your questions."

Indeed he took the time for Linda. Of course we wanted to know why he had not told us that she could expect such bleedings. He had said she was doing very fine instead. So... could he explain that?

His answer was that when he told his patients everything he could cause so much stress in them that this would do them no good. But then he added that he would do something for Linda that he rarely did, because she had his special attention. He would treat Linda every night from nine o'clock to ten o'clock with a team of astral doctors. The only condition was that she would have to lay down on a bed or a couch and move as little as possible.

Bianca added that this was something very unusual and it sounded as if she didn't agree with this, that Linda got way too much attention from him, not earning it. He must have quite a weak spot for her, she said. He said emphatically that Linda could get better but that she should have all the faith she could muster and needed to cooperate in every aspect.

At the end of the consultation Linda was allowed to stand right in front of him and she could hold his hands while he muttered a prayer. We didn't understand this, but we understood that the divine world would make every effort to help her get better.

What Dottore also wanted her to do was to start eating meat, red meat, and steak. We understood that meat is great for recuperation, but Linda was nearly a lifelong vegetarian. Then meat might no be that good, we remarked. We asked questions about it and asked if there was anything else that would stimulate her blood levels quickly. Eventually he admitted that very strong beef broth was sufficient.

We had been anticipating this conversation in fear. Suppose Dottore wouldn't continue helping her. Suppose he had ordered her to go to a hospital. Could she get better or was she doomed? Dottore's answer now had been given. As we walked down the hall towards the table were the drugs were sold Linda's emotions discharged and she wasn't able to restrain her voice. "I will be better," she cried. "I may get better!" She thanked everyone and was in a state of joy.

I went to the drug table and met Maria halfway. I exchanged some words with her with mixed feelings. After all she had dropped us, but despite that she had earned our respect too. She didn't share Linda's relief, but made a comment that worried me, "You still have a hard time to face."

During those days that Dottore stayed in Apeldoorn, we went to him several times, and during each visit Linda received injections, a lot at times. I asked Linda if she was going to eat meat, but the idea made her gag. "I don't understand why he requires this of me," she said. "There are many other means to recuperate, aren't there? He knows I'm a vegetarian!"

But he had been so firm that she agreed that I bought a jar of canned beef broth that needed to be heated only on the stove. When that had been simmering for a while Linda came down the stair but nearly fainted because of the smell. The idea of eating beef was so conflicting with all her principles that she finally said that she would rather die herself than ask animals to die for her to stay alive.

As discussed with Dottore we prepared Linda's bed every night at nine for her to lie down, so he and his team of specialists could do their work. She then had taken her medications, I had treated her and completed the entire ritual... we were ready. I hoped that the astral doctors wouldn't be bothered by my presence, and I imagined them working with special tools, removing all Linda's cancer cells, with accuracy only astral doctors would be able to do.

Linda even fell asleep during this hour. I was so exhausted that I lay down beside her and tried to sleep too. But twice that week something very weird happened.

Even while Dottore should still be at work with her Linda woke up with a startled outcry, because she dreamed that she was raped. The worst part was that I was the one raping her. This dream was so vivid that I needed several minutes to convince her that this was not real. Needless to say, the pain immediately returned. Dreams often have a symbolic meaning, and I trembled at the thought of the explanation that could be given for this dream. I hoped it didn't mean that I forced upon Linda my personal choices, which could be seen as some kind of energetic rape.

We just didn't understand this. She never had dreams, or at least didn't remember them. Maybe once a year, but now she had two nightmares in two days. Therefore I decided not to sleep beside her anymore, and since then the dreams stopped.

Something else happened during one of our visits to Dottore. At the end of that consultation we heard him saying something strange. He walked over to Linda and me in the middle of the room and stood before me. He was about to say something special, because it looked like he took a deep breath before speaking.

He started to say that he was seriously worried about my parents.

They had consulted him too that week and their health situations weren't well. They were pretty old and would not live that long anymore. He said that my mother's intestinal problems were under control for now, but that she worried way too much, which was not good for her. Therefore she should avoid all stress and it was better when we didn't ask her to help us. But he went on and added that it was also better that when we were talking on the phone that I should not tell her any bad news about Linda. Better tell a lie, he said, than having her needlessly worrying...

My father's health was not good either. His heart was in bad condition especially. For him too it was much better not to be confronted with Linda's problems. They should be able to spend their time left on earth together, to finish what had to be done now.

If we wouldn't do this, then my mother's intestinal problem could escalate and there would be nothing he could do to stop that. It would then become intestinal cancer. "In fact she's more ill than Linda," were his exact words. He appealed to us to do what he asked in this situation and sounded very serious.

Then he added something more. To Linda he said that she quickly panicked, which was not good for her health. It was important that she had more faith; she could get better, but she really should have that. Apparently we still hadn't enough.

To me he said that when Linda again was in such a panicky state of mind calling other people for help, I should leave her alone, because I should take care of myself, for my health's sake, because I was worrying much more than needed.

At that moment I didn't realize the full extent of what he was telling us, or I would have fired a lot of questions at him right there and then. Of course we knew about my mother's intestinal complaints and understood very well that we had to spare her as much as possible. But that was exactly the reason why we hadn't asked her to help us all this time. Only in February, when she and Mieke decided to come without our consent to wash some dishes, we had to accept her help, whether we liked it or not. And I really could use that bit of help all too well. To them it was important to be able to contribute some help, being part of it. And during all visits Linda put on quite a show to look as good as possible, so she shouldn't worry too much.

And now we were to understand that we should refuse all their help! Didn't he understand this?! Why didn't he know? After all he was an astral doctor visiting his patients every night. He should know!

I had my suspicions of what had happened... I think my parents had told Bianca, Maria and Dottore what they had seen at our home that night Linda was taken to the hospital by ambulance. They had cleaned all the blood that night and the following morning on the phone I had noticed my mother's panicky voice. She must have been shocked terribly. Apparently Linda always had put up such a good front that they never realized the seriousness of her disease until that moment.

I could understand their shock and also the fact that they had talked to Dottore about it. But what I couldn't understand was that *he* didn't understand the situation. Now we weren't allowed to welcome them at our home anymore to help us out. And I really didn't see myself paying them a visit for some small talk, leaving Linda alone at home. She was way too ill for that. And then skirting around the issue to make them feel comfortable while my head was full of only one thing: Linda trying to survive the terrible pains! So what choice did we have? Why did he ask this from us?

The next evening my mother was on the phone. I had expected it because I knew they had been to Dottore that day. But this conversation was to be very much different from what I anticipated. First she asked how Linda and I were doing. Dottore had ordered me not to make her worry, so I said all was fine. Dottore was very satisfied, blah blah blah. But as I spoke I suspected she phoned us for a totally different reason.

Then she started to say that they had consulted Dottore that day and that he had advised them to keep calm as much as possible. She was worrying far too much about Linda and it was important that she should think about herself more. I noticed she wanted to tell me something else, but she couldn't say it because she sounded upset. Then she interrupted herself and suddenly said, "You must understand that we love Linda. We love you both." She tried explaining exactly the same thing Dottore had told us, that she was reminded of her own health, because if she didn't, she soon wouldn't be able to help us anymore. That we did understand, didn't we?

What she was trying to tell us was that she didn't want to, or couldn't, see us for some time from now on. Not because she didn't love us, but because it was for the sake of her health as, which Dottore had told her.

I asked what she meant by 'soon'. Because 'soon' could be 'too late'.

She didn't answer that and said that Mieke would continue helping us. She would be an intermediary. So we could still keep in touch. I replied that we were told the same, but added that it couldn't be wrong for her to occasionally wash some dishes. Linda could stay upstairs, so she didn't have to see her. That would be good for my mother in fact, as it would allow her to feel she was helping us. Otherwise she would worry even more. Or was I getting it all wrong?

But she refused. I tried explaining it to her in other terms, but her voice sounded as if she was out of control and moments later she gave the phone to my dad. I tried talking to him, but wasn't able to reach him. He added that we also should not call them for some time. Dottore had stated that she should avoid all stress and had to keep calm and that Linda's illness was bad for her health. He too sounded very upset. Then he broke the connection.

I had never seen my parents like that ever before. I never knew them to be like that. What was going on here? What had happened? What had Dottore told them... in the name of God?

I explained to Linda what I had heard. She couldn't understand either. Never before in my entire life did I have such a strange conversation with my parents. They would never let us down. This was so contrary to their loving nature. Why did they do this?

So I picked up the phone again and dialled their number. My father came on the phone again. He sounded very defensive and didn't speak clearly. He wasn't himself. But I persisted and wanted to know what was going on. Why did they behave this way? They didn't have to obey Dottore in *every* aspect?

Then he reacted angrily, almost in panic. He said, "My wife is very sick and if she doesn't take care of herself, she won't live much longer."

In the background I heard my mom say something unintelligible in a strange high-pitched voice. Then my dad cut of the connection.

Two words got stuck in my ears: *my wife*.

After all... wasn't *his wife* not the same as *my mother*?

For the first time in my life my father acted as if I wasn't a member of his family. I didn't understand. I thought I had a sick partner, very sick. Now suddenly my mother was so ill that I wasn't even allowed to speak to her? Wasn't it much better for her health if she could occasionally do something to assist us? That certainly would make her feel a lot better, feeling useful. How can you deny that your son has a dying girlfriend, as if she doesn't exist? This didn't sound like them at all. Were these my parents? It simply did not sound right.

As Dottore was still in Apeldoorn, we made full use of the opportunity to visit him. Since my parents did the same it wasn't so unlikely that we met them at the next visit. They saw us one moment and I still remember my father's reaction when he noticed us. I tried greeting him, but he turned his head away and quickly pulled my mother into a room. I could hardly believe what I saw and felt like we had a dangerous, contagious disease.

That would be the last time I saw my parents for a long time to come, and how I would remember them.

Two days later, in the evening, Linda had a new very serious bleeding. Within half an hour she lost so much blood that again I was compelled to call an ambulance. I will not rewrite now what happened that night. The only big difference was that I didn't call my parents. I only called Mieke and was happy that she wasn't afraid of us. She was there for us. She was the only one we could call that night.

After the blood transfusion we went home halfway through the night. What else could we do in the hospital? But we had learned something this time, because they had given her a painkiller I didn't know, Dyclofenac. What surprised us was that the pain eased within the hour. We were given a prescription.

Had we now again been stepping out of Dottore's instructions? After all, he had told us that his astral injections were much better and that Linda didn't need any blood at all from the hospital. We should trust him. Had we betrayed that trust now?

Just to be on the safe side we did not show the audacity to make a phone call. According to Bianca he was always aware of everything, so I could guess her answer without doubt. But we now had many questions, so we decided to prepare a letter and send it to him. In this letter we said what had happened, and I described as best I could Linda's condition and how serious the situation was, because during the consultations I always had the impression that Bianca was only half listening while commenting that Dottore knew everything. We wrote that we trusted him greatly, but that we didn't understand this anymore. He had said she could get better? It seemed to get worse all the time. How could that be? All in all it was a really friendly, but also critical letter in which we asked for support and answers. At the end, we thanked them for all the efforts.

The following week Linda had recovered sufficiently to visit Dottore in Belgium. We felt it was important to continue the visits as long as he was 'here', especially now. So I called that morning to Belgium to indicate that in the course of that afternoon we would come, asking if Linda could be given priority. Then we continued with the preparations, but half an hour later the phone rang. I picked it up and heard Bianca on the other side of the line. She insisted that we should not come to Belgium, because Dottore could remotely treat Linda just fine. I found that strange, because if he even could treat patients like Linda remotely, then what was the point in coming to Europe at all? Then he may as well stay in Colombia.

She continued, "Linda has gotten so much strange blood in her body due to so many blood transfusions that there isn't a single droplet of her own blood in her body anymore. Therefore Dottore can't get through. He can't make her better anymore." And she concluded, "Linda needs to start preparing for her transition. Dottore will continue to take good care for her, even after her passing."

I was horrified. What was this? What had caused this sudden change of mind about Linda's chances?

She kept on talking for a bit, but I was so stunned that I was barely able to respond or ask questions. Then I interrupted Bianca bluntly and said she should give a message like this directly to Linda herself and not through me. I felt angry and apparently that was noticeable on the other side. "Then put her on to me," Bianca said reluctantly, and I handed the phone to Linda who was watching me with big frightened eyes. She saw that I was completely mesmerized.

She listened to Bianca and responded with some critical questions and comments indicating that there was a discussion, but Bianca broke the conversation quickly. When she hung up the phone it was as if we both had received a huge slap in our faces.

"Well, that saves us at least a few trips back and forth to Belgium," she said. But her face said something very different.

Bianca had stated that Linda had seen this coming for some time, so she knew this. That was a remark we didn't understand at all, because Dottore was the one who repeatedly and firmly had told us how well Linda was doing. Bianca had translated those words time after time! So how could she say this? From another patient that we knew well, we heard that very recently Bianca had said, "Linda is doing very well indeed, only she doesn't realize this herself."

This was what we had been afraid of all the time. Indeed, we had seen this coming, especially after the recent bleeding and the comments in the hospital, but *not* by what Dottore and Bianca had told us again and again. We just had not expected to be told this in such a blunt way. Why was foreign blood such a problem for Dottore? He had never told us this before. And what choice did we have? The blood loss had been extreme! Surely it wasn't forbidden to go to the hospital if necessary? Didn't anyone who came to him with really serious health problems had on-going connections with the GP or, if need be, the hospital? He could steer the hands of surgeons! He had said that himself. And during serious operations strange blood was used too. Then should we have stayed at home each time while Linda bled to death? Didn't we have enough faith? Was that it?! Did it all come down to that single word, FAITH!

The day after that phone call we were completely bewildered. Linda called her parents to give them the latest news. She called other people to release some of the pressure that had been building up inside her. But I couldn't call my parents. I felt like I had been hit twice. Now that I needed help from my parents more than ever during my adult life they weren't there for us. I called Mieke and left it to her what she would say to them. I didn't care, but we agreed that she would not say anything for the time being.

Linda's parents didn't understand a thing. Her mother was downright angry because of that phone call. She found it a very cruel act of Bianca and Dottore. We didn't know what to do and for a long time we only thought of that one thing, death. Even Dottore had subtracted his helping hands from Linda.

"He will continue to treat her," Bianca had said.

Yeah... sure... but we didn't believe a word of it now.

In the evening a few days later Linda asked for a notepad and a pen. She didn't say what she was up to, but it felt dubious when I saw her being so introvert like this, starting to write. She wrote quickly as I watched her and occasionally she deleted something. I asked her what she was doing, but she shook her head and continued. After a while she stopped, looked at what she had written, then turned a page and continued writing.

At first I kept out of it, but after a while I sat down next to her and looked sideways at what she wrote. She was writing letters, one for her father, one for her mother, for a number of people. The letters were brief, very brief. Most of them were only a few sentences and nothing more, as Linda didn't know what to write. All that time she said nothing, didn't look at me, but allowed me to watch her writing.

They were farewell letters.

For example, she wrote this letter to her younger brother Mark, who had recently become a father to his second son, Ilian, who recently had had big health issues to overcome:

For my sweet little brother, who for a long time now, is not so little anymore. Since you are quite a bit younger than I am, I always felt that I missed part of your life when you were on the Grammar Sat for example. And now that you live far away in the South I have seen you far too little. And during the time you had problems with Ilian I couldn't be there for you because I too had problems and I didn't want you to be more worried than you already were. All this time I myself believed that I would get better, but now it doesn't look like that anymore.

I am proud that you have achieved so much and when I was with you I was quite jealous of your big garden, but I didn't begrudge you that, because I love you very much, though I might have never said that.

Then she started several other letters, but she couldn't write more than a few sentences.

Finally she started a letter to me and she started with the words: "For my dearest dearest vriendje."

But then the pen ran dry. I quickly grabbed another one and read while she was writing:

Here should have been written 'and they lived happily ever after'. That has always been our promise. I regret that I have given all my attention to the school. That should have been for you. Yet we have done quite a lot of fun things together: Indonesia, Florence, and such. Few women can say they have a husband who likes shopping. With you it was always really nice and cosy. We have worked very hard together, and it is not fair that we have to give up this way.

Then she didn't know what else to write. She turned all the sheets over, "Do you want to hear?"

I nodded and she read the short letters one by one. I got a lump in my throat, especially when she read what she had written for me. I felt tears in my eyes, and didn't know what to say. I never cried, though I felt deep sadness, desperation and pain. She noticed and then looked straight at me and said, 'Yes! Show me you can cry for me!" But the tears didn't come. They were there, but all within. My emotion was totally blocked and it hurt so much! Meanwhile I was wondering about her remark. Was I so emotionless in her eyes?

I could barely do the things that had to be done at that time, because I was constantly thinking about what had happened. It did not let me go. At one point Linda was talking on the phone with her mum and I sat on a corner of the bed listening and looking at her, silently enjoying watching her, but I felt very, very sad at the same time. I heard Linda saying, "He's here beside me, crying. He thinks I'm dying."

Mediumship

It took a few days before things settled...

What Dottore had told us was *so* strange and *so* contradictory that we finally... finally began to wake up out of something that at best can be compared to being trapped in a cult where you have surrendered completely to a leader who can make or break you. That's how it felt for us, totally broken.

Having had so much faith in all that we were told. And yet all that we heard was that we didn't have enough faith. Never was it enough! 'Faith'... the very word made us sick.

When all along if there was anything we had in abundance, then it was that! We trusted Dottore so fully we did everything he asked of us. The only 'trespassing' was that we had called an ambulance on two occasions when Linda had seen litres of blood flushing down the toilet. That was a choice that had nothing to do with trust, only with acting logically.

Slowly all kinds of things started to fall into place and we began to realize how terribly we had surrendered ourselves to... yeah... who was it actually?

As a result of our realization we started to doubt everything that was said and done by Dottore. One of the key questions was, why had he not told us sooner that Linda had a tumour? After all, we had been consulting him for years. Only a few months before Linda was diagnosed with cervical cancer she had mentioned to him that she had secretion. If he was an astral doctor, after a whole lifetime of being an earthly doctor, now gifted with a wealth of astral and cosmic knowledge, X-ray eyes, sheer unlimited psychological knowledge, and all other things living doctors can only be jealous about, then he should have seen this coming years in advance. He could have healed Linda, or else have warned her so we could have taken measures. Or because of his warnings she could have consulted her family doctor then and the hospital would have made a difference at a much earlier stage and any surgery would have been minimal. That was precisely what we were consulting him for, to prevent this kind of problem!

Why then had he told us again and again that things went very well and that she would get better? And three times in a row the worst bleedings started within a few days after such statements. Why now did he tell her that she should prepare for her transition? Did our letter finally make them realise the seriousness of her illness? So we now asked ourselves whether Dottore *was* an astral doctor. Did Fiona actually go into trance? But, even if that *was* all fake... how could one say such things to a patient? You just don't do that!

What hurt us most was that he had scared my parents so much that they had panicked and broken all contact with us within this situation. And then he coolly told us that he wouldn't help Linda any further. What kind of doctor says *that* to his patients?

For us the consequences were clear, we were on our own; but for my parents? My father's heart was not okay, Dottore had said so himself. All his life my father always had trouble speaking about his feelings. What heart can withstand an internal conflict like this, in which he was practically forbidden to help his own son and daughter in law with a deadly disease?

My mother's health wasn't good either. Knowing my parents, this would eat them up. On the other hand, assuming that we were misled, we didn't understand how it could be that some other people we had spoken to, said that they were helped so well by Dottore. They didn't just dream that, did they? Apparently he did some good work too.

At first we felt a deep sadness. Then, when we started to look at it with a bigger perspective and saw through the whole thing - the conversations, his strange advices, some suspicious stories of other people, the fake looking light on his chest, and many details we now remembered – our feelings turned and we got very angry, and suddenly there was absolutely nothing left in our opinion that he had done well.

Only while writing this book, years after, I began to understand what had happened. This book is a book about love, a book in which Linda is the central person. In such a book condemnation doesn't fit, even when it seems so justified. However, I do write down what has occurred... or as we have experienced the things that occurred. But that's always a coloured version, seen through my eyes. I try to be neutral and while writing I try to place myself in someone else's mind. And the longer and better I succeed in this I find it all the harder to condemn anyone. I must admit that the feeling of condemnation was very strong in the days thereafter. But now that I can oversee this period I see clearly the fears that clouded our thinking, fears that made us surrender to an astral doctor. So I let go of the idea whether Fiona is a psychic or not, or that Dottore is an astral being or not, because I can't judge it. I simply can't.

Also, I now see the fears that led my parents into making the decisions as they did. They too had completely surrendered to Dottore and accepted blindly everything he said. It may seem strange to you, the reader, that people can be so blind. But don't forget that many of their friends went to him, with good results so it seemed. They were so frightened that they thought it was in everyone's best interest to keep a distance from us.

If there's anything in this book that I've given a lot of thought to, as to whether or not to mention it, it is this business of my parents and us breaking contact with each other. Should I write this down, so everyone can read, and judge? I risk picturing my parents as loveless people, which they definitely aren't.

In the course of writing this book I discussed the situation with my parents, and asked them what they thought about the situation being published. As could be expected, they weren't happy at all for starters. "You don't need to hang out our dirty washing for all to see," was my father's immediate reaction. My mother, who had had good experiences with Dottore, didn't want to abandon him that easily and said that he'd told them that 'the contact should be maintained'. She suggested that the translation could have caused a misunderstanding.

But let me talk about our reaction, Linda's and mine. We were very angry. The proper way to clear up a misunderstanding is to communicate, listen to each other, talk, try to place yourself in the other's position; that way you can begin to develop understanding so wounds can be healed. But to do this you need to give each other the chance to talk. At first my parents didn't give us that chance, but the other side of the story is that when they started realizing the consequences of their actions, and after Dottore had said that the contact should be preserved, they tried to connect to us, but we weren't giving them that chance anymore. My mother tried to call us on many occasions, but I kept those conversations as short as possible. This attitude caused much pain to my parents and surely wasn't good for their health either. A train was divided into two parts and each train was on a different track at full speed towards an uncertain future station. How and when and if those tracks would meet again was impossible to predict.

I am sure all of us, including you the reader, sometimes do things which we, in hindsight, would have done differently... or not at all. Sometimes circumstances work together to make us take that one single unfortunate step in our lifetime, in which we let ourselves be misguided by ego or worldly desires; in our case by fear and anger. Later, realizing what you have done, you want to undo that, but unfortunately this is not always possible. These are very difficult times in your live, because it really does hurt when you see the consequences, and that there's nothing you can do to change anything. So next you look for arguments to re-justify your actions. If you can't find them or your inner voice is telling you that there is no justification, next you wish to forget that it happened, you want to suppress the memory and you run from what you did. But sooner or later you'll discover that running won't work. You will be reminded of it all of your life as long as you deny it, because your soul seeks harmony and love.

Gradually you discover that the only option in order to be at peace with yourself again, which sets you *free*, is to face what you did and accept the lesson being presented by it. Then you can continue. That's not easy, but it is part of our life on Earth; you fall down and you get back up again. We've all been there, no one excluded.

So... then was what happened a good thing?

Let me say it again: no one is to blame; no point condemning either party. It's done. To condemn would be the same as blaming a Level 4 student for not understanding the textbooks of Level 5. Perhaps then it is good what happened, because it is by learning from our mistakes that we make progress on the Two Roads, so beautifully described by the Indian holy man Nicholas Black Elk[3].

On Earth we have the choice of two roads, he says... The good red road, which is the spiritual road, and the dark and difficult earthly road. Where the two

---

[3] *'The Two Roads', by Eliza White Buffalo,* http://www.thetworoadslightfoundation.com

roads meet, there is a holy place. For spiritual growth we have to walk this difficult road as well, but it will challenge you greatly. It's by going back to the centre every time, by listening to the voice of your heart that you will be shown in which way to walk, preventing painful steps. Apparently this was such a moment in which we forgot to do just that, forgetting our Selves.

But whatever choice we make, the two roads move on, allowing us choices *all* the time, and even the worst things that happen can be transformed into something beautiful when we choose to accept and forgive... the other one *and* yourself. It's the path of a soul towards perfection.

Anyway, after many intense conversations with my parents they understood that, because by allowing me to write this down, their actions and our actions can be *giving*, a good example of what can happen when you deny your responsibility, depositing it outside yourself. That was what my parents did and it was exactly what we did! They weren't different from us. Then how can I blame them for what they did?

The fact that finally they gave me the freedom to write this down at my own discretion is therefore a very precious gift, one for which we all may be very grateful.

But in the days immediately following that telephone conversation we were not ready yet, we weren't centred in the holy place of the two roads and so we couldn't see what we were doing. We were sad and deeply disappointed. Then our grief turned into anger and indignation. That too might not have been the right attitude, but through her anger Linda overcame her disappointment and started fighting again. Instead of a victim she again became the pugnacious fighter who would stop at nothing when it came to getting better.

So after a few days she took the pad of notes, tore them all out and shredded them to confetti tossing it all around on the bed and on the ground with a grand gesture as if to say, done with it! I thought that was a shame, because these notes really meant something to me. The scraps lay there for a few days until I casually put them in a box with old newspapers. But in the shed I fished all the scraps out of the box and put them safely away in a secret place.

What we hadn't done for quite some time now were the visualisations. So we started that again. Linda longed to be reconnected with Amà. Fortunately she wasn't gone and she quickly appeared on the beach without us asking for her. Nothing else was necessary, only to start the visualisation, bring Linda to the stone circle and let it happen; no steering, no summoning, just doing what we always did to support Linda's healing.

There were many questions Linda wanted to ask Amà. The conversations and asking questions and receiving answers went very easy, but I watched her closely, because we had added a very painful experience to our memories and I was looking for insight on a specific problem I spent much time pondering: how dangerous was this anyway? Because if Fiona and Bianca were cheating people and Dottore wasn't who they said he was, then we had walked into an open trap, such as those sceptics would warn about... a justification of everyone who opposed alternative and spiritual matters.

So who could assure us that communicating with a creature that doesn't exist in the Earthly dimension wasn't exactly the same thing? Was Amà an angel or was she a demon entity? Or was she nothing more than a product of Linda's imagination? How could we know for sure? Who could advise us? Should I stop her? Were we making the same mistake all over again?

I could think of only one thing that might help me discern between right and wrong, and let that determine if I wanted to go along with this or not, and that was, What role does Love play in what happens? Are the things being said from Love? Or is there a hidden purpose behind it? But still... how could I tell? How could I discern between truly loving words and deeds, and everything else in which there is no real unconditional Love? How do you know if someone is meaning well with you? How do you know that you are deceived? How can you tell if someone is pure?

These questions have always kept me busy, my entire life in fact. Because in the 'regular' world, everything is regulated legally by training and education and qualifications, yet in the 'alternative' world there is no uniform standard.

But for the regular world too 'what role does Love play in what happens?' is a relevant question. Because for us this was the main reason we had decided to go our own way, not listening to the proposals of the hospital. If we had felt that the hospital and all the people in it were guided by Love and out of Love made their decisions, then certainly we would have agreed with the surgery and wouldn't have chosen such an extremely lonely path. Then Linda would have been much less fearful about that surgery. But we neither felt that then nor later.

Not that the people individually weren't loving; of course there are many people working in mainstream health care because they feel it's their calling, who are putting all their love into taking care of others, but how about the many extremely well-paid surgeons, specialists and other skilled medics? And how about the big pharmaceutical companies with billion dollar budgets?

So as a whole the regular route presented itself to us as extremely sterile and unloving; and if there is something patients like Linda need most of all, then it is the safe feeling of being surrounded by loving people.

As I said before, Linda was also guided by fear, and fear is definitely not a good counsellor; it was fuelled by stories of people with bad experiences in the regular health system, and don't forget, what happened to her brother Arjen had significantly contributed to her decision. This fear was the reason we had surrendered to someone like Dottore in the first place. We had done it ourselves! No one else was to blame.

I realized that my decision as to whether or not to go along should not be based on fear, so I would have an open mind for every other possibility, face everything, and also be prepared to act according to the information being presented to me. Listening within to your inner feelings, to your heart that is, means to have an open mind for *all* roads, to look at *all* options, and not let your eyes be blurred by fear, desire, greed, anger, to name just a few challenges on the dark earthly road. This way you are clearing your mind, your senses. But it truly means that *all* options should be taken into consideration, the one you don't want to hear *and* the ones you do wish to hear! Don't make decisions based on, "This is bad news, so it will be right." That's the typical attitude of a pessimist.

Now then... how could I tell if this contact with Amà was the real thing?

I felt it! We let it happen. We were completely free. We didn't steer the way it would go, and no one steered it for us. I saw how delighted Linda was when she was with Amà, because I could feel her joy, joy that I had rarely seen in her, despite the situation. It made me happy too, really happy, and that was a feeling for which I didn't have to do anything. It was just there! Amà triggered this somehow, and so it came from within. My heart resonated to something that I can only describe as... Love. For me that was decisive.

Linda started asking Amà questions, and her first one was very significant: Why hadn't Amà warned us about Dottore?

Amà's answer was as unexpected as it was simple. She said that we wouldn't have listened to her. That was true. We relied entirely on Dottore, so much so he could do no wrong in our eyes. We would therefore have pushed Amà away, thinking she was a malicious entity trying to mislead us with beautiful words, luring us to our doom. And the contact with her would have been lost. Of course I will not write down everything we heard during the conversations we had with Amà in those days that were mainly to do with Dottore. I heard everything from Linda in turn, and so now I would write that down, albeit from my own recollection of that time years ago, and since then so much has happened. So how would I recollect every word without making changes? But because what happened has made such deep scars on all of us, being so central in this book, I wish to go into this in more depth; however, not only based on Amà's words, but also based on the many thoughts and experiences since then and what I have learned, heard and read about mediumship.

On Earth psychics and seers are held in high esteem, at least by the spiritual minded people. However, many people assume that a medium *owns* the wisdom and that, as a medium is in trance they are not responsible for what is spoken. In this way you as a listener not only put the responsibility for what is spoken beyond that of the medium, but also beyond yourself. You accept all too easily what you hear, because it's told by heavenly entities, intelligences, ascended masters and cosmic beings, isn't it? But... *you* will always be responsible for all that you allow into your own mind, and what you do with it. There are significant differences between mediums, depending on the developmental level of the soul of the medium. We all are here on Earth to learn, even mediums. We are on Earth to learn what true unconditional Love is, and to let that Love become part of our soul. Some of us are way ahead, and there are others who are at the beginning of this school. Being at the start of a school doesn't mean 'still not good enough', but it does mean 'still ignorant of the knowledge the school can give'.

Because Earth is a planet in the physicality, it is subject to the laws of inertia, and thoughts will not materialise immediately as is the way it is in the Spirit World, for in the Spirit World 'thought creates', immediately that is. Therefore Earth is an ideal playground in which to cope with different aspects of life. Thus it is possible that in one incarnation maybe you are to learn to deal with money, which is a form of energy, and you may be impoverished that whole life, so you learn to realize how important that energy can be to stay alive. And so, in another life, you may learn the opposite aspect, being very wealthy, which is also difficult, because with money you can do a lot, but it can make you lazy too, and it allows you to make big mistakes. Maybe you need to correct those mistakes in a next incarnation, so you learn the consequences of both your negative and your positive actions. Simultaneously, you experience the consequences of what other people do to you in both their ignorance and in their wisdom. Never is this a matter of dumb luck. There is always a reason when you are the one in the line of fire. Coincidences do not exist, because everything is interconnected in all places and throughout all times. So you learn to see everything from different viewpoints, and you learn to be creative, to think out solutions to bring yourself back into balance. Slowly you begin to understand that condemnation makes absolutely no sense and that only Love is able to heal wounds. That is the process of growth for us all.

Mediums too are people on their way to the Light. At the start of the school you can already have psychic abilities, be allowed certain gifts, but how pure will your channelled messages be? At the end of the school you'll be a much better medium, but maybe there are still a few aspects you need to face. Maybe you have been given only one aspect of mediumship, because that allows you to act according to your plan, learning certain lessons, doing certain things at the same time. To whom will you tune in? To whom will you listen? Do you wish to listen to the impulses of your own, truly loving spirit guide who is your guardian angel showing you the way since your birth? Or do you rather choose to listen to other beings who are also fumbling their way around?

What's the agenda of the latter? Maybe they present themselves as guides or as wise and ascended masters, cosmic beings with big plans for you and the Earth. Precisely, that one weakness of yours makes you vulnerable; your anger, your unhappiness, your hastiness, your greed, your ego, your fear...

Maybe that's their job, the job for which you have selected them, to help you bring that weakness of yours mercilessly to the surface and into the light and by experience it can and will be made strong and light. May you then condemn these entities for the fact that they were on your path? Or condemn yourself because you weren't able to make the distinction yet?

It may also be that someone isn't a medium at all, but is fooling him-self and others, with all the consequences. There are very few really good mediums, real way-showers to the Light, being clairvoyant, clairaudient, Clair cognizant and clairsentient. They are used by perfected souls in absolute freedom with unconditional Love for all who seek truth. The people who call themselves a medium will likely say that he or she belongs to the few per cent because they themselves may not know where they stand. There's even no need to know that, as long as you stay attuned to the highest universal, unconditional Source of Love.

Guardian angels work from Love; otherwise they are not guardian angels. And also, an angel is a being of Light. They always respect the free will of humans on Earth, and in every action they take into account the road we have to follow. All their actions and words are fuelled by the love that they have and that they feel towards us. They will not remove the blockages that we need to learn and grow out of our way, but they will help us to overcome them. That way you get stronger and wiser and so you grow!

Today, many people call themselves channels, but the same applies here; being able to channel but hardly being able to perceive by whom, from where and for what purpose the things are said, means you only listen to *some* source of information, nothing more. For how unconditionally loving are the words being said? How do you know? You might hear a lot of wisdom. Surely you get *some* useful information, very useful information maybe. But slowly, without you noticing, you start trusting this source of information and you start living by this information, you're surrendering yourself to it. So, when finally the words and advice are changing slightly you don't notice it, and you live by them too. If there are doubts raised by others, you may even defend it. Slowly you are 'guided' off track, and your path will be guaranteed to become much longer and harder than it was already.

So, in short, whether your source of information is earthly, astral, stellar or cosmic, from the 1234th dimension or whatever, how good a medium is said to be, how sympathetic and well meaning he or she might be... everyone has their limits. Ultimately, the responsibility for what you let in and what you do with it is always yours and yours alone! Do not hide behind the words of another, not even as a medium. Always keep thinking and feeling!

That was what Amà was pointing out to us. Not exactly in the way I have just said it of course, but it's what it boiled down to. At least... this is my interpretation, contained in my words. I also should not make this very mistake and say that these words are Amà's responsibility and hide behind her.

The tentative conclusion Linda and I pulled out from this was that Fiona may have made herself dependent on a source of income she could not live without anymore. She lived in Colombia, and was collecting money for a children's home with dozens of orphans, so she and her colleagues said. A lot of money was needed for their shelter, education and training of course, and they came to the Netherlands to raise this money. That in itself is very good and one must be very loving to do this and keep working for this. That was what impressed us. What also convinced us was that Dottore worked under the umbrella of the Roman Catholic Church. Moreover, there were many relatives and friends consulting Dottore, and the consultations were free of charge... weren't they? All in all we had donated quite a lot of money for the good cause. But now I'm not sure about the word 'good'. While preparing this book for print, I surfed the Internet for new information about Dottore and I discovered an article describing Doctor José Gregorio Hernandez as a Venezuelan man, not Colombian as we were told. So they had told another lie.[4]

_____

[4] _A version of this article appeared in print on September 30, 2014, on Page A4 of the New York edition with the headline: As Church Seeks Proof, Hometown Sees a Saint. He died in a car accident in 1919 in Caracas. In this article it is written: "... (his picture) can be seen all over the country -_

It was only when Linda and I came in contact, during the visualisations, with a being like Amà, it occurred to me how much love could go out from such a contact and how Linda and I were enlightened during those times. Zebra too had this in him. I felt the good it did me, the joy from within me, while I did nothing for it. It made me just completely happy! And as I thought of it again, even hours after, the feeling of joy and happiness came back to me. That feeling was very strong and it came naturally. This was a contact from freedom, from Love.

If I compare the contact with Amà with our visits to Fiona and the translator, I realize we never felt something like that there, not even close to it. I felt amazement. I found it mighty interesting and that Linda was in good hands. I was *mentally* convinced that something good happened. But I felt no joy, not that deep feeling from within. It wasn't that special. It wasn't that feeling of... Love. For me, that feeling has since become crucial in contacts with 'the other side'; whether it's through a medium, trance medium, a channel or whatever they may be called. There is a large 'grey' area that our normal senses can't perceive and we are very easily fooled by words and mental thoughts that are louder than the silent pure voice from our heart.

Amà told us to never again make ourselves dependent on an astral entity, doctor or cosmic being, not even to herself, or to anyone else. It was a difficult lesson that had a deep impact on us, our parents, and who knows who else. Later we heard that same comment in different words: "Always keep both listening to your heart and thinking with your mind! Only then your own loving guide can reach you."

---

painted on walls, reproduced in small statuettes, and displayed in roadside shrines or simple altars in stores and homes." He was indeed a doctor of the poor, and he performed so many, sometimes miraculous healings, that now attempts are made to run a sainthood effort conducted by the Archdiocese of Caracas.

Freedom...

Because of the recent experiences we now even feared Dottore and his 'team of doctors'. After all, Linda had dreamt she was being raped, on two occasions, and so we wanted to protect ourselves and our cats against possible attacks from that side, whether the fear was realistic or not. Linda was very vulnerable in those days and was terrified of re-bleedings. She asked Amà how we could protect ourselves, and Amà's reply was that if our thoughts were positive, preventing negative thoughts to enter our minds, we would need no protection at all. But as we had trouble doing that she advised us not to think of Dottore and instead think of good things. Also, she suggested we remove from the house all things that had to do with Dottore.

That was a job for me because Linda didn't want to touch anything anymore that was related to Dottore. That was a lot. All the papers with questions and answers, mini-disks with recordings, all pictures, brochures, computer files... I searched the whole house and threw everything into a box, which I put in the shed. It took me days to find and collect it all, but finally there was nothing left that we could think of.

Very early the next morning, around four o'clock, I put everything that could burn into a large earthenware pot, which I placed close to the pond behind our house. I lit a match and fanned the starting fire, so that everything went up in smoke.

It did indeed go up in smoke, because very little oxygen was getting into the pot to feed the fire, and so this created thick oily smoke, fed by paper and the plastic of the discs. The clouds of smoke drifted over the grass field and enveloped several blocks of houses at the edge of the park. It was a warm night and most people slept with the windows wide open. This was all wrong! I could have alerted the entire neighbourhood, and I imagined fire trucks with sirens driving through the park awakening everyone still asleep, and causing an uproar with me having started it all. Semi-panicking, I grabbed the pot and tried to turn it upside down but meanwhile it was so hot I immediately burned many fingers at once. It was a stupid move. I uttered a loud cry of pain... very clever... If it wasn't because of the smoke, the people would certainly be alerted now by my screaming. So I kicked the pot to turn it over and immediately it rolled the last metres downhill leaving a smoking trail of unburned papers and notes, after which it dropped in the pond where the rest of the contents started floating on the water surface... out of reach. What a bumbling!

Linda said we were to make a protection around the house and garden. This happened during a visualisation in which I too participated. Linda did it with Amà between the stones while I was lying next to Linda on the bed with my eyes closed. Amà instructed me through Linda what to do.

First I had to visualise the tiniest piece of the strongest material I could think of and put all my strength and love into it. I practically needed to create this tiny piece of super strong material atom by atom. "Make it stronger!" I heard Linda saying. "Concentrate! Stronger still! Do your best, you need to protect me, remember!" I concentrated and concentrated and finally succeeded imagining a very tiny piece of some rare special material, indestructible, ultra-light, translucent and impervious to all negativity. Such a hardly visible small piece was just within my abilities to imagine.

"Okay," I finally said. "I have something that is incredibly strong."

"Can you see it well?" Linda asked. "Keep seeing it, don't let go of it. Now, stretch this material horizontally until it is as wide as the path to the front door, a few metres in front of the house."

"Won't this weaken the material?" I asked.

"No, to the contrary. You make it bigger. Have you already done this?"

In my mind, I extended the tiny bit of super strong material horizontally to the width of the path, resulting in a narrow strip. Then I had to stretch this strip of material vertically until I had a plate of this stuff as tall as a door. I found this a very convenient method to materialize anything, by starting small and making it larger. Visualising such a powerful door at once was way too much for my inexperienced mind, but in this way I learned how to overcome my limitations.

"Now grab your airbrush and on the outside you spray the most beautiful violet light that you can imagine and as you spray it creates a thick layer of violet cotton wool that sticks to the door" Linda continued.

I imagined that I airbrushed the entire door, providing it with a heavenly glow of violet light, and I was impressed with the results myself. Next I had to spray the inside with the most intense white light, so bright that I was unable to look into it.

"Now you take one side of the door," Linda said. "There's a handle that you can grab, hold on to it. Now pull that door behind you and walk around the house. Step by step you walk through the front garden, through the wall next to the neighbouring house and so on in the direction of the back garden. And as you do so you create a wall of the same material as the door that you pull behind you around the whole house.

I started walking and spoke aloud to say where I was, because I found it hard to do it silently in my mind. I needed to imagine every metre as I walked and it worked much better when I said aloud where I was. Finally I ended up where I started at the front door. At that moment both ends melted together and at the same time above and below the wall extended into a transparent sphere around the house in which we would be protected against all negative influences that we, rightly or wrongly, feared.

Was this fantasy? Maybe so, but at that time we needed something that we could do ourselves, and this helped. So for us it was no fantasy. It was fun to do. Amà later said she had to laugh at me. Because when I left the house I opened and closed the wall to go through. She found that very funny.

Every day I had to re-visualize the wall by again pulling the super door around the house. I didn't need to start from scratch, because the door was well made.

Now as I write, I realize that that really made a difference. The big difference it made was that we were focusing our minds on purity and light. Amà helped us in this playful and humorous way to overcome our own darkness. That made the real difference. The wall itself was unimportant in fact, the real protection came from within and from that viewpoint the wall was very important at that time. Strange that is... It was an illusion, and yet this illusion had very realistic effects! Thought creates!

During one of these visualisations we were paid an unexpected visit from a girl who came along with Amà, a little girl with a big bunch of long dark brown curly hair, very cute to see, a real darling. But Linda was completely stunned when this girl said she would like to be born and with us as parents. This surprised Linda so much that later she told me how she had even started having second thoughts about her conviction of never ever wanting to have a baby. She actually said, "If there's someone who I would like to have as a child, then it's this girl! She's so sweet!"

Unfortunately, we were completely back to square one, six-hour days. But with one difference, namely that Linda didn't take Paracetamol after the Cyclokapron, but Dyclofenac instead.

The first few days of taking those pills worked very well and took away a lot of pain. But after about one week a weird side effect began to show itself. Immediately after taking them her pain increased to extreme levels for about three quarters of an hour. Then the pills started to work even better than Paracetamol, but not for longer. That extra pain was really something. First of all the Cyclokapron triggered it, and then it was tremendously increased by the Dyclofenac, so much so that Linda went out of her mind because of pain.

So she again started pacing the living room, moaning, and sometimes with her head nearly on her knees, she trudged for hours up and down the room. When she sat or lay in bed she couldn't keep her arms and legs at rest. She would suddenly wildly throw her arm or her head away, or shake her entire body completely out of control. She couldn't stop it, she said. 'Shaking' we called this. Especially during the night the pain was so bad that sometimes she couldn't help herself from screaming so loud that my ears hurt, making me wonder what the neighbours must be thinking about what happened here in the middle of the night.

I pulled out all the stops to treat her in any way I could think of. Over the years I had taken several courses, like working with the Egyptian Ankh, or colour therapy and chakra healing. But most of this was useless because she could hardly lie quiet for ten seconds. As I realized more and more that limitation only exists in the mind, I grew more creative and kept coming up with new ideas, sometimes with astonishing results. I could be really amazed what at what I came up with myself.

One day I picked up an empty glass and asked Linda to lie on her side, so I could treat her back. Concentrating, with my fingers spread just above her skin, I 'pulled' so to speak, all the pain in her lower back to a point near her tailbone. I held the glass just below that spot and let the pain fill that glass.

When the glass was 'full' I covered it with my other hand and quickly walked to the sink where I flushed it away with lots of cold water. As always I told her what I was doing, and if it worked she would let me continue, otherwise she would bluntly tell me to stop it because it was useless.

This time she said, "Do it again. I think it works."

I noticed that if I concentrated well enough, I could lighten her pain a lot in this way. Exactly that it was: enlightening her pain, bringing light into the painful area. However it also was a drop in the ocean... yet... it worked! It contributed in calming her. Naturally, this treatment became part of our daily ritual before sleeping.

What also became part of this ritual was me working with the Egyptian Ankh over her body, sucking in pain. I had been taught that, in the early days in Egypt the Ankh was used by priests and pharaohs, so this felt quite special. And the results were incredible.

At first I found her responses exaggerated, and I didn't really believe her. I thought she was trying to please me or that she imagined it all. Putting pain inside a glass or sucking it up with an Ankh kind of goes against your common sense. Then, when I kept the Ankh above a certain spot for more than a second while she lay on her belly with her eyes closed, she immediately yelled, "What are you doing! That hurts! Stop! Stop!"

It appeared that the effect of the Ankh could be far too much if I didn't move it. And then I needed to wait for several minutes before I could remove that pain again.

One day a thunderstorm started while I was working with the Ankh. I was holding it nearly one metre away from her body when suddenly a bright flash of lightning lit up the room. Linda screamed and was angry because the flash had struck her through the Ankh into her body at the point to which one of the arms was pointing to. We were shocked and I was unable to take away that pain. It cost her one period of sleep and that spot hurt for several months afterwards. And so I learned never to work with an Ankh during a thunderstorm unless you can perceive the energy being conducted through you. In this way you act as an earth, a ground, or an Ankh itself if you like; advisable too to believe that your Ankh is a strong enough ground for a lightning bolt.

The pain relief that could be achieved with those treatments was hardly matched by any painkiller. I didn't understand, but when she said that it worked it was worth all the efforts, even when it was for the thousandth time, even when it was three o'clock in the morning, and even if I hadn't slept for forty hours and was sick with fatigue. It was worth it. But how could it work? Was it a placebo effect? I had trouble believing that suddenly I had the gifts of magnetizing. But on the other hand, Linda could tell me exactly, and blindly, what I was doing, or that I, just to check, did nothing at all. So I simply had to accept the fact that my hands were capable of passing this divine energy. I'm pretty obstinate, but sometimes you finally have to stop being stubborn and just accept what happens. So unknowingly, I was given almost fulltime training in becoming a healer, using my hands, my imagination, my voice and sometimes an Ankh or an empty glass.

However, there was something really nasty about this pain, for there was nothing that had a lasting effect on it. Everything we undertook, whether I did it, or other people from a distance did it, or medications from whatever source, swabs, anti-pain-devices, hot water bottles... everything worked for only a few minutes or only a few times and that was it. That was the reason why I always had to think of new things, to keep being one step ahead of the pain. It was like fighting a very intelligent opponent who was out there to create pain, undermining all our efforts.

For starters, we of course searched for this opponent outside ourselves, blaming the diabolical entities of the Club of Dottore. But slowly I started to suspect that it had something to do with Linda herself.

People like Linda, who are seriously ill, having so much pain that painkillers aren't effective anymore, are dealing with what sometimes is called 'soul pain'. Well now, the soul is the inviolable spark of God, of Creation. It experiences no physical pain, but what is meant by 'soul pain' is that pain sometimes is no physical thing anymore, but originates from a much deeper level, as if coming from the soul itself. It is a battle with themselves that these people are fighting. Everything, really everything is pulled out of the closet and the anguish is revealed one way or another. And this is a battle no one can win. Fighting this pain, running away from it, is impossible, because how can you run from yourself? This pain asks for recognition, not to be ignored or risen above if you like, but to be entered into fully; how absurd it may sound, because that's the last thing you may want to do. The very idea alone! But... to do this you must not struggle, for it is in facing what underlies the pain, in accepting *all* your soul's experiences, that the beginning of a solution is to be found. That sounds simplistic and I do not pretend that I would do it just like that if I ever were to face the same thing. But when every way out is blocked, when every single creative solution you come up with is counteracted... then isn't that the time to stop struggling and to open your senses to what the pain is trying to tell you?

So maybe what I gradually began to suspect was true, which was that Linda herself, something in her sub-consciousness, was holding on to the pain, blocking real solutions; as if she didn't want to get rid of her pain, her disease, needing it for something. It was a radical idea, which I didn't feel was a good idea to tell her, because you don't say something like that to a person in Linda's position. Yet, I got increasingly convinced of it.

In her despair she had a great need for contacting people who would listen to her, hoping they would give her some advice. She spent many hours on the phone. Sattia was one of those people who were always willing to listen patiently. Sattia answered Linda in a quiet way and he treated her every night from a distance during his daily rituals or prayers, with energy transfers. I really can't tell what the effect of his treatments was, but the conversations alone were very comforting and healing for Linda, and he didn't ever give the impression that she was overwhelming him.

Truly, such is a very difficult battle. And while the answer seems very simple it is not easy... and yet it is. If you're in the middle of such an inner conflict it really doesn't feel simple at all. I didn't realize it, but Linda taught me this truth; she guided me during all those endless nights. Maybe she did that so I can tell you these things now.

Lesson One

Last year when we consulted Jacob with his high-frequency resonance equipment, one of Jacob's questions to Linda after the first treatments was, "Have you cried already?" But it hadn't happened; during the whole year before the first bleedings she had hardly cried, and if at all, it wasn't as a result of his treatments. I had my thoughts about this, as I knew Jacob's question was an important one. From the first moment I met Linda, now more than eighteen years ago her eyes fascinated me. Eyes can radiate so much pain, if you are willing to see it. Linda's eyes did, though I particularly loved them; after all, you don't fall in love without a reason. It was striking the way her pupils were surrounded by so much white, even below the pupils too, giving gave her a piercing look. This phenomenon, which is called 'sampacu' or 'three-sides-white', is a significant observation in physiognomy. I've heard that it is a relatively rare phenomenon, and as long as it isn't caused by hormonal or other physical conditions, only extraordinary people in extraordinary situations have this. It has been observed in humans during deep trance, or in certain kinds of people facing imminent death, like in very violent criminals, moments before they come to their end; but also in very enlightened beings. In other words... in people who are not 'normal' in the earthly life.

I saw a lot of pain and sorrow in Linda's eyes, though showing emotions had never been her strongest point. Her experiences before she knew me, all the bad events to which no end seemed to come, had never triggered many visible emotions in her. Given that even Jacob's powerful treatments didn't make much emotional difference, I suspected that the lid on that emotional pit was very tightly screwed. What was hidden underneath must be very intense and very deeply hidden, perhaps with roots in past incarnations.

Being able to let go of emotions is very important because a disease like cancer has to do with serious blocked feelings. Not that blocked feelings automatically lead to cancer, but it can have an invigorating effect. If those emotions are unleashed by the misery of the situation, the confrontation with the finiteness and the meaning of the earthly existence, through pain, through death, fears and whatever, then it *seems* that the whole disease process becomes much worse. In such cases people often are prescribed all kinds of painkillers, anti-depressants, sleeping tablets and other means to suppress the emotions. But in fact the unleashed emotions are a very important step in the right direction. In Jacob's practise most of the people who came to consult him had been through a long track of hospitals, surgeries, chemotherapy, radiation-therapy and very many disappointments. Often the hospital had given up on them, saying they had only weeks or months to live. In such situations, as a by-product, people are deeply affected in their emotional state of mind and it is nearly guaranteed that tears will come.

Linda and I did it the other way around; we first went to Jacob. She hadn't experienced any suffering from chemo, surgery and radiation; in fact she hardly had any intense hospital experiences at all. So the lid on Linda's emotions was still firmly in place. The tighter such a lid is fastened the more it takes to release it and that was what worried me. Linda had been in control of her emotions all the time, even the first six months with all the bleedings. What is hidden underneath that lid, I sometimes wondered warily.

Only the massive impact of Dottore's actions had touched her so deeply in her soul that Linda lost control of her emotions. Anger, pain, sadness, frustration went hand in hand and, sitting in her chair, tears streamed down her cheeks. And in those times I often had to think of Jacob's words, 'have you been crying?' She was crying now. Not for a few days or even a few weeks, but for months! So much that I seriously worried about her drinking enough water to replace the abundant moisture coming out of her eyes and nose. I couldn't comfort her; it was hopeless. She didn't care that she wept, how she looked, what I thought, what her parents were thinking, what someone on the other side of the phone was thinking. I could only talk to her. She heard me and sometimes she responded, but I could only guess what my words were doing to her, or if they reached her at all.

Had she now been treated by specialists then they would undoubtedly have given her countless painkillers and a variety of tranquillizers and anti-depressants. Nobody wants to suffer pain and no one likes to see his or her loved one to suffer. Specialists are no different. But I'm convinced that

Linda's deep hidden emotions would then have been expertly concealed much longer, suppressed by synthetic means, and that this rare opportunity, that had been precisely orchestrated and created by the cosmos, would be missed and that it would need another incarnation for Linda to unleash what was now presented to us... We had, unaware of what we were getting ourselves into, chosen this road, because deep down inside we knew it was the right one.

Dottore, or better said... Fiona and the translator played an important role in this, without justifying their deeds. Everyone plays a role in each other's life plan, a life plan selected and approved by you, together with your guardian angels. And all the people, including the good, the bad and the ugly so to speak, play their role, a role for which you have selected them. When you start unravelling this ingenious cosmic plan, even if you see only a fraction of it, then you realize that condemning makes no sense at all, because we are all on the *Two Roads*, the one road of higher wisdom, along with the other road of personal choice. I expect the Lakota holy man, Black Elk would say: We are One!

Yet it was only too right that no one had been standing at the beginning of this road with a video screen showing us scenes of the road ahead. That certainly would have complicated our decisions. Anyway, if Linda's pain had been suppressed by strong medications, we would never have gone through what now was to be expected...

Since *this* started it... because the lid on her emotions had been completely broken away there were no brakes, there was no restraint.

At times she suddenly would utter words that came from nowhere, out of the blue. Children often behave like this, thinking of fancy words and names while they are playing. Children can easily show what they feel. Well, Linda certainly wasn't playing, but soon I was no longer surprised when she, turning restlessly in her chair, suddenly said a word like 'esnachkiya'.

I paid no serious attention to it anymore. Anytime she had been ill, with fever or that, she would have made up funny songs that made no sense. To her it was a kind of lightning rod to think of something else rather than being sick and not being able to do anything else. She made fun of it and sometimes grinned about it herself. "Family ailment," she said sometimes.

Her grandmother had taught her to make up funny words like: "putting, cutting, shining, missing... " and put them in a made up song too, though in her native Dutch language the words would all rhyme and seem to be imaginary. Then she would complete the rhyme with a funny line like "the rabbit has gone fishing." That way you can think of countless variations. Her grandmother always had this strange humour and together they could have a lot of fun, laughing about things no one understood. I let her do it, because it distracted her attention, and I liked hearing her voice in a different way for a change.

Because her back hurt so much that she couldn't lie normally I called a home care aid shop in Apeldoorn. There must be many people having back problems, so I thought. And indeed in this shop several solutions were for sale or for rent. I bought a piece of synthetic sheepskin. Indeed this worked pretty well for a few nights, but like everything we tried out, then a counter effect started; the skin became too hot for her back. Naturally! Nothing could have a lasting impact. That had happened with my hands too. They became too hot when I was treating her. So I now treated her just *above* her skin, and strange enough... it worked just as well.

The problem was she was underweight. I had heard that obese people with cancer 'have something to fight with'. I now understood what this meant. A layer of fat is the best cushion for aching bones and a good backup for weight loss. From the beginning Linda hardly had anything like that to fight with, apart from her great fighting spirit. At the beginning of this year her weight was only forty-two kilograms and it took a huge effort to avoid further weight loss. It was as if her body couldn't seal in any extra calories.

She was often nauseous and some medications worked best on an empty stomach, which wasn't helping very much. In these modern times of dieting and weight care diets, I discovered that most products contain few extra calories. In no time I could fill the shopping basket with semi-skimmed milk, low fat cheese, a whole variety of low-fat and light products and more of that stuff, simply because it is hard *not* to pick those items. I just wanted products with phrases like 'fat good' or 'heavy stuff' instead of 'ultra light'. Or 'weight gaining cure', 'three times more calories' or 'the ultimate solution to underweight'. There was no way that I could find these products in the normal stores. Should you then eat whipped cream and cream butter instead?

Apparently I couldn't think clearly at that time, because for starters I did just that; enrich her food with more fat. To casseroles I added a good dash of cream and over it I doubled the amount of cheese. When her parents came to visit I made cake, of course with extra whipped cream and cream cheese. I was happy with every morsel she took and silently I kept a record of all the calories. But the result was that she didn't gain a gram, and after two months couldn't bare the sight of another pie. And she got angry at me when again I asked, "Do you want something to eat?"

So I was advised to bring in a dietary expert. Our physician had no objections against this, so a couple of days later a nice young lady came to visit us 'on prescription'. She brought with her a range of free sample packs from the two main manufacturers of nutritional replacement foods. If Linda liked any of those she could order them directly. Suddenly there were a lot of people facing the same problems: weight loss after severe illness, hospitalization, chemotherapy, anorexia, etc. Moreover... this lady would compose a diet especially for Linda.

We began with the brought packets of soup and drinks, and after one week of testing we had a list evaluating each product with a digit from one to ten, ten being the highest score. No product came higher than a seven, or 'drinkable', but most didn't even get a five saying 'one time, never again'. Again we wondered: who had invented that stuff anyway? Most drinks truly tasted like cardboard and to camouflage this they had a synthetic raspberry or other fruit flavour. After as few as two sips Linda felt her body react in protest and put them away with the words, "urgh! Am I supposed to drink this?"

Apparently Linda was 'an ounce too heavy' as the Dutch say goes, meaning that she simply was too hard to fathom for this woman, who certainly seemed committed to us. Presumably no expert in this area would have come up with a real solution for Linda. Real solutions weren't handed to us, or weren't recognized by us, resulting in us making the 'wrong' decisions all the time. Linda's road was a very bizarre one.

I understood, pretty late, that we had made a big mistake. Again! The dietician and every pharmacy were only allowed to provide us with the scientifically tested and approved foodstuff. And what's the result? Drinks, puddings and soups that contained every enzyme and vitamin up to the last officially approved insights, perfectly balanced and supplied with a fresh and fruity flavour; and for soups a crisp and creamy taste, but... totally undrinkable. The point now was not that she should consume the healthiest stuff, but that she was to start to gain weight as quickly as possible.

Eventually, somebody came up with the brilliant idea to inquire at gyms. Bodybuilders and sports enthusiasts want to add extra high-calorie diets, because they wish to show off with their mass; for inflated, shiny muscles supposedly determine your masculinity or femininity, depending of course on where they are located. What a crazy world this is anyway! Then I discovered that there's much to be had in this area. Mega mixes, super powders, weight gainers, energy drinks, power bars... and optionally also in Linda's favourite chocolate flavour! Even these products were scientifically tested and examined for their effects. Why didn't the dietician come up with this, realising that her usual ammunition supply was inadequate? These products were a very welcome addition to Linda's diet, and especially one soon became Linda's favourite: Crash Weight Choco. But I had to take care of one thing, namely that she didn't use this as a replacement for, but as an addition to her normal meals.

This discovery made me very sad too. How many months had I lost now? Very many... too many in fact, because I could only offer her one, maybe two mugs of this energy-rich chocolate drink a day, and in fact she needed twice as much the least. Last year this wouldn't have been a problem at all because she was able to eat anything then. But now? Her biggest motivation was her love for me, because I tried so hard for her. Why hadn't I thought of this before? I felt like such a fool.

Lesson Two of 'Wim's Nutrition for Malnourished Sick' if you want to gain weight... first of all you need to take care that your daily diet should be well balanced, containing no deficiencies. Here the dietary expertise plays an important role.

Lesson Three is that you shouldn't always be guided by the idea that every ingredient should always be healthy.

But unfortunately I never mastered Lesson One: do not insist endlessly that a sick person eats if she does not want to. Not only that doesn't work, instead it only causes annoyance, with the result that eating becomes a struggle. This has to do with acceptance, which was playing such a big role in our situation, Linda's big issue.

But what about me? Should I have to learn to accept things as they were too?

When I looked at my list tracking her weight I had that strange feeling again of swimming very hard, but still losing ground. Whatever we tried, her weight wasn't stable in the long term. She came up with many reasons to explain how she would have lost an ounce that day, and tomorrow she would eat enough to compensate for that. But after several months she didn't want to see that list anymore. Not with me standing around that was.

What I also learned was that money didn't make the difference between life and death, because we spent a lot of money. Not everyone in a similar situation can afford to buy and try as we did. I found that, within your reach, all options are available to accomplish your goal. Perhaps you will have to look for them, and maybe you'll need to ask for help. Some people have lots of money. Some have lots of time. Some have specialised skills or knowledge. Some have plenty of weight. But often it is your friends and family, the love that surrounds you that helps. All that you really need is in reach somehow, or it comes your way, sometimes through the strangest ways.

We were fighting Linda's pain, trying to move heaven and earth for the ultimate cure against it, not realizing that you *can't* fight this kind of pain. The solution then was not to engage the battle, but to face the pain. What do you think?

Acceptance is called for. We didn't accept what was on our Dark Road, the road that we had selected ourselves, but which we now considered too much of a burden.

Rituals

One of the most effective remedies that we had at our disposal was within ourselves... visualisation! What you need is often closer and easier to achieve than you realize, and easier, cheaper and closer than within was not possible.

During our 'visits' to the beach Amà joined forces with us sometimes against Linda's pain. That pain was like a living, smart and elusive monster, or else it consisted of countless small pain bugs. But... pain bugs can be caught! So we all started catching them. 'Watch that one! He's trying to escape! Ah... got him!' - 'Trying to hide in there? Not this time!' It was a kind of agility game. Left and right we caught the small creatures and threw them in a large box. If one of the animals escaped Linda and even Amà, would run away at full speed over the beach, then the bugs had to face Taksi who never lost a race, returning them in no time. When the box was full, then Linda had to focus her eyes on the tiny animals so they would shrink until nothing was left.

"I find that sad," she said.

That was the difficult part, because Linda said that these animals had such beautiful eyes when they anxiously looked up at her from the box. But Amà made clear that in this case she didn't need to have sympathy with them. It was her own pain.

Crazy as it seems... this worked! Physically it was only a drop on an overheated plate, but spiritually this was extremely important.

My condition was jacked up quite a bit these months, hardly sleeping, if at all, not eating enough, never sitting down, running wherever I could, tremendous stress all day long and always an oppressive feeling of despair and painful sorrow in my chest. By now I wondered how on Earth I was able to keep on going like this. That simply is impossible when you come to think of it. What I also didn't understand was how Linda kept on going so long with so much pain, not sleeping, hardly eating and still losing weight so slowly. Gradually I got the feeling that our prayers must indeed be heard somewhere.

Over the previous week the strange words and songs Linda made up changed. She began to sing more and more and no longer was her vocabulary limited to a musical 'la la la', because she now created complete songs with funny and often strange words. Usually only short songs, pure fantasy based, but funny to listen to. It became kind of a hobby for her and I enjoyed hearing her voice this way, listening to her experimenting with sounds and words. Sometimes she became very enthusiastic and started something like an opera. She might start whispering the first words, humming the melody, but slowly the words started flowing effortlessly from her mouth. At first singing softly, then slowly, her voice showed more expression and she sang faster and wilder. Then there was tension in her voice and she whispered the words as she sang about the danger in front of her, holding her voice back, until suddenly she escaped the danger and melody and her voice joined in a loud climax of joy and laughter.

"What am I acting like, crazy, eh?" she said to me sometimes. But I wouldn't be surprised if the audience had given her a standing ovation. It was fun when she was like this.

Together, hand in hand, we sang every day for a while and we repeated several mantras and prayers, asking for help. We addressed this not only to the Almighty, but also to the archangels, our guides, whoever wanted to help us. Always while doing this I had this specific feeling that I didn't understand. We were putting so much effort in healing, then why didn't we notice anything? Why was this happening? Linda asked me this question countless times, looking for a meaningful answer that I might be able to give her.

"How can I carry on with this? I would love to live, so why is this happening? Them above must understand that this can't continue forever? Just a little easing of the pain please... why can't that be? Why? Have I made all this up myself? Is this karma? THIS?! I can never have invented this. Why does no one help me?"

It seemed indeed as if she was learning a lesson that was so incredibly important that for this lesson everything imaginable was brought into position. It was as if we had to go through the most extreme part of the extreme. And when finally we had reached the bottom of the deepest pit on Earth, then it appeared that there was a secret trap door through which we could fall much deeper. Almost everything we tried to fight her pain with stopped working after two or three times. Everything effective was beaten out of our hands. Yet I thought it ridiculous to think that our spirit life guides, or God, wanted to test us or something stupid like that. But if not... then what was it?

There were rare moments that I had a strong feeling of being part of something... great. I didn't understand that feeling, and it was gone as swift as it came, but whatever it was it must be pretty important if God allowed this to happen.

The bed on which Linda lay was equipped with an eight-inch super soft foam layer, but that wasn't enough. "What can we do to change that, so I can sleep better?" Such a question she could ask me at half past midnight, shortly before trying to sleep.

I might then look at her with a weary sense of 'oh dear... not now please!' But then I asked her a counter question, to which she of course knew the answer, just to start it, "What spot hurts most?"

"Well yeah... that place above my coccyx. I can have nothing against it. Even the touch of a feather hurts."

I thought for a moment and then said, "If we could cut out a hole in the mattress, so that this spot doesn't have to touch anything?"

"How do you want to do that?" she asked. "Cutting out? If you could cut out the pain, now that would be something!"

But the idea appealed to her, so I cut out a piece of foam from the mattress the size of a hand and then we placed the mattress back on her bed. On top I put a soft flannel sheet that we had baptized 'granny sheet', because it had been a gift from her beloved grandmother. That felt a lot better, but inside the hole that sheet still touched her painful spot. So we were fiddling for a while until she was happy. "Yes... let's keep it like that. Let me lie for a few seconds."

I watched and waited.

Then she remarked, "There's still something that needs attention. I think I feel the mattress below this one."

"I think we have two old mattresses that my sister Mieke gave us recently," I said. "One of them felt pretty soft."

So I dragged that one from upstairs and we pulled everything from the bed. Then we rearranged the bed with first the old mattress, then Mieke's mattress and finally the super soft foam mattress. And on top of that the granny sheet... and wow, *that* was a soft combination! I wanted to try it out and was impressed with the result. But when she tested it for a little while she said there still was something that needed to be fixed. We also had this quilt that her mother had brought us, now didn't we? That too was amazingly soft. Couldn't we... ?

Meanwhile it was half past two, but that didn't matter. Again we pulled everything from the bed. Old mattress, Mieke's mattress, foam mattress, quilt, granny sheet and... yet it wasn't quite that. What could we think of now?

"You know what the problem is," she said after testing again. "I am lying on my back a lot, but my leg is stretched and it causes tension in my belly. I should have something to support my knee, something soft.

Apparently the mattresses were approved for the moment, but now we had to find a solution for her knees. We tried all kinds of pillows, blanket rolls, wraps, some clothes strapped together with a belt, but always there was something with it. So at half past three we were still rebuilding the bed, but... while being so busy she still hadn't asked for the painkiller. Obviously this wasn't about finding the ultimate solution to kill the pain, but merely about killing the time. I wisely kept my mouth shut. Had she forgotten about the Paracetamol?

But just at that moment she said, "It's going pretty well, huh?"

I agreed with her, only had to pull myself together to show a bright smile on my face before starting to rebuild the bed all over again for the... I lost count of that. I couldn't walk straight anymore and had to grab the railing along the stairs tightly to prevent myself from falling down. Always there was something not quite right. She could have outdone even the famous princess on the pea, because she was able to tell through a layer of six mattresses and sheets and whatever more we had, that way down below that pile on the floor a grain of sand was crooked.

"Gee, guys," I thought more than once, "It's half past four already... everyone is asleep and what are we doing? - totally re-making the bed for the thirty something time."

Finally at half past six or so we agreed that for the next night we had invented a reasonable solution to sleep on.

This kind of bed rebuilding we did at least twice a week. If only she could sleep for more than a few minutes... But even sleeping pills were no option. They made her feel so weird and sick that she refused them all together. No solution again, of course.

Another part of the ritual was I holding her hands when she finally had closed her eyes, the last part of hours of work. I kept her right hand in my left one, visualising refreshing white light flowing into her body, while in my other hand I held the Egyptian Ankh on which her other hand laid, and through it negative energies were pulled from her body, to be purified and transmitted to the cosmos.

Only I was so tired that I had big trouble staying awake. But when I wasn't concentrating anymore she noticed it immediately saying, "You have to stay awake silly! Don't fall asleep! Otherwise we've done it all for nothing."

Now that I write this I can barely believe that we could keep this up. Am I exaggerating it all? No... that is what happened, it even was a lot worse than I could ever express. But it convinced me of one thing and that was one way or the other we were helped tremendously to accomplish whatever we needed to accomplish.

But why? Why was all this? What was so important that all this was needed?

Your Friend Is Close By Your Side

Your friend is close by your side
And speaks in far ancient tongue

'Somehow I'll find my way Home'
John & Vangelis

Linda's weight was dangerously low and this naturally led to serious deficits. She could hardly see anything with her left eye anymore; it had been sensitive for quite a while, probably a side effect of the Cyclokapron that, in combination with her low weight, increased the symptoms.

Another consequence of its condition of underweight was that her body was unable to create endorphins, body chemicals with a narcotic, analgesic effect.

Her singing and expressing of strange words began to change in nature. For a time all the words she used seemed to originate from German, with this typical 'angular' accent, like 'Ordnung muss sein'. But she could speak that language, so why this strange 'look-alike' of the language? A week later she changed the style and was experimenting with French and English sounds en songs. After that she started with Hebrew sounds, not so strange because she lived in Israel for a year and a half. Finally she started using a language that I didn't recognize. Remarkable too was that the melodies of her songs change nature, becoming hauntingly realistic and convincing. It was as she went through the same stages a baby does, mimicking and experimenting at first, uttering sounds and gibberish, slowly mastering the language of its parents - fake it till you make it. But were did Linda 'hear' this language? It was so realistic! What was her example?

Distraction! That was it! After a while I paid no attention to it anymore, feeling glad that at least she had a bit of fun while experimenting.

But a week or so later I had to admit that the language that she had mastered somehow sounded very much as if originating from an Eastern European region. I hadn't seen it coming, because quite suddenly I realized that her fancy words and slogans had disappeared completely from her vocabulary and now she spoke a language. And not just a few words now and then, but all the time. She never stopped! For days she sat talking on and on. Not just talking, but also an endless monologue spoken in an impatient way, at a frantic pace, hardly taking time to pause and breathe. With a small recording device, I took some clips and was thus able to write it out phonetically. It sounded something like: "Munàma mostokòha kostoch tajàha togtog teja kahára... "

It was a very musical language, but I couldn't pin it down. It sounded like she was irritated, angry even, or desperate. As if she was saying to everyone who would listen, what kind of miserable situation she was in, throwing everything out that bothered her.

I let her go with it and if I had to ask her a question she answered that normally, but immediately thereafter the flow of words continued to come from her mouth. During the sparse moments that she paused she might say something like that she herself got tired of doing this - but she couldn't help it, she said. It just happened, as if by itself.

Not far from our town we discovered that there was a pain clinic. That sounded like what we needed; people who specialize in treating pain. I made some inquiries at first and learned that the pain was treated through injections. Linda sighed, "Injections for pain... if that doesn't work... !"

So we made an appointment and a few days later we were welcomed into a large, clean room where several nurses were at work. The head of this clinic began by giving a series of small injections around her entire abdomen. Linda let it happen passively, but the injections must have hurt her a lot. The syringes were small with short needles. The doctor explained that he first had to anaesthetize the skin and the tissues underneath the skin, so later he could give deeper injections. We looked at each other and didn't know what to think of this.

After fifteen minutes he returned with slightly larger syringes. The needles were longer. He gave her a new series of injections. Now Linda had great difficulty keeping calm, and I thought, "Can she feel this? How can this be?"

Some time later he returned again, this time with syringes with incredibly long needles. I looked reluctantly at them. That long! I hoped the precious injections had done their job sufficiently otherwise this might be yet another painful disappointment to overcome. Linda feared the injections very much and was all over the place.

The pain clinic experiment was indeed another total failure. It had only caused Linda lots more pain. And what's more, she still felt the needles sticking inside her abdomen! She had had quite a few of them, all over her belly. I didn't know the precise number, but she was given at least seven injections with the super long needle. That needle was so long that it must have gone almost till her back!

I expected that the pain caused by the injections would soon disappear, but not so. The next day she felt as if the needles were still inside her belly and she asked me if I could take them out. I hardly could believe what she was asking me, because how on Earth was I to remove needles that weren't there? But I promised I would do my best and that night I went to work. It was half dark inside and I started with treating her like I usually did, magnetizing, Reiki, healing with my hands, preparing myself.

She lay on her back and I sat on the floor beside her, with my hand hovering over her belly. She couldn't see what I did close to her skin and besides that she had her eyes closed. I tried to feel and see where the needles were exactly, but that was not easy. Of course not! You have to be a psychic to be able to do that. But I didn't intend to give up that easily and so I closed my eyes to slits, concentrated like never before and after a few moments I thought I could see something at the edge of my perception, barely visible. Carefully I moved my fingers to that spot, trying to touch the transparent 'thing' and suddenly she screamed out in pain. "What are you doing!?" she screamed. "That's it. Right there! Get it out!"

I suppressed my surprise and kept focused. Did I really spot something there? Had I seen it? Perhaps it was my imagination, but I thought I could see it and again tried to touch it with my fingers, trying to grab the needle. Linda couldn't see what exactly I was doing nor where, but her reactions made it clear that she didn't have to see it... she felt it immediately! "Ouch Ouch!" she said, "You must catch it! Not just *do* something!"

I concentrated again, focusing with all I had, and suddenly I felt very confident and I knew that the needle was right there where I looked. Like picking a needle from a pincushion I took the tip of the needle between my fingers. Her reaction was immediate, a loud outcry of pain, confirming that

I hit bull's eye and with a swift move, and a short outcry from Linda, I pulled the needle from her belly.

"And... ?" I asked when it stopped.

She was still feeling if the pain was gone, but then said surprised, "The pain is gone! Yeah... my belly still hurts like always, but that needle is gone. I can't feel it anymore.

I didn't understand, but was relieved that it had worked. So I went looking for the other needles. One by one I found them and pulled them out. Very bizarre! But it worked. So the extra pain caused by the treatment was neutralized. I had still trouble comprehending what I had done somehow. My rational mind told me this was nonsense, but meanwhile I had seen more things that my reason couldn't deal with.

Her funny talking began to take on a life of its own. So it could happen that when her parents came down for a visit and we all sat in the garden, she could suddenly say something aloud like, "He mesh keme!" or something like: "Uztabija hebe spàgkija". Quite loud and easy to repeat what she said, but totally impossible to understand.

At first we found that odd, but we got used to it as usual. So after a while it occurred to me that she could say the craziest things in between a conversation, but no one took any notice of it. After saying such a sentence or word she would join in the conversation like nothing had happened.

Of course those remarks she made were far from normal, but the stressed, hours long monologues at full speed had gone. And I was happy about that because it made me so tired to listen to it all day long.

It was obvious that whatever she said, it was not her own thoughts she expressed. It was like somebody else was talking through her, and after a while I began to see that even subtle facial changes could be seen while she spoke with that voice. Sometimes she was telling a whole story and while listening I could study her, and I observed how her whole attitude changed. But it took me a couple of days before I really saw that.

Was it possession, foreign entities taking over her body? That was what we were thinking for starters. Being so weak and having so much pain, that idea seemed pretty conceivable. We had never dealt with such a thing, but after a while we rejected the idea. Whatever it was, it was certainly a good distraction for us, because the voice didn't at all sound aggressive or hostile. Impatient perhaps, or capricious, but that wasn't bad. When we talked together about this, we referred to it as 'her voice'.

Singing was something her 'voice' could do very well! The songs were not those strange made up rhyming kind of songs anymore, but now they were real songs, with a beginning and an end, with choruses and often hauntingly beautiful melodies that were different with each song. I wished I could have recorded them, but every time I tried to do that her voice kept silent.

Even though this wasn't possession, yet it seemed like a personality saying things like this through Linda. Actually, we thought it was Linda herself, but how can that be? How can you be yourself and at the same time someone else? Actors can do that, but this was nothing like acting. This was a language spoken by a personality that resembled Linda in a certain way, as far as you can tell such from just intonation and posture. We couldn't yet figure out if it was a male or female personality, but the jargon was singing, seemed to stem from Eastern Europe and was a very beautiful and fascinating language to listen to.

One fragment that I was able to capture on time sounded roughly like this:

Kiemèsh keme mijbéka bijtos togtejéboch.
IJmesh spoike he spogpocht.
Hie mesh keme.
Uztabija hebe spagkija.
Hè... Bijmas mija kespastia.
Bweès meke mjas bijéweg."

Words she uttered very often, usually apart from other things she said, were 'snacht', 'esnachkija' and 'nasja'. Especially that last word 'nasja' she could repeat very clearly and emphasized, and it sounded always very emotional. Most of the time she called it more than she said it - "Nasja... nàsja... naàsja... NASJÁAaa... "[5]

It was amazing how much pain and sadness she could express with just that one word. All the pain, loneliness and sadness, so many months now, that

---

[5] *Though few, there are some recordings of Igor. You can listen to them on www.akaija.com*

I, even after so many pages, still can't really describe... and she was able to express it all in just one cry, nasja!

We were both wondering what it meant. But how were we to find that out? And what language was it? A Russian dialect? After a couple of days we concluded at least one thing. Her voice was a male personality. I think Linda just knew it, because I couldn't tell.

Our cats naturally often came for a quick check of what we were doing, walking over the bed, and eating cat food in the hallway. They didn't elude the attention of her 'friend' as we gradually started calling him. The Birman, usually downstairs, got a name from him: Pusj Maika. Our black cat was called 'Kleine Pusj', meaning 'Little Pusj'. The latter name we understood, because Charonna was one year younger than Liselle and we sometimes nicknamed her Little Puss. But he didn't pronounce that word Puss well, making it sound Russian with the sj-sound.

But why did he call Liselle, Pusj Maika?

In any case, her 'friend' seemed to be very familiar with animals.

Because it was impossible according to us, we rejected the idea that this phenomenon could have something to do with past lives. We were convinced of reincarnation, everyone having multiple lives, based on the immortality of the soul. But Linda's past lives were over and done with, so it had to be something else. But then what?

Linda parents were friends of a clairvoyant woman who said that she could retrieve information from the 'Akashic records'. The Akashic records can be described as the Chronicles of the Cosmos, an infinite recording of everything, in which absolutely everything that actually happens, even every thought, is stored. Not in written or spoken words, and in its entirety never comprehendible for the human mind, but to a certain level it can be accessed by a very few gifted people. Her parents gave this woman Linda's details and informed us later, but we soon forgot about it. We didn't doubt this woman could do such a thing, but we had other things on our minds.

Often in the early hours we sat at the window waiting for the first light to arrive from the east, the Sun projecting her first rays in the low sky over the horizon. Then it was light! And for Linda that was the best time to go to sleep.

Something for the Pain

Maybe it was the nice weather, so we could often sit outside, making her feel comfortable in the garden. Maybe it was the treatment of the various people who were distantly working on her health, sending energy and such. Perhaps there was another cause. Anyway, the bleedings occurred less and less and her condition seemed to slowly stabilize. And mid-August, in the last week for her birthday, the change announced itself for which we had been waiting for all those long months; a real improvement on all fronts. I had already suspected this for a couple of days, because everything seemed lighter, the days were easier to pass and she looked better, subtle changes that you only become aware of when you look back over the last week and compare. Increasingly, I thought, "Hey, it looks like this is going a little better now!"

In the room above our bed was a poem that I once had calligraphed. Because of the gradient background from light to dark, the bottom lines were increasingly difficult to read for weak eyes, so that was an ideal eye test. Every morning Linda tested what she could read with her bad left eye. She used to have hawk eyes, but her left eye had deteriorated over the last months, probably due to medications. With that eye she couldn't read a single line of that poem, it was a blur.

One morning she was practising again and I saw her react differently than usual. She looked with one eye kept closed at the poem and then looked at another object. Then she looked at me, alternately closing her eyes and finally said, "I must tell you something."

"Your eyes?" I asked.

"Yes. I wanted to wait a few days until my parents arrive. But I want to tell you now... I can see better with this eye!"

"Oh?" I replied happily. "Can you read that poem again?"

"Not quite, but it's getting better."

She explained. "For a couple of days now I can read the first two lines. And now... " And almost effortlessly she read the first half of the poem, while she kept her good right eye shut.

"Wow!" I said. "That sounds good!"

"And what's more," she continued, "You know that I have trouble going to the toilet, my constipation, and this morning... it just went!"

She was happy, as happy as a child. I never knew that from her, always so guarded, protected, tough and strong. And now she was emotionally happy as she looked at me. The fact that she couldn't wait to tell me until her parents would arrive, telling me in advance... she couldn't keep secrets anymore.

"And you know... The pain has been getting less... for a few days!"

She described all the changes over the previous days. The pain was located in the bottom of her spine. Her lower back was always on fire with pain that was now disappearing. It was still there, but now restricted to the bones in that location. Around it all was improving.

Now that was what we had been hoping for so long, an improvement like that! The pain was going away. Sleeping was still a problem, but when she continued to improve that would follow automatically. YES!!! When I listened to her describing all the changes I finally had that feeling for the very first time, this is a real improvement! Not just hearing reassuring words from people that she was improving, but now it was by our own experience! That's what counted!

From that moment we were more cautious, to do nothing that was dangerous. This improvement had to be nurtured terrified as we were something might go wrong. We strengthened the protection around the house, because who knows, there could be evil forces at work wanting nothing less than to make her suffer in pain. They wouldn't get that chance. We took care of that!

Even at night things went better. She rested more and even slept a little longer. The Dyclofenac was still crap, so she used that less and less, but even a quart pill could cause intense pain responses.

We rearranged the bed for the thousandth night, but now we were hopeful. It felt more comfortable for her to lie on her back, so finding a good solution was easier. We also started experimenting with warmth again, but we had to dosage the amount of heat very precisely. A hot jar should have exactly the right temperature. I also had a couple of hot and cold gel packs that I heated in a continually boiling pot of hot water. I was running up and down the stairs all day long, but it had effect. But we needed a better solution. So we a tried an electrically heated seat, and an infrared lamp. But those were not really good solutions.

In the pharmacy I had discovered heat patches, which you could easily apply at the right spot. They could provide warmth for a long time, as the name suggested "warmth bandages'. It looked okay, but how did they work? I thought they needed to be kneaded for the warmth to be generated by a chemical process, or maybe that as soon as air got to the exposed bandage that it started to produce warmth. I knew that mountain climbers used such things against frostbite.

I made some inquiries in the pharmacy and the lady behind the counter told me that they were completely safe. They even had the normal bandages and the hyper sensitive version, especially for people who were over-sensitive. She had never heard of anyone ever having any negative reactions to them. It really could do no harm. Before buying them I tried to find out on the Internet if I could discover anything about the active ingredient 'nonivamide', but apart from a scientific report full of scientific terms I couldn't find out anything worthwhile. The Internet was in its early stages then.

We hesitated, but finally I bought both types. We would wait till the next day, because then her parents would come over and with the bandage she probably would be able to talk to them for a longer period of time.

Meanwhile she was getting better all the time. The next morning she read nearly the whole poem, only the last lines in the dark background were just a bit too vague. "The colours are getting normal again too," she said. "With my good eye the colours were totally different, but now they look nearly equal again. And the flickering in my eyes is less. That made me so tired."

One hour before her parents arrived I started preparing the hypersensitivity patch. It was a rectangular piece of material with an adhesive foil. I cut a small piece of it and put it on her skin, not on, but close to the painful area on her back. Putting it right on top of it didn't feel like a good idea. It would need half an hour or so to start working, so meanwhile I could prepare a few things for when her parents would come in. This news would make them happy! This was Linda's surprise for them.

Fifteen minutes later Linda said it felt weird. It wasn't warm under the patch, but it began to burn. I lifted a corner of the patch to see how it looked. Her skin was all red. I didn't like what I saw and Linda said, "Take it off quickly! This doesn't feel good at all. Take it away!"

But it was too late. The skin was very red, like sunburn. It began to hurt terribly, not only there but also everywhere in her body. So much so that shortly afterwards she felt like going crazy because of the pain. We tried to cool the place with wet washcloths, but it had no effect. She was dying of pain. Meanwhile, I railed against the manufacturer of that heat patch. Linda said it felt like the matter was going all through her body. What in Heaven's name was it! Hyper Sensitive? What nonsense! I had expected that the patch itself would start getting warm, applying warmth to her skin, but instead it caused the opposite. It made her skin react to it, generating some reaction inside her body. But that wasn't the intention! Nobody had told us that! Maybe that information could be found somewhere and I had totally overlooked it. Of course it may have been better to apply it first to a totally other location on her body, but if this was an allergic reaction that that would have made no difference. Maybe I should have tested it on myself first. Why had I not thought of that before? Stupid stupid stupid!

By the time Linda's parents arrived she was sat in the garden, crying. At the door I explained to them what had happened minutes before and shocked they walked to the garden. They sat quietly beside her. Her mother tried to comfort her, but Linda said, "I'd like to surprise you! I'd like to tell you things went better. It went so well the last few days. I could even see better again. The pain was less. It was going so good!"

She bent forward in the chair and was barely audible between the sobs. Her father looked at me and asked what exactly she said. I explained what had happened and how she had advanced so well this last while.

"But perhaps it is still better, you are just not feeling good because of that patch," her mother tried.

"I have been upstairs," she said. "I've checked. I can't read the poem anymore. Everything is again vague. And the pain is back!"

And how intensely it had come back indeed! The pain was so great that she conked out and lay totally stretched motionless in the chair. She wasn't even breathing it seemed! I simply gripped her hand, recovering her, and immediately she came to, completely dazed.

"What just happened?" she asked. I saw fear in her eyes like I had never seen before. The pain was so severe that she lost consciousness again a short time after.

It was such a disappointment! Months of work completely destroyed, offset by a little patch of a few square centimetres. Her eyes were bad again. She couldn't go the toilet again. She slept as bad as ever. The pain had returned, worse than before. Also the bleedings returned in full force. But although there was more than enough reason to, we didn't call an ambulance.

At the beginning of the summer we had been passed on a message from the family physician in which the hospital obstetrician informed his colleagues about Linda's choices, doubting the usefulness of any future blood transfusions. So what was the point of putting Linda in that situation again, regarded by the specialists as totally nuts. We were better to save ourselves from that.

We were pounded into the ground. Whenever there was an indication of improvement we were kicked down. It just wasn't allowed! Every way out was cut off. What was going on here?

No matter how bad the bleedings were, Linda stayed alive. When I later did find more information about Nonivamide on the Internet I discovered that the same stuff was used in Australia in painkillers. Painkillers work by widening the blood vessels through chemistry, hence...

I called the manufacturer of the patches in Germany, but I got nothing but denial, ignorance and especially distant reactions. What was I expecting? I was angry, very angry, and wanted to do something, but what could I do? It had happened. It wouldn't change a thing. Swallow it and continue fighting.

But this was a very bitter pill to swallow.

Her birthday a few days later, we skipped. Mieke, and also Linda's parents came for a visit, bringing a birthday card, "Just another year to flush through the toilet".

I had no gift for her, but when I asked what she wanted her reply was simple, "Something against the pain."

It is Light

Once again we were beaten down. Those are moments when you feel that you're deprived of your breath and your heart is totally blocked. This was true for me, but I could only guess what it did to her.

A few days later I got an idea of how that was. Because of my hasty running and racing I didn't always have a clue about what was going on inside her. I think that she would have preferred crouching away in a corner crying as hard as she could.

What could I do? Sit beside her and hold her hand? Touching her anywhere else was unbearable for her. Sometimes her grief expressed itself in impotent anger, and she screamed out, making my ears ring.

"I can't!" she said. "I can't! Do you hear me! I quit!"

She paused, a dubious silence.

In a low voice she continued, "If you suddenly find I'm not in bed, then there's no need to look for me because I will be gone."

She looked at me and I feared the sudden change in the tone of her voice. "I love you." She looked at me very urgently. "You know that. You have done well. No one could have done better. But I can't keep up. Now you must let me go. Don't go looking for me"

"What are you going to do? I asked, with a sense of fear.

I shuddered at the thought and visualized me finding her. That scared me, perhaps most, because in the end I wouldn't have been there for her. It scared me that she would decide to end it in solitude. I would have failed to protect her, and the thought of her being all alone at the most difficult moment of her life was unbearable.

So I said to her, "Then I have failed."

I tried talking to her, to make her realize that this was not a solution to her problem. But I didn't reach her.

Fear around my heart...

It was August and the days were very hot. Even during the nights it was warm. I had become a seasoned 'mother', being able to distinguish normal and alarming sounds while sleeping. So, when after a short while I heard something strange, I became fully awake. I pricked up my ears but remained silent. It seemed that the door latch had been gently opened. She was trying to go downstairs then? And obviously she didn't want me to hear it.

"What are you doing?" I asked in the dark.

At that moment she opened the door quickly and went down the stairs. I quickly jumped out of bed, put on my jogging pants and followed her.

"You must stay here!" she shouted when I came up behind her. "I must go alone!" She hadn't put anything else on her this time and didn't even do something with her hair. Downstairs she had switched on the kitchen lamp and was looking for the house keys... but I already had them in my hands.

"Only if I can come with you," I said, showing her the keys. It was not right to use my authority, but I couldn't think of anything better.

"I must go alone," she said again. "What are you *doing!*"

"Coming with you... I won't let you go alone" I replied.

She tried to work herself past me to the front door but I could easily stop her. I felt awful. This wasn't good. I felt compelled in my strength and agility and I knew in this condition I would always win.

She was angry, but couldn't express it. She didn't want to talk about it, only to leave. She reached for the spare keys but I had those in my hand too. "You can't come!" she spat at me. "Give me the keys!"

"Then what are you going to do? Commit suicide?"

"Give me the keys!" she said again. "You have to let me go. Don't you understand?"

I shrugged my shoulders, decided to let her have her way and gave her the keys. She immediately turned and walked to the garden door. In the middle of the night she walked out of the door, quickly pulling it closed behind her. It was pitch dark in the park behind our house. I saw a faint blur disappearing into the night through the darkness.

She had expressly ordered me not to follow her but what could I do? Let her go? What was she up to? Would she jump into the pond in the park? Throw herself under a car? But at half past two in the night with no cars on the roads, that might prove to be some challenge.

I decided not to follow her straight away but to go out of the front door. So first I had to go round the block, but were would she go to? I was half panicking, couldn't think straight. Should I go into the dark park? That's were the ponds were. I ran around the block, softly calling her name. During such warm nights all people would sleep with open windows. The advantage was that she wouldn't suffer the cold that fast, let alone freeze to death.

As soon as the houses were behind me I raised my voice calling her name louder: "WHERE ARE YOU?!"

Of course, no reply, but at least she knew I was looking for her. Perhaps she would hear the panic in my voice. Who knows that would make her see sense. Who could tell me what to do and where to go? I *had* to do this, didn't I? I couldn't let go of her just like that?

I walked into the dark park following the bike path and called her every now and then, straining my eyes to see in the dark. Somewhere in front of me I heard a croak of a solitary invisible duck. Our friends... Would she be under water already? Would I be able to save her? How long was I walking now?

Half running I moved on and suddenly from a corner of my eye I caught a glimpse of a different colour on a bench in front of the elderly nursing home. Someone sat there. Was it her? Thank God. I went to her. She sat hunched over, crying.

Without saying anything I approached her.

"I *can* do this, can I?" she said softly.

At least she wasn't locking me out with silence.

I sat down beside her and talked to her in a low voice; simple comments, I don't remember what, but it didn't matter. She said she had wanted to go to the roof of the nursing home and jump. "But I can't even walk that far. I just can't!"

I looked behind, saw that we were right in front of it. Here and there a few lights were on – old folk not able to sleep too. It was only a few more steps.

She cried again. But this crying wasn't from frustration, despair, anger and whatever; this sounded like real sorrow, intense sorrow of disappointment upon disappointment. This came from very deep down inside. This was real crying.

Very carefully I put a coat that I had hastily grabbed over her back. It wasn't cold, but the bench was wet and cold, and with her skinny body she would quickly cool. But I didn't urge her to come along.

"I love you," I said. "Maybe I should tell you more often. I don't want to lose you, but I also don't know how we can do this."

We talked and eventually we went home, slowly, while I supported her. But it didn't feel safe like going home. And when we entered there it wasn't like coming home enjoying the comfort and peace together with our two cats. This was no victory, no solution. There was no consolation. What was there in fact? Another night, again more pain? Would she ever get better? And if not... ?

As difficult as it was, somewhere she found the strength to fight again. And again I was impressed, and admired her. She didn't give up, disappointed maybe, temporarily maybe, but never permanently. Do not give up. Never give up! Where did she get the energy for fighting like this?

Her funny language wasn't affected. Her 'friend' could sing very well, because almost every day now I heard her or him sing songs, and always it was new songs, and not fantasy songs anymore, not in the least! She sang intricate lyrics and I noticed that there were often repeated choruses, which, as far as I could distinguish, were verbally and melodically exactly the same. They weren't just songs, because they were so nice! Some were reminiscent of Cossack songs, which I strangely enough had listened to a lot to in my youth. Roughly speaking, there were two kinds of songs, lullabies and marching songs. The difference between them was obvious. The marching songs had a sleek and measured pace, with simple and repetitive texts.

There was one such marching song, unlike any other, that Linda repeated very often, probably because it sounded challenging and was easy listening. That's why I remember the text. She always sang a few sentences in which something was said or remarked and then came a brief chorus that she sang very exuberant and joyful:

"Kiru la fanái! Kiru la fanái!
Questa questa questa questa...
Kiru la fanái!"

As with almost every song long before the end of it, her way of singing really emphasised it. At the end of this song, the text of the narrative singing became exciting, softer and softer. She stretched it as long as possible and then shouted loudly, "KIRU LA FANÁI!"

The lullabies were quite different in character. These were always hauntingly beautiful. And always one word would show up in every song, nacka nacka. Linda said that this word meant 'sleeping'. Sometimes only at the end of the song it could be heard, but when she sang it, we knew it was a lullaby.

Her friend kept calling that one word 'nasja'. We wondered whether 'nasja' could be a name. Could *his* name possibly be Nasja? Then suddenly he added some other word to it, saying 'Nasja uzbekija'.

When the mail fell on the doormat I picked it up as usual without looking and brought it to Linda, so she had something to do. One day I had just done so and was back in the kitchen again, and while I was at work I suddenly heard a loud outcry that had me running to the stairs. Only when I went up the stairs I could make out the words. "That's him! That's him! Come on! It's him! You see... I didn't make it up! That's him!"

I saw her sitting upright with a note in her hands, crying with wet cheeks, but this was different. She was excited and gave me the note. It was from the woman that Linda's parents had been consulting for her ability to access the Akashic records.

I read:

"1532, Russia, a former life. You were a soldier and fought with swords and axes. On the battlefield you were injured. Your bowels lay out, but you had lived to survive for five days. Sadness, anger, pain... everything came out."

There was some more, but when I read it I got a lump in my throat and suddenly I began to cry. Now what! I never cry. What is going on here?!

A past life? But what else could it have been? We already knew it was so for a long time now, without understanding it at all. Apparently there was a link with lots of pain to that battlefield of long ago. Maybe the pain during these awful months had triggered something that made Linda jump back and forth between two incarnations.

I was reading the letter over and over again with tears in my eyes and suddenly I knew something else: "I was Nasja!" I said. The feeling was so strong. "My name actually was Natascha."

This letter thoroughly shook us up, because it reactivated centuries old memories and emotions that hadn't been processed. For me it was a very strong sense of finally getting confirmation that she, or he, had been killed in some battle of long ago.

That same evening she called me again to come up, "Come quick... come, come. He's showing it all to me... come quickly!"

I ran upstairs and saw her on the bed. She was seated on her knees, leaning forward with a blanket pulled entirely over her and it appeared that she was in the middle of a conversation. "She's here," she said as if talking to herself, which in fact was her friend. "Nasja is here. Would you say it again, to her?" she asked softly. Then she fell silent.

To me she said: "You have to be here. I don't know if I can do this again, but you need to be here. He's showing it all to me!"

I sat down beside her on the ground and she started telling me what she had experienced, and then, with me present, she relived it again. They lived in a small town in Uzbekija. Nasja was his wife.

"She's very pretty, isn't she?" Linda asked with a particular voice, as if talking to a child.

Her friend then replied immediately, through Linda, "She's the most beautiful girl in town." He said that in such glorified tone and repeated it again, "the most beautiful girl in town." He was so proud.

"What was his name?" I softly interrupted him.

"Igor," Linda said. "His name was Igor." And I knew immediately, yes! Igor. That's his name. That's right.

In some ways it now was possible to communicate in Dutch with him, and Linda immediately understood what she saw and heard. After this we got the entire story, while we, Linda and I occasionally asked questions to Igor and received answers to them right away.

Igor and Nasja had lived in a small village somewhere in Uzbekija. They were married and apparently he had come to live with Nasja. They had a cat, Maika, and with the cat in his arms he was singing songs, many songs. He was practicing with Maika because Nasja was seven months pregnant and soon he would be a father. He was so proud! And so happy! While holding Maika in his arms he walked through the house, sang lullabies, and also created new songs for the upcoming baby and love songs for his beloved Nasja.

They had three geese. "Honk Honk Honk," he mimicked them. The people in the village however found them weird, because Nasja was talking to the geese. And to geese you don't talk, you eat them. But... if you talk to them you start loving them, and so you can't eat them. Then they just cost you money and that was strange. But this didn't bother Nasja and Igor.

He also had a mother or grandmother who still lived, Ìrina, whom he loved very much.

One day men came to the village, soldiers. They were searching for young men for some distant war going on (it probably was the time of Ivan the Terrible, that's why). All men had to come. It was promised to them that when they would return, they would be rich and the people would be proud of them. Igor said with a scornful laugh, "Yeah... if we come back." Those recruiters knew perfectly well that probably no one would come back, so that was an easy promise. Nobody wanted to go, but when the other goes, you can't stay behind. That's just wasn't done, so Igor went along too. They were all braggarts. They didn't let others know their feelings, didn't show their fear, they acted brave, but in fact they were all very frightened.

I asked if Nasja gave him something from her as a love token, to remind him of her. I knew somehow that would be the case.

"Yeah... a beautiful blue headscarf. A blue headscarf." He was very careful with that and showed it to nobody. But he said, "The others have things too, but they don't talk about them. They keep them hidden, but I know, because I sometimes see them pull out something and look at it."

Then they had to walk a very long way, visiting other towns along the way. During those long marches they sang songs, marching songs. On that trip he also got to know someone with whom he became friends, staying together for the rest of the trip. Finally, after many days, but probably it was weeks, they arrived at a large house, more like a military base. They only stayed there for one day and they were handed swords and axes. The next day they were marching again, but almost that same day they encountered the enemy. This enemy was very well trained and they hadn't had time to exercise with their weapons, so they were massacred, slaughtered to the last man.

Igor was quickly wounded in his leg by a stroke of a sword. Linda had suffered for years from a vague pain in her right leg, exactly at that spot. He fell and for the moment he was left alone, but after a while he tried to crawl away. Linda hurriedly said to him, "Do not!! Stay there! Lay down. That way they don't see you!"

But he didn't listen, because a little further he had seen a tree and wanted to hide under it. When he had nearly reached the tree they found him. All his friends were probably dead or severely wounded and the enemy had free reign. Apparently they were quite sadistic, because with a sword they cut open his belly, so that his intestines bulged out, and then they left him there to die.

In Igor's voice, I heard how miserable he felt. He was able to drag himself the last metres to the tree and there slumped with his back against the tree with his hands against his stomach, not even strong enough to lift his head. Whenever I think of Linda, how she hung in her chair when she was in so much pain, I still see that same hopeless position. The rest of the day he remained lying there. He heard his comrades around him calling for help. But nobody was able to do anything. There was nobody there, and nobody came.

Igor started to cry, "Nasja! Nàsja!... NASJAAáááaa!!!"

"She can't hear you, can she?" Linda said to Igor. He continued to call Nasja, just as I had heard her do so often.

It went dark and around him his comrades' voices fell silent one by one. Silence on the field. Only he remained alive, calling for Nasja. Sometimes he shouted her name in the darkness. Because the night was so dark and he felt so lonely, he started talking. Maybe there were wild animals in the neighbourhood, who were attracted to the smell of death. And the night lasted so long that it seemed endless.

Finally the light slowly returned. "It is light," he said hopefully. "Now they are coming to get me. Now they come! It is light."

But no one came. He continued to hope and to prevent getting mad he kept talking, rapidly and busy, endlessly, all day long. He spoke out everything that was bothering him, what he had done, what had happened, all his sorrow, his frustration that he couldn't be with Nasja, that Nasja didn't know were he was, his main concern. He called for her. He had to go to her. How could he get to her? Where was she? He had to take care of her. She was pregnant and he was to be the father! You don't leave your wife alone when she's about to have a baby! She could give birth any day now!

This repeated itself for days. Whenever it was light he hoped that someone would come, as he was so pleased that the night was over again. But never anyone showed up. When he told us this I was completely lost in my sense of Nasja. I felt the despair and sadness of the time. But now I felt a strange relief... that was Nasja's. Finally... finally knowing what had happened to him. But this was a terrible discovery.

However he didn't say that he had died on the battlefield. We tried asking him what had happened thereafter. "What happened next?" we asked him. But he went no further. He had to go to Nasja, he didn't die. He was fighting for survival, but he went no further. His story stopped there.

How much alike were he and Linda!

Linda could never sleep at night and now that she was so sick she would never switch on a lamp at night, because when you do that then outside it is really dark, and then it really is night. Every morning very early, when it was still dark outside, we often waited until the light of the day showed, and then we quickly switched off the lights, so we could see the rays of daylight gaining strength. For her that was the signal that all was safe to sleep. "It is light," she then said with a weary, hopeful voice. "It is light."

Ring Ring Nasja

Finally we understood what was going on, why this was happening to her. But how could a life of almost five hundred years ago act as a living thing in the present?

In fact, Linda and Igor were one and the same soul, but they didn't act as one. When Igor was speaking he acted like a 'third' person in the house and he did this so convincingly that it never felt like I was talking to Linda. It was like a fantasy movie about time travelling, in which a person from a distant past accidentally had been transported by a time machine to the twenty first century.

Igor now kept talking and singing in his own language. He had told his story to Linda; now he spoke through her, but it was as if he were a third party in the house. It was as if there were now two people within Linda. Usually we didn't understand what he was talking about, but he interacted in everything and was aware of all that happened. Even if he hadn't been talking for a long time, it appeared that he knew everything that was going on.

He wanted me to invent something that would help him and Linda. He didn't regard himself as being a part of Linda, but as Igor, a unique living being. It was beyond his comprehension. I was indeed inventing new tricks and means to help Linda fight the pain, and I had become very creative at this. The only problem was that all that I had come up with lasted only for a few nights at best. Igor understood this. I noticed this when he, at a certain moment, tapped with Linda's finger against the side of her head, looking empathically at me, and said "Peakagh, Peakagh!"

He expected me to think of something new against the pain, because he was worried about Linda. She needed something new, even if it only worked for a few days. I could do that; he had seen it.

One day, while working with the Ankh Igor suddenly repeated a specific same sentence, saying, "Uzmabe be stokje Ankh."

I thought it was funny first, but then Linda said, "He agrees that you treat me with the Ankh! He's worried about me."

But a few days later he went even further. Again I was treating Linda with the Ankh when he interrupted me saying the same words and even more. He had taken over Linda and was gesturing and speaking at the same time, but I didn't understand him. So I was relieved when Linda came back, saying, "He says you're doing it wrong. You need to position the Ankh differently in your hand."

What! I was taken by surprise. Did he even know how to use the Ankh for healing?

"Let him show it to me then," I said.

Linda couldn't control when Igor was taking her over, but I had discovered that I could elicit this by uttering some Uzbekija sounds, so I said: "Keme mish mish Uzbekija?"

That worked and immediately Igor took her over. I held up the Ankh and said in plain Dutch, "How do I have to hold the Ankh then? Show it to me."

From that moment on I was educated for half an hour how to work with the Ankh, and how to make moves with it. Sometimes he took my hand and that felt very different compared to Linda doing the same. He put the Ankh in my hand, and closed my fingers around it in a very special way, very loosely. Most of all I noticed that he wanted me to work a lot more respectful like with this instrument. And I had to make the movements over her body much slower, starting far away from her body, moving very slowly towards her, gently continuing the movement along her body, and very slowly moving away from her, preparing for the next move. My movement had to be very gentle, slow and respectful, following certain patterns. And he was right! I used to hold the Ankh firmly in my grip, metal is metal, what else can it be, but that was totally wrong.

He took my hand again, opened my fingers, laid the Ankh diagonally on it and pushed only my thumb softly over the central part of the Ankh. Then I moved the Ankh along her body, but no... I moved too fast, and I already thought that I was doing it really slow. I had to start the movement from far outside her energy field, then move the Ankh very close along her body, without hesitating a single moment, continuing the movement every inch of the way.

Every time when Igor had explained something, I had to exercise it, and Linda then lay on her back while he carefully checked all my doings from the corner of his, or her, eyes. Sometimes Linda came back explaining something in Dutch, but most of the time that wasn't necessary, because I understood him very well.

It was very bizarre to get a workshop from someone from the ancient past, in a language I had never heard before, coming from the mouth of my very ill *vriendinnetje* that had never done anything with the Ankh in her entire life. Try explaining that!

But I immediately felt... this worked a lot better! Reiki, magnetizing, aura healing, and working with the Ankh are after all treatments using divine, universal energy, Love that is. That was the most important thing he tried to make clear to me: Be respectful when you work with this and then do it with conviction, and no doubting, because you can!

Sometimes Igor could be downright annoying, because he interfered in everything. I wondered whether he was capable of taking Linda completely over. There were times when she was barely able to say anything and then I only heard her say weird things, complaining, singing, but also being silent while still being Igor.

But mostly Igor said something very quickly, followed by Linda with a reaction to what he had just said.

There was a lot of power in his voice and also Charonna, our black cat, Kleine Pusj, was to experience that. One time Linda was sitting behind a table sorting out papers, bills and notes when Charonna came in the room after eating in the hallway, still licking the corners of her mouth. She jumped on the table and, like cats usually would, walked right through the papers that Linda had carefully been sorting out, and sat down right in front of her, preparing for a thorough wash, pushing papers aside. That's how things should be done. Aren't all cats like that? You can't help hating them when they do that, but you also can't stop loving them, even though they regard you as lesser beings.

Linda tried to push her away, but Charonna looked at Linda's hand irritated as if to say 'that is not an option', and continued washing her belly with even more concentration, indicating 'don't even dare touch me again'.

Then suddenly Igor stepped in between and without touching Charonna he spoke a few sharp hissing Uzbekija words and pointed to the door. Charonna didn't see this coming and immediately jumped from the table and made her escape.

But Igor was in fact really kind to animals and could deal with them very well. I myself hadn't been there, but Linda described to me what had happened during my absence buying groceries. Igor had sung a song to Charonna! She showed me how he had embraced Charonna while she was sitting on the table, bending over her so she could go nowhere. Normally she would have gone berserk trying to escape, but not so this time. All the time during the song she had been sitting silently, listening, as if she knew this was meant for her.

It was very nice with the three of us. It was one of those special things we were given during this awfully difficult to accomplish task, because the visualisations with Amà often were not possible because Linda had trouble concentrating when she was in so much pain. It was a very good distraction for both of us.

I began to love Igor. Linda and Igor were two totally different personalities and of course I loved Linda, but I felt a great love being born, or should I say 'reborn', for Igor in an amazingly short time. The love I felt in this life for Linda of course was very related to Igor, but maybe our love was much older even than Uzbekija. Who could tell? It was a very strange sensation. I learned that love does not die, given the fact that five hundred years didn't make any difference at all.

Only thing was that Igor didn't see me as the reincarnation of his beloved Nasja. His understanding was that of a simple farm boy from Uzbekistan. He continued to call for Nasja, especially when Linda felt so miserable. At one point we were sitting behind my desk and Igor tried to get me do something for him, but as usual I didn't understand. He called Nasja, wanted to go to her, and I had to help him with that. Why didn't I want to do that? That couldn't be such a big problem? Then suddenly he grabbed the phone and pushed it awkwardly against my chest. "Ring Ring Nasja," he said.

I was stunned. Should I call Nasja by phone?

"Nasja Uzbekija. Ring Ring Nasja!" he said again and pushed the phone even harder to my chest. Obviously he had seen me, or Linda, talking to invisible persons not present in this room, so talking to Nasja in Uzbekija shouldn't be any problem at all.

I tried to explain him that Nasja was dead for a long time, almost five centuries ago. But that wasn't what he expected to hear from me. Every time when I started explaining that, he interrupted me saying, "Nasja Uzbekija." He didn't let me finish my sentences. Finally he said raising his voice, ""NASJA BEI UZBEKIJA!" telling me that the discussion was now closed.

Suddenly I had an idea and I said, "Nasja is born again. Nasja is here. I am Nasja!"

He had been looking downwards, a posture he often kept, unlike Linda's normal posture that was facing the world without any fear. But at hearing these words he lifted his face, looked thrilled and had a happy smile on his face.

"Nasja!" he said hopefully. "Nasja?"

Then he looked at me a little better and with Linda's fingers he touched my short beard as if to say that I never could be Nasja. The joyful gleam faded from his eyes as he lowered his head and with a sad smile he whispered, "Nasja nai... Nasja Uzbekija!"

On another occasion he had discovered something else. A few times over the past weeks we had been going to the therapist in Arnhem by car. He had learned something from that. When Linda and I sat late at night to discuss something he suddenly came in between and said, "Vroom vroom, Uzbekija. Nasja Uzbekija. Vroom vroom, Nasja!" He wanted me to drive him to Uzbekistan! Then he could go to Nasja and he would be home.

He was very convincing and I'm absolutely sure that if I had gone down and had stepped into the car, he would have followed me all the way. Probably he would be able to tell me exactly which way to go once we would arrive in Uzbekistan. Of course that was no option, but how should I explain this to him? I tried to point out that Uzbekija was very far away and that it would mean many days of driving. I didn't even try mentioning Nasja no longer being alive, since I wasn't able to get that into his mind anyway. But he kept repeating 'vroom vroom Uzbekija', so finally I picked an old atlas and searched for a large map of Europe and Asia. I showed him the map and pointed to the Netherlands as a small dot on the far Eastern end of the page and to Uzbekistan all the way on the other side of the page. He refused to listen to me and after a few attempts he pulled the atlas from my hands and threw it angrily across the room against the cabinet, after which he withdrew into himself and sat down huff-like, "No one wants to help me!"

After that Linda took over and she was pretty angry with this latest behaviour from Igor. "He gets very brutal!" she said. "He's not the boss here!"

Although this was very special and even fun most of the time, sometimes I felt really uncomfortable, because he could be very impatient and Linda sometimes was away for a long time. She too could be impatient, but she was much more reasonable.

Igor was indeed trying to master the Dutch language, and thus it could happen that suddenly he said a recognisable word. One time we were behind the computer surfing the Internet for painkillers when I suddenly heard him say, "Come pootrr." He had an understanding what we were doing and that this computer-thing gave access to distant locations and information. So when he gestured and started talking in his language I quickly understood that he wanted me to find Uzbekija on the Internet. "He wants to see pictures," added Linda in between. But no matter how hard I tried, there wasn't much more than a few statistical data on population numbers and boring descriptions available in those early days of Internet. There were no photographs in any case, and Igor showed no signs that he could read the present day written language of Uzbekistan, the Uzbek. However I was amazed to read somewhere that Uzbekistan spelled in the Uzbek language indeed was written and obviously spoken as 'Uzbekija'.

But this gave me an idea and I picked up a sheet of paper and a pen and started to make a drawing of a woman with a skirt and short blouse and I said, pointing to the drawing, "Nasja? Did Nasja look like this?"

He laughed when he saw this, grabbed my pen and started to change my drawing. The buttons on her blouse were no good and her hair was different. The skirt was longer, and Nasja needed more belly, because she was pregnant. Because I had not put feet under the skirt he managed to draw some badly shaped lumps under it. Then he drew a goose and gave Nasja a forked stick in her hands and showed how she led the geese with that stick. The result would never win a contest, especially with Nasja's weird feet, but he laughed out loud when he saw the results of his efforts.

The Fifth Day

Linda's pain was so extreme and she responded so poorly to analgesics that we were constantly looking for an answer to this one question: Where does this pain come from and what can we do about it? We asked each therapist the same question and because of our asking and searching we finally came across a classical homeopath that said that this might have something to do with a mild form of arsenic poisoning in the past, having been stored inside the fat cells and now released into her body again because she had lost so much weight. On the Internet I discovered that arsenic works on the end parts of nerves and so can cause pain.

We made phone calls to many therapists in the Netherlands and even abroad, and we finally found a man in Putten, a town not very far from Apeldoorn, who was said to be a specialist in neutralizing poisons in the human body. He had a busy practise and was unable to treat Linda on such short notice, but he knew a woman who worked with the same equipment he owned. She wasn't very experienced, but he could give her instructions on this specific problem. It so happened that this woman lived only two hundred and fifty metres away from our home. Telephone-searching all over the world to end up as close as that was almost absurd, but it served us very well, because Linda was extremely weak and her weight had dropped to thirty eight kilograms.

That same evening this woman came to us with her equipment. Marianne was her name, and her kindness and genuine interest were a relief for us. Her method of diagnosis was well known to us, because it seemed exactly like what Roberto did. We had never heard of the device she used but it sounded good. It was called Health Angel.

Marianne's tests revealed that Linda's energy levels were almost immeasurably low. She tested only thirty percent while healthy people normally go up to sixty percent or eighty percent. The fact that Linda was alive was a miracle in itself.

Marianne could not only measure with this equipment, but also treat, which was very welcome, because Linda had trouble taking in food and medicine. The first thing Marianne also decided to test for was the presence of cancer related frequencies, and she found them immediately. The therapist in Arnhem didn't have the right test ampoules then. So now, for the first time we got a clear, be it alternative, answer to our question of does Linda have cancer or, like she often said herself, infections. I suspected that she necessarily wanted to believe the latter and that nobody was allowed to shake that belief.

Marianne told Linda what she had found, and Linda seemed to accept that outcome, so Marianne was allowed to treat her against the cancer frequencies. But only that first time, because during all subsequent treatments Marianne was not allowed to treat her against this again. Shortly after the first treatment Linda had had a small haemorrhage; nothing special, but she was unsure and thought it was related to the treatment. Imagine the danger this device could do sending cancer related frequencies through her body, no matter if it was only neutralizing them.

Because I would pick Marianne up by car and bring her back home with her heavy suitcase, I could talk to her for a few minutes without Linda hearing what was being said. Marianne didn't understand Linda's refusal to be treated against the cancer frequencies either. It even made her sad. She mentioned that she had even toyed with the idea of treating Linda unknowingly against the cancer, but she had abandoned the thought right away. Linda had asked me about this too, wanting my thoughts about it, but I felt that this had to be her decision and her decision alone, and that I would support her all the way. That was very important to me.

I felt how important this device of Marianne's was, and so her refusal was very hard on me, to even support her in this.

There was something else at work here, which was the bigger plan behind this. It was related to her soul, with the higher goal of her incarnation, her soul's destiny. As soon as we discovered anything that would really make a difference, anything capable of healing or powerfully suppressing her pain, then it was taken out of our hands. Or, as in this case, she thwarted it. It was her own soul that directed her decisions. Marianne was allowed to help, to give relief, but *not* to remove her cancer. The road itself was important. *That* was decisive. This was the movement of the cosmos, and her moving through the cosmos, following her... Two Roads.

When I try imagining what the reason behind all this could be, the first thing that comes to mind is that Linda and I were connected in a rare way, and we were together because of this. It is possible much more than that played a role, but at that time I didn't have a clue.

You may also wonder why Marianne came into our life at all, if she wasn't allowed to contribute anything substantial, but maybe her arrival had another reason.

Igor, as always, was often present, and in his voice I noticed how worried he was. At a certain moment he expressed this in a very special way. He grabbed one of his fingers and said, "Bir". He looked straight at me and then picked another finger saying, "Ikki". He continued with the other fingers and summed up the words that belonged to each of them, "Uch... Turt... Besh... "[6]

I looked at him in surprise and asked what he was doing. He did it again; taking his fingers one by one and saying the word that belonged to each. He was very serious I noticed by his facial expression, but it did not ring a bell in my mind. I tried to imitate him and repeat what he said, but I succeeded only partially.

Then Linda came in between, saying, "He's counting!"

"He counts to five," she added.

I shook my head uncomprehendingly. "So what! Why does he do that?" I asked. "Are we going to learn his language now or... ? What does he mean?"

"Don't you get it?" Linda asked, eyeing me urgently. "He has been fighting to stay alive on the battlefield for five days. He's counting the days! He counts to five!

He means... something decisive has to be done quickly, or else I won't make it!

It is the fifth day...

... and on the fifth day he died!"

---

[6] *The words written here were found on the Internet and represent the present day Uzbek language. The real words Igor spoke probably were different, but I wasn't able to remember them exactly. However the sound of these words reflects my feelings of that moment exactly.*

The Healing of the Soul

Hadn't we already tried everything we could think of? What more could we do? Our reserves were depleted; physically and mentally we were totally finished. The fact we still kept going was a miracle, but the moments in which Linda wanted to give up and put an end to it were becoming increasingly commonplace, and so I was confronted with a very difficult dilemma because I saw exactly how terrible the road was that she was following. I could easily understand her desire, but I didn't agree.

Each time she said it I refused to comply, but each time I also wondered, "Can I stop her? This is inhumane! This should not be!" And every time I *felt* that it was not right, no matter how bad the pain might be... suicide or euthanasia was not an option.

Once I had been taught a ritual which was said could separate the physical body from the soul, breaking the silver cord, the invisible connection between the soul and the body. This act was intended to help already deceased people to release their body faster. I had done this ritual for a knocked down cat I had plucked minutes before from a crowded crossroads in a big German city. His back was broken and he was dying of pain. My actions had had immediate effect. However... I now think that my earthly actions were only the reflection or at best, an excitation of what the spiritual beings did at the right cosmic time, but I didn't realize that when I was taught the ritual. And I now have serious doubts about this ritual being a good thing to use, or even that it would be effective at all. However, for now that didn't matter. What mattered was that we *believed* I had this capability.

Linda had asked me several times to do this on her and I had always refused, saying it was not right, but her demands became more persistent every time. I kept refusing, but with what excuse? I had no defence. It was a feeling, a certainty that this was wrong.

"If I was to do this... " I tried, "then you would be very happy here, now, on Earth, but from the other side you would curse me." Maybe I put that a bit too extreme, but at least I had made my point. Still her request kept coming back and finally I made her a promise. I promised her if after four weeks she had not made a real improvement, I would do it. I could see that Marianne's treatment indeed was having some effect and that Linda's energy levels kept improving, although her pain was still very bad. And if that were not the case, then she wouldn't survive another four weeks in my opinion. I couldn't stand it anymore and wanted to have something for her to hold on to.

Together we tried persuading Igor to look at what happened on the battlefield. We knew he had died there, but he didn't continue his story. When one time we were both pushing him to move into the light, Linda said to me, "He stands before a door through which shines a lot of light. He just needs to go through that door, but he doesn't do it. He refuses." She added, "If I was to go through that door, then I'd die." I was surprised when she told me that, because... why hadn't she done so already? She asked it of me, but didn't do it herself. Slowly something began to dawn on me...

Igor had been a singer or storyteller, a Russian troubadour maybe, in that incarnation. I wondered whether the national anthems such as the Russian Cossack choirs nowadays perform, went back to the time of Igor. The melodies and the lyrics had a lot of resemblance. Maybe Igor had written one of the present day Cossack songs himself, he was often experimenting with words and melodies. He could repeat a certain line or a few words for a long time, experimenting with them till he had it like he wanted, like a poet searches for words in a poem.

"Are you experimenting again?" we then asked. "Are you making another song?"

On another occasion Linda was sitting at the table in the living room while I stood in the kitchen. We were talking to each other and while I was speaking I suddenly saw her face change. Her eyes softened and her attitude changed to a more reserved posture, humble even, which certainly wasn't Linda's, but belonged to Igor.

Then he started to sing a song, and right from the start I knew that this song was made and sung especially for me. I couldn't understand the words but halfway through the song I recognized the words Nacka Nacka. Linda pointed up her finger, as if she gave me a wink and a meaningful smile, because we both knew what that meant. So now she was even able to give me signals while Igor used her voice!

I understood that the words 'nacka nacka' didn't always mean a lullaby. This particular song was a surpassingly beautiful love song, such as I had never heard before. Maybe Linda had asked Igor to do this for me, I don't know. The melody and the words I may have forgotten, but the feeling and emotion of that moment I will never forget.

'Nacka nacka'... I love you.

Despite those beautiful moments there was something strange going on here and it was obvious that we had to do something about this, if possible. So finally we looked for a reincarnation therapist in the yellow pages, one who was willing to come to us. Our goal was to help Igor accept that he had died and should go into the light, and to know what precisely had happened on that ancient battlefield.

The man we contacted was a friendly and experienced man, and right from the start I noticed that he was well capable of dealing with Linda's expressions of pain and misery. He didn't ask Linda to lie down as that would cause too much pain, but that wasn't even necessary. It needed only one question from him and she was there, totally absorbed into that life.

He let her go through the whole story, just as we together had done, and finally Igor arrived at the last of the five days on the battlefield. There he stopped speaking. The therapist asked Igor to move on, meaning to let him go through the process of dying, but Igor refused, saying that he had to go to Nasja, and for this he needed his body.

Linda and I had never succeeded in convincing him that he couldn't stay there, not knowing how to deal with such a situation. However, the therapist's training and many years of experience came into play, because he knew exactly how to deal with the situation. He asked Igor to look at his own body, not accepting no for an answer. He asked him if this body would allow him to go to Nasja. Igor fell silent for a while and the tension in the room rose. Then he shook his head and started to call for Nasja like I had heard so often, "Nasjáaaa!"

Slowly and asking the right questions, the therapist guided Igor through the last moments of his earthbound life and finally Igor abandoned his body, and was able to look at his body from above. Indeed... that body was in no shape to bring him to Nasja and his grief was almost palpable in the room.

Now that he was deceased and facing that fact, I expected that Igor would go into the Light, retrieved by his guardian angel and other deceased loved ones, and hence the session would be over, but what followed next totally surprised me.

Igor might have deceased, but that didn't mean he would give in to that. Instead of going into the Light he went straight to Nasja. He didn't accept that he had to leave his love Nasja. It appeared that for years afterwards he remained around her. But not as a poltergeist or as an evil entity, because he sang songs for Nasja and for their baby, and he took care that no harm would be inflicted on them. Nasja wasn't able to see him, but occasionally Pusj Maika perceived his whereabouts.

When a woman in the village became pregnant, Igor saw his opportunity. He aligned his spirit with the body of the unborn foetus and was born some time afterwards. Remarkably quick after being born, as soon as his vocal chords allowed him to speak recognisable sounds, he said that he had to go to Nasja. "I am Igor," he said. "Take me to Nasja! I need to go to Nasja!"

The people laughed at this strange little boy and said, "No, you're not Igor. Igor was a big and strong man, but he is dead. You are Pjotr."

Around his seventh year Pjotr started suffering from severe abdominal pains and pretty soon afterwards he died of whatever it was that had made him sick. He was buried, but even then, standing beside his own grave, he said that he didn't want to be buried under the ground. He was Igor, not Pjotr! He had to go to Nasja!

We didn't hear what happened immediately after that, because after a question from the therapist Igor suddenly was engaged in another incarnation. He, or Linda, or her soul, was now a woman who lived somewhere in the mountains... in the Swiss or Austrian Alps. She was married to a farmer and they had lots of cows. They were happy together, but at an early age her husband died and she was yet to live for many years thereafter, growing very old. In her old days she lived high in the mountains and led an isolated existence as a hermit. She was now ninety years old and had only one cow left, with which she lived in the same room during the winter. Schnibbili, the cow, was ill and could not stand well on her feet. Linda, the old woman as she was, tried to keep her standing, pushing against the vast body of the cow, crying, "No no, don't die! How should I go on living without you!" but Schnibbili wasn't able to stand and fell on top of her. This broke her hip and because of that and the heavy weight of Schnibbili, she couldn't get away. Again she was pinned down on the spot, suffering terrible pains for days in a row, till she died.

But this time her husband who wanted to take her into the Light retrieved her. This time she obviously allowed this and happily agreed to come, but... under one condition: she would only agree if Schnibbili were allowed to come with her. That was no problem and together they went into the light. And thus the session was ended.

Years ago, a psychic woman had told Linda that in a previous incarnation she had been a farmer's daughter during the time of the colonization of the Americas. She had been a cow whisperer then. Even as a little girl she was consulted by farmers from all around when one of their cows was ill. The psychic described how Linda, as a girl of maybe eight or nine years old, sat in front of the cow on a small stool, talking with them. Then after a while she would know exactly what was wrong with the cow and what needed to be done. That story now fell neatly into place.

After that, Igor never returned again. He had gone to the Light. He finally had accepted only then, that life could be integrated with his soul, and therefore with Linda. But what had it taken to make this possible. What had to be experienced before it was compete? So much misery, so much pain, so much loneliness! The grief that I had seen in Linda's eyes from the very first moment we met... I now knew were that came from.

Acceptance...

It was quiet after that, very quiet. I had fallen in love with Igor and it felt like I had lost a friend. I missed his unintelligible comments, his remarks and especially his poignant songs. Linda too thought it was too quiet now. It was good, we understood that much, but very silent.

Silence... before the storm? Now that this was completed in a good way, I shuddered at the thought of the future.

The promise I had made Linda haunted me, because she kept reminding me of that. "When the four weeks are up I will hold you to your promise," she stressed. "I'm gonna hold you to it."

That sounded like a threat and I hated to hear that from her. Something had come between us and that was the last thing I wanted.

Although her condition seemed to improve slowly, it was not comparable to the improvement we had seen after the summer. I felt my stomach contract whenever I thought of the promise I had made. I felt that I should never have done that, and it was impossible to bring it up with Linda now. She wouldn't even begin to talk about it.

The dilemma kept me so busy that I asked my guardian angel Amiris, whose name I had learned when I was a boy writing my first short stories about ethereal beings protecting nature, to help me. How he could help me with this I didn't know. After all I had made a stupid mistake. His wise answer came one or two nights after my question in the form of an eerily realistic dream.

In this dream I had done exactly what I had promised Linda to do. I had just freed her from her body while she was still alive. She seemed out of misery, but I saw myself facing the consequences. She was deceased as a result of my actions, and as I looked at her lifeless body I was in total panic, panic that had nothing to do with grief or mourning. I was choked to have done something incredibly stupid and irreversible. There was nothing I could do about it anymore, no matter how much I wanted. There was no way back!

This grabbed me so much that I woke up trembling with fear and it took many minutes before I even started to realize that it had been a dream and that Linda was still alive and lying next to me. Even then, being fully awake, it took me a long time before I lost that oppressive feeling. Not that waking up in the daily nightmare we were in was a relief, but I was very grateful to my guide for the understanding that the dream had given me.

When the four weeks were more than over and one night things went very bad, she started again, looking at me with this one question in her eyes, "Will you keep your promise?"

I hesitated long and then tried, "I think that it's not as bad as it seems. You're making progress."

"Do you think this is not-so-bad!" she cried out angrily. "If you felt it yourself then you would do it immediately! You just don't want to keep your promise. You never intended to. You just want to keep your hands clean! You're so mean!"

Those words hurt.

"I really intended to," I said. "But I now know that it is not right. I should never have made you that promise. I'm sorry. It was incredibly stupid of me."

"So you won't do it?" she asked again. There was a reproach in her eyes that really hurt me.

"No," I said with a sudden certainty. "It is not right. It's not good." I had been pondering on an answer, endlessly searching for a good argument, without result. But suddenly I knew what to say. I said, "I would rather break the promise than do something we both will regret terribly for sure."

No more excuses. Just accept that I had made a mistake and take responsibility for it. I had always looked for a justification, but there just wasn't one. Finally I faced that, and I took back my words. Better I had to live with her being angry and disappointed at me. If that was what it takes, then so be it.

But I continued asking myself, had she been right? Did I really want to keep my hands clean? Did I really want to keep her with me at her expense? Or was it a deep inner knowledge that the Great Spirit in all his or her love lets no one suffer without a very good reason; that no one transitions at the wrong time and that it is not up to us to determine that moment? It's a very ethical issue that undoubtedly has perplexed many. I couldn't figure it out, but I kept to what I felt. But it also felt as if I pushed my love away from me at a time that she might only have weeks to live. It was horrible.

Later that same day she threatened that she herself would make an end to it, so I asked how she was going to do that. She didn't answer immediately but said that she would go away as I slept. Maybe she would force an accident, or drown herself, anything. I was so tired that I wouldn't notice a thing, she said.

That same night I *knew* she would carry out her threat. She always had been kind of unfathomable for me. Perhaps some might have called her mysterious, but that wasn't the case anymore, not to me. I saw right through her. Still, mysterious or not, my love for her wasn't suffering in any way. On the contrary!

Now I knew without a doubt that she would carry out her threat that night, and funny enough, I wasn't worried at all. I felt a certainty that I would be awake in time.

I don't know whether I had slept or not, but I was awake before she was at the door. I didn't move a muscle. It was pitch dark in the room, but I heard her going to the door as quietly as possible and then I heard the latch of the doorknob. After she went through she pushed the door closed as much as possible, and only when I heard the soft creaking of the stairs, I stood up without making a sound. Then quietly I went to the stairs, but didn't go down, only listened to the sounds and stared down at the faint glow of the light coming from the living room two flights down. I stood there for a while, ready to grab my trousers and sweater if it was necessary, but then, to my surprise, the light was switched off and I heard her going up the first staircase again. What?

Puzzled, I waited a few more seconds and then went back into the bedroom, and quickly crept back into the bed.

When she had been in bed for several minutes, while I pretended to be asleep still, I heard her softly say, "I could have just walked away and you didn't even notice."

I acted as if I woke up from a tired sleep, mumbling if she had said something.

"You didn't even know," added her voice in the dark. "I could just have left. You didn't even notice."

I left it at that and it felt like the right thing to do. She didn't need to know I had been very ready to follow her. It was good like this, and I'm very grateful to my guardian angel for the special help he had given me. Still puzzled, I kept thinking about what had just happened. Everything had happened exactly as I had 'known'.

It would take a long time before I understood why this event felt so important. The only thing I had done was... nothing. I had let her go.

Since that night she undertook no more attempts to try to make an end to her life, nor did I see her crying as frustrated as she had endlessly been doing. There was a fundamental change in her.

Now, in retrospect, I know why I had felt like that then. It was the moment when she really hit rock bottom, and finally... *finally* began to accept. I now believe that you should accept that you are sick; accept that not everything can be controlled, no matter how much effort you put in and no matter how much money you spend; accept that it is ultimately not the doctor or the therapist who determines if you heal or not; accept that you might die even... as part your healing. I don't mean to say that you shouldn't attempt to heal yourself in case of any illness. Of course we all want that. But when time after time things work out differently... can you then make that change and accept a different outcome?

Not only did Linda go through this change, as this was also true for me because I had come to accept that the cosmos followed roads that I as a human thought undesirable. This acceptance was the turning point, the lowest point of the downward spiral of her illness, for true healing... of her soul! But what a path!

I could barely leave her alone anymore, because she needed me nearly every second of the day and the night, so whenever it was possible for me to go to the grocery store I acted like I had won a five minute shopping spree. I ran through the store with the shopping cart, grabbing things of the shelves left, right and centre. Perhaps she would like this, maybe that. Could this be something? No idea, throw it in the basket. Better too much than not enough, so I could compose maybe ten meals with a combination of what I brought home. But even then she managed to ask for that one meal precisely for which I didn't have the ingredients. Because she had less and less understanding for maybe the fact that something wasn't there she could verbally be very angry with me. Normally she would never do that unless there was a good justification for it, and I forgave her this same instant, but it still hurt. A woman working in the home care shop that I spoke to told me that this was quite common behaviour of very ill people. "They can't help it," she said. "But they do it only with those they love the most," she added. "They can only do it with them really, and so it is good that she has you."

Those words brought tears to my eyes, because that's exactly how it felt. Actually it was a very big compliment that she felt so safe with me, that she could be angry with me, because she couldn't let her frustrations out otherwise, resting assured that this wouldn't affect my love for her at all.

Because we wanted to know more about the how and why of her illness we wished to find an experienced and trustworthy psychic. A couple of years previously we had met such a woman during a small-scale psychic fair in Apeldoorn who had made a profound impression on us. Everything that she had said was to the point, no guessing, not a single doubt. With her we really felt we had met someone who did exactly what you expect from a psychic, making contact with the Hereafter, bringing through crystal clear messages that you simply can't ignore; each word's a hit. She described herself quite surprisingly, saying, "I'm just a fax."

We had taken her business card, but unfortunately had lost it. Now what was her name again? No matter how much we tried, we couldn't remember her name exactly. Judoka? Judesca? Something like that. At least a name with a 'y', a 'c' and an 'a' in it. And... she had a striking Amsterdam-accent. I surfed the Internet, phoned with organisations of psychic fairs, but without result.

We knew another clairvoyant woman in Apeldoorn, Vera. Linda said that recently she had been thinking a lot of her deceased brother Arjen. She felt very connected to him and felt that Arjen wanted to tell her something. So I made an appointment with Vera. She lived not far from our home and for this purpose I was allowed to be away for the one hour that was needed. What she told me for Linda I have now largely forgotten, but most important was that Arjen said he had started something that Linda now was finishing. Indeed, was his illness, which was also a cancer, comparable to hers? He too had suffered extreme pains, though for a shorter period of time, and against which no painkiller had an effect. Vera couldn't know these facts. The most important thing Arjen said was that all was about one thing only and that was Love. He had now seen and experienced this and mentioned it several times. Hearing *him* particularly saying that meant a lot.

That evening I asked Linda what she wanted to eat. She didn't know, and for minutes I summed up all that I could think of. That was no good, because valuable time was lost that way. "You have to think!" she said. "Not just name anything at all! You sit there and say nothing. You gotta help me!"

Just imagine this...

Because this particular food was too much for her, or that she couldn't swallow, or this needed too long to prepare. Maybe that she had had yesterday or something else smelled too much. Maybe that particular meal had made her nauseous and was on the black list now. She said that in a way indicating she thought it ridiculous that I even dared mentioning it. But my list of recipes grew thin that way! And so I preferred to keep my mouth shut instead of saying something stupid, but that too was the wrong thing to do, of course. Preparing food now had become a major problem, but in fact the answer was that there wasn't really *anything* anymore that she could eat. We had reached the end of the list.

Then she had an idea and suddenly said, "Floepskakkers!" Floepskakkers (*roughly translated: Slipshitters, a childish dirty word*) is a combination of two words, made up by Arjen, who as a small child fantasized over an old recipe: Drie-in-de-pan (three in the pan). They are like mini pancakes with juicy fruit jelly.

That was easy enough, and while I was baking them I brought the plates and spoons in to Linda, and she said that it smelled so nice in the house. She knew that smell from her youth, when her mother had made floepskakkers so often for Arjen, who was crazy about them.

We both believed that it was Arjen who had given her this idea. He knew of our hard struggle and handed us something that helped us a few more steps on the road, a recipe that brought back the times of early days: Good old times, days of laughter and carelessness.

If the urgency was at its highest, then there was always help, another light pole on our lonely dark Road that gave us the courage to keep going a few more steps.

After that I made them often: floepskakkers.

One drop of Water

Mid-November we received a tip from an acquaintance who suggested we should consult an Ayurvedic doctor. The doctor she proposed was not just any doctor but a prominent physician in India. To prepare Linda for the first consultation, he advised Linda to use a special kind of oil, which I already had heard of before and of which I had high hopes. I bought this oil, and for two weeks it sat on the kitchen table. We didn't do anything with it because we were afraid to try out yet another medication that might cause a serious problem; we had experienced that too many times now.

Then the homeopath contacted us, announcing that after months of studying he had found the definitive remedy, but it had to be diluted in a lot of water before taking it in.

Linda wanted to know my opinion and I instinctively leaned towards the Ayurvedic means, and that was what I said to her. But I added that it had to be her choice. And whatever her choice was, I would support her.

She opted for the homeopathic remedy. Lachesis it was called, rattlesnake poison. She had had it before, but in a very low dose. It didn't feel good to me and reluctantly I diluted the remedy as prescribed with ten glasses of water. Then I gave her only one instead of the prescribed ten drops in a glass of water and tried to reassure myself. What's the big deal, I said to myself... one drop of water in a glass full of water... nothing more.

Within two hours she developed severe abdominal pain, different than what she was used to and in a part of her belly that was never painful. During that afternoon the pain got worse and over the next days her belly grew thicker till it was about as round as football. I suggested she go to a hospital, which she allowed. So I brought her to the ER. The doctor in duty immediately suspected what was going on and showed us with an ultrasound that her bladder was blocked. The solution was therefore very simple: a catheter to drain the urine.

That wasn't so bad. A nurse returned a little later with the catheter and then we had to wait until her bladder was empty, which was set to go very slow, as a wise precaution.

We were asked whether Linda wanted further treatment in the hospital. With the nurse still standing next to us, and with serious consideration for me, Linda asked me what I thought. "It would be easier for you if I could stay in the hospital for a while," she said. "Then you can finally sleep," she said, "and catch your breath."

That was very sweet of her, acknowledging that she knew very well how hard all this was for me. But I didn't like the idea.

"Do you really want that?" I asked her. "Don't worry about me not sleeping enough. I managed for over a year and I can still do this. It's not about what I want. It's you! You decide."

"Well... if I can choose, I'd rather be at home," she said, and I heard a huge relief in her voice. We agreed. What could be done in the hospital that we couldn't do ourselves at home? Blood tests? What for? The results wouldn't change a thing. Surgery? We had abandoned that road long ago. For me to enjoy my sleep? Come on!

No matter how this would end... this too we would do together! Imagine if she died without me at her side... after all these months. We asked if I could handle the catheter at home. That was no problem. Maybe not the most obvious option, but this gentle nurse fully understood us. In the course of that night her bladder was empty and her belly looked normal again.

I was sitting next to her bed, regularly checking the tube of the catheter and all the time I had seen the ordinary yellow urine dripping in the bag. Just before the nurse disconnected the catheter I saw a very slight colour change in the tube close to her belly. The nurse didn't see it, or didn't find it interesting, because while she was handling the bag and the tubes, she commented, "Looks good doesn't it? Shall we remove the catheter now?"

I couldn't judge if this was anything serious or not, but it seemed as if a tiny bit of blood was darkening the urine. I didn't mention it. We wanted to go home, be in our own wee house.

In the days following that it appeared that Linda still couldn't urinate. I tried applying the catheter as was explained to me, and when I finally succeeded I was shocked, as it seemed as if I had made a wound in her skin, because the tube suddenly filled with dark blood. I hastily pulled out the catheter.

I didn't dare experiment, afraid to hurt her even more. This took someone with experience was my opinion, and I told her so. She was disappointed and insisted that I kept trying. I was shocked and concerned, but I didn't voice my concerns because I wasn't sure. Linda protested and preferred not to see a doctor again.

"But the only thing he needs to do is insert the catheter" I said. "That's what they are trained to do. Something has to be done now, or else the pain will come back again." Normally I would respect her wishes, but now I stuck to my opinion; I wanted a doctor to confirm my suspicions.

Fortunately the man who came to us later that evening was very friendly. He shook Linda's hand and introduced himself. Linda explained herself what was going on and, still in his raincoat, he tried to affix the catheter. He was easy going and wasn't angry that we were adding to his already burdened evening.

I felt a vague satisfaction when I saw he too had difficulty. Apparently my failure was very understandable. Then the same thing happened as I had seen before. Suddenly the tube was quickly filled with red liquid and like me he was terrified, not immediately understanding what happened. He took off his coat and began to ask me questions. Had she had blood in the urine before? What complaints did she have? He added that he hadn't had the opportunity to check the patient's files before. It was a very busy evening.

The bowl rapidly filled with blood-red urine. The physician said that this was quite common. "Sometimes some blood comes with the urine," he said. "In a few moments the colour will change to normal." But when, after a minute, the bowl was more than half full with dark red urine and blood I saw his confusion and I knew that this was indeed not good at all. He asked if he could call an ambulance.

Linda responded shocked and defensive. "If I go to the hospital I will not get out!" she said.

I didn't understand her refusal at first. It was obvious that she had to go to the hospital now, wasn't it? If she stayed at home her belly would be round again within days. We had been so occupied fighting her disease we never had discussed a certain outcome: the possibility that she could die. I think she had a hard struggle to discuss the real situation with me. But now she couldn't avoid it any longer.

So I said, "Even if I have to abduct you! I will not let you die in the hospital! I'll stay with you as much as possible and if it's clear that the hospital can't do anything for you, I'll take you right back home with me!"

That calmed her down enough to agree with the GP to start making some phone calls.

The Movement of the Cosmos

Another ambulance...

This time her eyes were wide open with fear when I looked at her through the windows of the ambulance. Maybe my eyes looked the same, I don't know. I was indeed very afraid of what would happen next, and watched the ambulance from the parking place driving away. My throat was closed tight. Another ambulance... again... in the hospital... again... in the ER... back again to all the misery and the explaining to doctors and nurses nodding 'yes' and 'amen' while you could see in their eyes that their thoughts were totally different from their words. She couldn't handle this anymore... always so tough and strong, but not anymore. This was too much to endure.

The results from the blood tests came in, but nobody dared explain the scores to me, which was understandable but very annoying. When we were left alone for a few minutes I checked the paper. On it was typed a mass of measuring values and behind them it showed the maximum and minimum limits for each score. I noticed that there was a lot of values way outside the normal parameters. Even in my ignorance I knew this was all wrong.

This time there was no question of her going home straight away. She was given a separate room on the second floor. I was not planning to go home and reckoned that I should have to spend the night here. She was much too sick and there was no telling how things would go, but I didn't dare go home for fear that she would die. She was now alive well enough, but with this bleeding and her extremely exhausted body, I wasn't sure.

Another nurse came in and introduced herself with a cheerful voice inquiring how we were doing, and said, "I have something really tasty against the pain!"

My mind went into overdrive... Something tasty to treat the pain?

What did she mean? Morphine maybe? By itself maybe not a bad idea and, given Linda's pain and the consternation she had caused in the ER, the obvious choice, but should you introduce that in such a funny way?

"Who do you think you are," I thought. "You aren't talking to a toddler here!"

She had a syringe containing a large amount of liquid and wanted to inject that into Linda. Now I intervened. This was way out of line for me. Absolutely not, without consultation, inject... whatever!

"What's in this?" I asked the nurse. "I had expected a doctor to explain things to us first."

So now the exact thing was happening that we had always been afraid would happen, the reason why we had refused to hospitalize Linda: other people making choices about your life without consulting you first. At least we could be involved in such decisions! If it was discussed!

At least what the hospital staff did ask us was whether the doctors were allowed to intervene to the full extent to save Linda's life in case of serious complications during medical procedures. And there was this nurse coming in with a big morphine syringe. No questions, just act. Why should it mean that as soon as you're hospitalized, your life isn't yours anymore?

Because of my refusal to let Linda commit suicide, and my broken promise to her, we hadn't talked about this. There was no tense atmosphere between us, but we had avoided the topic. Maybe that was the reason she had panicked, saying, "If I go to the hospital I will not get out!"

Did she want to stay home then, waiting till the bleeding was uncontrollable? Then why was she fighting to survive? All was irrational to me. I didn't know what to do and asked Linda how she felt about morphine. That it *was* morphine was at least acknowledged by the nurse.

She shrugged. "Then I finally can get some sleep," she sighed. "That, I would love... sleep." But her tone was wrong, kind of 'well whatever, what do I care!' That was nothing like Linda. Still I had to resign. Normally she wouldn't have pondered a moment about morphine, but now... It was wrong, but what choice did I have now but to accept?

The nurse looked at me, silently asking my permission.

"Okay," I said. "Go ahead." With dismay I saw how she injected a large amount of morphine. This felt like having to surrender under duress. It was not good. Then Linda and I talked a bit. She was too tired to say much, but I wanted to get some answers to a few unspoken things, knowing that when the morphine was fully working she wouldn't be able to clearly think and talk anymore. Who knows, we may never have got the opportunity again. But again we didn't get much further, because after a short time she said, "I don't want to talk about this."

A while later she told me, "I think I may fall asleep now. I feel sleepy, so you might as well go home now. Then you can call my parents, and sleep, and then tomorrow morning you can come back again. I'm fine. I won't die now."

"No?" I asked.

I think my voice sounded timid, because she looked at me and smiled and said with warmth in her voice, "No, you silly. How can I abandon you and our kitties? I'm going to get better! But you must wait until I really sleep."

When, after half an hour, she indeed slept, I packed my stuff and then walked straight to the department counter. I wanted to make sure that they had my phone number just in case. I trusted no one anymore.

At home I called Linda's parents and told them about the latest developments. I also called Rob, her oldest brother, who repeatedly had asked if they could do anything for us. I knew he very much wanted to do more, but I didn't know what Linda would allow. Apart from me and her parents, no one was allowed to come near her. No visits and no help. For Rob and his wife Martha this was very difficult, as they were accustomed to taking action. Now they were lost as to what to do. He asked if it was okay for him and Martha to come now, because Linda always had told them not to come. You see, there was never an opportunity to speak with them without Linda listening. All my time was spent with her. I told him that they now shouldn't ask for permission, but that they simply should come. I was certain Linda would appreciate their presence very much, but she would never admit it beforehand.

As soon as I had put down the phone it rang and suddenly I heard my mother's voice. That surprised me, because we hadn't seen each other for over half a year. She had tried to phone us many times, but that was very hard, because most of the time our phone was disconnected to prevent Linda waking up by the sound of a ringing phone. The few times I had spoken to her she was always very apologetic about the state of affairs that she wasn't happy about at all. Those conversations were always very short. Linda and I never contacted my parents directly, but only through Mieke. I guessed my mother was torn by this situation. Regarding my father, I knew from Mieke that he really sympathized with us and that he too didn't know how to deal with the situation. In fact, the big problem was that he actually found it more difficult to deal with than my mother did. That the situation had done him no good whatsoever showed from what I was about to hear next...

My mother asked how it went, and as usual I said all was quite okay, that there wasn't much improvement, but that we were coping; something like that. I didn't tell her that Linda was in the hospital again though keeping that a secret was very hard on me, and I may have seemed to be coping, but I was only just. In fact I was completely upset.

"No need to be alarmed," my mother said, "but your father is in the hospital."

Well, that was a blow! Since my childhood my father had never been in hospital. At the same time I was surprised that she now was doing what we weren't allowed to do by Dottore, but that indicated the seriousness of the situation.

"It's okay," she quickly continued, "but the doctor ordered him to go the hospital just to be sure."

"Then what happened?" I asked, seemingly calm. I already was totally upset, so this made no noticeable difference in my mood. Things were as worse as they could get; there's simply a maximum that one can deal with at once. She told me he had had a minor stroke and was now in the CCU. In the same hospital...

I had to digest this for a few moments. And I thought 'well, just add it to the pile; it can't get any worse than this.' I asked my mother how serious my father's situation was, what had happened, and if I could visit him.

"Do you have time for that then?" she asked.

It was then I said that Linda was in the same hospital.

"I hope it's nothing serious?" she asked worried.

I didn't want to keep pretending. Now she had to hear it all, so I told her briefly how things were, and that Linda would survive only a few days.

She responded shocked. I couldn't soften the shock for her now. And to be honest, I didn't want to, because deep inside I was still angry, or disappointed, I couldn't tell the difference anymore. This was a moment for truth and to finally abandon Dottore's advice of no contact with my parents. They had done so much harm! I am convinced that his advice not to see Linda in combination with my father's inability to express his feelings had been one major cause of his stroke. However, this incredible situation had one big advantage. In the hospital I only had to go down one staircase to see my father. My mother expected that it would make him very happy. "Do you want that?" she asked sounding uncertain.

I wondered whether she thought we were actually against them and that I never wished to see them again, because that certainly wasn't the case, but because we hadn't properly communicated for over half a year the idea might not be that hard for her to believe. Whatever... with what my mother was asking me it was clear that she too felt it was so good to be talking to one another again, without Dottore's shadow over every conversation. So now, the misunderstandings between us could be eliminated for good.

Sleeping that night was impossible. For the first time I was in bed without my *vriendinnetje* being there. I was haunted by many images and I was worried and very scared. Maybe I did sleep, but it didn't feel like that, so when early in the morning the alarm went off I got up immediately and went to the hospital as quickly as I could.

Then I discovered what miserable stuff morphine is. Linda was totally unconscious, or so it seemed. Her arms were moving and she ran her fingers along her eyebrows all the time. Her eyes were half open and rolled back and forth. Her facial muscles moved continuously. I told her I was with her and she responded to my voice, so obviously she wasn't really unconscious. There were even words on her lips. It was as if she couldn't use her body to talk to me.

I stayed for a while with her, but nothing changed. She kept moving without being able to connect with the world around her. Was this morphine? What an awful drug! In any case, the urine in the catheter bag was no longer red. So in any case, the bleeding had stopped.

As she still seemed to be far from regaining her consciousness I had an opportunity to see my father. I found him at the end of the cardiac ward, with masses of wheezing and squeaking equipment around him. Fortunately he wasn't totally draped with tubes and wires, so his situation apparently wasn't that critical. He was so delighted when he saw me that he even had tears in his eyes.

"I'm so glad that you're here, boy!" he said. He smiled broadly. His whole attitude spoke such relief. I believe a huge burden fell from his shoulders that moment. Somewhere 'Above' some really smart guardian angels must be orchestrating and bending even this situation to our advantage.

So finally we could talk to each other for a few minutes. Luckily his situation wasn't too bad and it was expected he could go home very soon, maybe even the next day. And the next day was his birthday, he told me happy.

Jeez... Yes, that was true. I had not given that any thought. I promised him that if he still were in the hospital I would come to see him.

In the evening Linda's parents came, together with Rob, Martha and their daughter Sonja. In the hall outside Linda's room I informed them about the current situation, but then what was I to say? I didn't know. I saw concern on their faces. Sonja especially had a hard time. I thought she was very brave and I was happy that she had come too. Sonja and Linda had a special unspoken bond with each other, but alas didn't see each other enough, and in the past year, not at all.

They offered to do the dishes at home and that I liked very much. Then I didn't need to take care of that. I did not dare go home with things as they were now, how she reacted; I had never seen that before. I suspected that they had given her way too much morphine, putting her out of it completely, probably because they hadn't taken into account her extremely low body weight. Wasn't it supposed to only relieve her pain? Not to bring her into a coma... I hoped... or what?

Only in the course of the next night did she start to come round, and then it was possible again to talk to her a little. The past twenty four hours had completely eluded her and she was surprised that it was the next day.

That night I stayed with her most of the time. Fortunately she didn't get another injection, but only a morphine patch. At least that didn't make her unconscious. The last few hours of the night I went home for the kitties, to return in the early morning.

Later that morning I was invited for a talk with the head of the department and a specialist, in a separate room. I would rather have had Linda with me, but I understood that was difficult for them. In very cautious terms, they wanted to make clear to me what their expectations and findings were, but I interrupted them and said that I very well knew the situation.

What surprised me most was that they were worried so much about me. Did I look that bad? I couldn't tell. They tried to clarify to me that I had to think about myself, meaning that taking care of Linda was best left in their hands.

No way! I knew very well what we both wanted and that was to go home as soon as possible. Could that be arranged?

Their main concern was whether I was capable of taking care of her. Was there an arrangement with the home care aid? Was there enough other help? Well, not really so. Such was our situation now and we had managed to do this for fourteen months. We had done everything together, and now that things looked so bad I wouldn't be prevented from doing whatever I could, not by anyone or by anything! I would do anything to take care of her, even if I died trying.

For starters that meant us going home... as soon as possible. Fortunately I was not argued with. Once the transport was arranged she could go home. They wanted to arrange an ambulance, but I didn't want that either. I would drive her home myself, in our own car. I knew this would be the very last time that she would sit with me in the car; one more time together in the car... almost like in the old days. Her parents came that morning and that was a good thing. They could take care of all the extra stuff so I didn't need a second trip to get it.

When I went downstairs to pick up the car I suddenly saw Marianne, our therapist, coming through the entrance hall. I concluded that apparently she had found out that Linda was in the hospital, but she was as surprised to see me, as I was to see her. It turned out that her father was in the hospital too. He too had had a stroke and he was in the same CCU as my father! This was unbelievable! The fact alone that both our fathers were in the same condition and that we met in the few seconds it took to cross the hallway... coincidence? I don't believe in that anymore. Yet I was glad to see her, even though the conditions were absurd. We had little time to talk, so we wished each other strength and agreed that next Saturday she would come for a treatment.

With Linda's parents following us on the way home, we drove along Linda's school that stood across from the hospital. There we stopped, because Linda wanted to show them something. It was her last project at school, one that had given her lots of headaches. It was not her own creation, but she had put a lot of energy in it taking care for the school to have an original art project, now to be seen at several locations on the roof of the school. But she was unable to step out of the car and she wept as she told them about it.

On the roundabout near our home, we also drove along the pond were all our friends, the ducks and moorhens, gathered together. She watched them closely as I drove by as slowly as I dared... our children.

Linda had been given morphine patches and those worked a bit. They helped her to sleep, but didn't do much against the pain so it seemed. They made her feel drowsy.

The next day another bleeding started. She still had the catheter, but yet the bed was quite red. I didn't know where all the blood came from. The washing machine had broken down many months ago and we hadn't had time to buy a new one, so Linda's mother took care of most of the laundry, but now she wasn't there. And so I washed the sheets by hand.

On Saturday Marianne came and the look on her face told us that she couldn't do anything. Linda's energy levels were even lower than the very first time. I could see how Marianne was seized by our hopeless situation. She could only support us. The treatment itself had no meaning. I saw tears in her eyes. She sympathised with us and understood. Recognising so much love in her was very special.

When I walked her to the car carrying her suitcase, she asked, "And who is there for you, Wim? Who is there for you?"

I was surprised, because nobody had asked me that question before. I thought about it... tears in my eyes. I didn't know the answer.

That night Linda asked me again. "Will you do it now?" she asked. "Will you?"

I paused and felt that it was good. I nodded and said, "Yes, now it's okay."

She seemed relieved and I now knew that whatever had come between us, now it was going to be cleared away. We didn't know if this would work, but we went on the understanding that it would, and so we first discussed a few things that were important to settle. Then I brought the kitties one by one to let her stroke them. She cried when she expressed how sorry she was for me.

"We did everything we could," I said.

"Yeah," she said. "We have done everything. I would have loved so much to stay with you and our cats. But you shouldn't stay single, though. Shall I help to find another woman for you?"

I smiled faintly. "I don't think I'm up to a new relationship for quite some time. How could I? Yet I have two sweet kitties and you leave me some money and a house full of little things that mean so much."

"Yeah," she said, "a house full of those things."

That was true. Over the years we had always bought things that made our home into a whole in which we felt very at home together. Everything matched the energy of the rest. We had never bought anything just for having it, but always considered if it contributed to the rest. This gave me a reassuring feeling.

"But you shouldn't stay alone," she said. "I might not like it very much... but I want you to be happy."

Then she asked me a memorable question, "I probably will be allowed to visit you some time. *What can I do to let you know that I still exist?* Shall I turn off and on the lights?"

"Nope," I replied. "Spend your energy for something more useful. I know very well that you'll sometimes be with me."

I thought for a moment, got an idea, but hesitated to say it. It had gone through my head a few times these last days. Then I said, *"But if you would like to inspire me now and then... if that were possible... that I would really appreciate."*

When I had finished saying that I felt joy, almost a sigh of relief. I was glad I had given that answer. As if I, like in a fairy tale, was granted a wish, and that I didn't simply choose wealth. Linda didn't visibly react to my request, but I knew she had heard it. Then she clutched her arms as usual very tightly around my neck, amazing me how strong she still could be. It must have taken a lot of what little strength she had to hold me like that. "I love you," she said and I replied with the same words.

I carried out the ritual carefully, like I had been taught to. But it didn't work. She said she did see strange flashes around her. I did it again, but again nothing happened.

"I really am doing my best," I told her. "But it just isn't working."

That was the truth. She believed me.

So it would never have worked. That promise of mine therefore was of no use... at least not for that purpose. But I had, albeit late... kept my promise; that was what mattered. For that was what it really was intended for, as part of the plan to teach her acceptance; it had already fulfilled its function. Also my acceptance had joined this. Yet, even though the purpose was fulfilled, my broken promise had to be healed, and that had just happened.

Wearily she laid her head in the pillows. "Let me go get some sleep now," she said.

In the following days she had one bleeding after another. Actually, I think it was all one and the same bleeding. She lost blood continuously. The catheter didn't function properly, it hurt and so I removed it. At least twice a day I had to change the sheets. They were always wet and red with blood. I washed everything by hand. There weren't enough sheets to wait and have them washed by Linda's mother and in fact I only needed to rinse them. But no matter how many times I rinsed them, the water was always so red I couldn't see my hands under water. There was so much blood in the sink that it didn't function properly. It didn't bother me anymore. If the sheets were orange, but useable, then that was fine.

Linda didn't allow me to be with her very much. I didn't understand at first, till she said, "I have to leave everything. That's not easy you know!"

I understood, but it really hurt... especially now.

Some time later she told me she would like a mushroom sandwich. Contradictory as it was, because bread was hard to swallow, she had loved eating mushroom sandwiches for days now. I had snatched every mushroom sandwich from every store in the area, but this time there was none to be got. But then I realized that I had all the ingredients to make them myself, so I went to work. While the bread was under the grill and I was cooking onions and mushrooms I suddenly realised that this was exactly the same dish that Linda had made for me the very first time after we had spent the night together. I started crying when the significance of this dawned on me...

This would be the last time I would cook for her. I knew it. I knew what would happen and I wouldn't be able to avert the course of events now by not cooking. Whether I liked this or not, it wouldn't make any difference. The choice offered to me now was to join in and accept, not place myself outside the movement of the cosmos.

She ate only a few bites, but that wasn't what this was about.

The next day it was the fifth of December, known as Sinterklaas[7] in the Netherlands. On this day we had always decorated the auditorium of Linda's school with artistic artwork, which we had put together with her colleague and friend Marijke. It was a time and energy-consuming tradition that was greatly appreciated by the students.

Linda's parents came again for a visit, along with Rob and Martha. They wanted to do so much more for Linda, but never got the opportunity, and had a difficult time with that. They came every day now, something they *could* do, fortunately. And not only did they come but Mieke, my sister, of course came too. She had tried to help us wherever she could, but couldn't do more than what she already did. It's good to have such a great sister. And Marco, Linda's youngest brother came, and though he had to travel for many hours, he had come several times. His support alone meant a lot to me. And Saskia, the love of her deceased brother, came; she knew what it meant to go through this.

Linda wasn't so happy with all the attention, but I couldn't and wouldn't spare her. Not now. This wasn't about her alone, no matter how ill she was. But despite her sputtering she was very happy and sad at the same time to see them. No wonder.

She had selected music. She wanted a particular song to be played. A song that she, since I knew her, had loved to hear: "Somehow I'll find my way home." That song described precisely how she had felt her entire life. I never had expected that song to play such an important role when we, many years ago, had copied it ten times in a row on a cassette tape and

---

[7] *Sinterklaas is the original Dutch name of the man that now is well known as Santa Claus. The date then changed to Christmas, but the original date is December the 5th.*

played it very loud during the long car trips. I had already prepared the tape and, while Rob and Martha and her parents listened, she sang the words while the music played. Her voice was broken and was nothing like that of Igor, but she made at least as much of an impression.

Then she was talking a little with them. I was watching everything from a distance and observed her. I noticed that the blood vessel in her neck had a very fast beat. I roughly counted along and kept an eye on the clock. Her heartbeat was 150 at least!

When they were leaving her mother asked her, "Do you mind if we come back tomorrow?" She replied, "Do you mind if I die in between?"

Half an hour later she said in a faint voice that she wanted a bath. I had a plastic tub in the bathroom in which she could sit upright. That she could just bear. I tried helping her to sit up in bed, so she could stand. I had already noticed that without my help she couldn't walk to the toilet, but now she could barely lift her arms. She tried to lift one knee and I helped her with it, but she couldn't keep it in place. "My arms feel so weird," she said. She tried again to lift an arm but could not. Then she wanted to turn back, leave it like that and lie down again, but I bent over her and put her arms around my neck and pushed my arm under her shoulders. I wanted to lift her up like that.

I couldn't see her face in that embrace, but at that moment I felt something strange happening. Her breathing was very strange and I knew right there what was going on. I continued to hold her and said softly to her, "Are you dying, love?"

I said this, because I wanted to make her aware that this was happening. Sometimes people don't realize that.

"You may, dear. I love you. You're free to go. I let you go free. Go ahead. I love you."

It didn't happen easily, and all the time I continued holding her. Just as she had often said she wanted, in my arms... out of loneliness, she wasn't alone this time.

It was 5 minutes to four in the afternoon, 15.55, 5 December... the fifth day!

It was still light!

Into The West

Don't say
We have come now to the end
White shores are calling
You and I will meet again
'Into the West'

From the movie "Lord of the Rings - Return of the King"
Fran Walsh, Howard Shore, Annie Lennox

How do you cope with the death of your love?

What do you think about?

For a while I kept holding her. Then I sat behind her and laid her head against my belly so I could caress her face and her hair and express my thoughts. Always I had the greatest difficulty in feeling anything. Feelings of love... for sure they were there, but why could I almost never feel them clearly before? For if there was one thing that became clearer to me at that moment than ever before, it was the great love that I felt for her. So intense! And I said to myself, "Remember this feeling. Never forget it! What ever will happen in the future... this love for her is a part of me and always will be."

Only now... *now* it was that I could really feel. At the same time it was as if I had been struck a huge blow, slamming me to the ground. And I was surprised to discover that my body was still functioning; surprised too that from one moment to the next my life had gone through the most radical change I had ever experienced.

The twenty-four hour caring, running, despairing and being out of breath to catch up, in just one moment, was no longer necessary. And eighteen years of living intimately together, rarely having time and rest to be at peace together, had now suddenly come to an end.

While many impressions and thoughts went through my head I had the feeling that there was a lot of light in the room, that she still was around her body, that she could hear me should I say something. It was very quiet in the room and it was slowly getting dark outside. I didn't put on a lamp.

On the bedside table I looked at the things that she had used: a box of Paracetamol, a glass of water, the box with morphine patches, a small clock... They didn't move; they weren't necessary anymore, and it seemed there was no life left in them too anymore. I was uncommonly silent in the room... very quiet... very special... quiet.

Finally free of that horrible pain, just like that... from one moment to the next, free of the pain.

She had sustained her life. All that time she had sustained her life, with help, of course, but *she* had sustained it! She had accomplished something amazing. I wondered what would have brought her on now. Where would she be on the 'other side'? Who would have picked her up? Arjen? Her grandmother? Her guardian angel of course! And Amà... yeah, Amà! She would be there! Now they could really meet each other. But surely Linda wouldn't be in her frayed jeans and old red T-shirt. Would she now wear the same dress? Would they run along the beach together?

A funeral had to be arranged, people had to be called. Still much had to be done. That evening we gathered together, her parents and Rob and Martha. Everyone who should have been there was there. All important phone calls had been taken care of. Everything was arranged and put in motion. Lost, we sat together. I put on the music that would be played during the ceremony: "Somehow I'll find my way home." It seemed most appropriate at that time.

That first night it was impossible to sleep. The doctor had suggested prescribing me a sedative or even a tranquilizer, but I had refused that. I *wanted* to feel the pain and grief. I didn't want to push it away. I wanted to experience it! This grief, which was so total and so overpowering, it was the confirmation for me that I could actually feel. Finally I could feel! Would I have deprived myself of that then I would have become a zombie, always fleeing from pain and sorrow.

I lie in bed and the house is empty.
It is totally beyond comprehension.
My vriendinnetje is dead!
Not just a little bit dead, but totally and for real!
She isn't there anymore.

I shall never see her again.
No more doing something together, no more shopping, no more making
decorations, no more sleeping together, no more talking, washing dishes,
brushing teeth, sitting in the car, dancing...
No more... no... more...
Never!
Yet today she was still with me.
Today...
Only a few hours ago.

In the following days, we arranged everything for the ceremony. That ceremony had to be something special. We hated the black dress etiquette that seems compulsory, emphasizing the sombre mood, notwithstanding the respectful intention of the people. So we asked everyone to wear bright and colourful clothes. We wanted to express a feeling, and dark clothing wasn't part of that. For us, those left behind, it was gloomy enough as it was. For Linda this separation might have been as difficult as for us, but apart from that it was her victory, her liberation, a party, because she had conquered! She was back home! She had really accomplished something and that was what we wrote on the card:

We have fought
Heaven and Earth we have moved
Lost the battle, but yet victorious
She's free!

Idiosyncratic as Linda and I have always been, we wanted everything different than usual. The ceremony had to be something that people would remember. And so it would be...

Linda's body was in our home, in a beautiful white coffin with flowers all around, but the day before the ceremony it had to be brought to the ceremonial room. I insisted that I would help to carry her coffin into the car. I had carried her over the threshold when we moved into this house, and so I would carry her body now. But while I did this I realized that now, instead of an ambulance, there was a black funeral car on the parking place, and everything came back to me from the other times we said goodbye. It could be even more horrible yet.

The car took off driving slowly, and I walked behind it till the bend in the road. There I stopped and saw the car moving towards the main street. In that car was my vriendinnetje, or her body was, but that wasn't how it felt at that moment. She would never come back. This was the last time I would check on her. I didn't wave.

We had arranged the tables and chairs in groups, like a circular cafe almost; no boring straight rows of chairs. Linda's white coffin was in the middle, between the people, and flowers were all around her. On every table candles were burning. Instead of the usual boring slices of cake and cheese rolls I had brought petit fours. No pastor. We never went to church so why pretend now? I wondered if I would be able, being one of the speakers, to say what I wanted to say to a room full of people. Especially that evening I wanted to be strong internally, and so I asked for help. I had written something on paper and while I read it, but also during the entire ceremony, I felt worn. The last words I spoke, I had carefully thought about, before 'allowing' myself to speak them out loud, without realizing what these words would bring one day:

It is my desire still, to go with you very often, and find together what we are both looking for.
To be one.

There was alternate music and speeches, and after this we had asked Mark and Josée, our Argentine Tango teachers, to dance an Argentine tango. They had refused first, which I could imagine only too well, but having given it serious thought, they had nevertheless agreed. They could dance excellently and gave a precise expression to the feeling we all shared: a mixture of sadness and yet joy for Linda, to have passed all this. This modest tango was very special to see.

Marianne, the therapist who had treated Linda at the end, and who was sensitive to impressions, later said she had had a vision of a moving light in the room, seeming to dance.

To conclude the evening we had asked a friend of ours, Bert Smits, and his Klezmer band to play. The four members played on their instruments: a violin, an accordion, a bass and a guitar. Even the music, a kind of gypsy music with Israeli and Eastern European influences, had both sorrow and joy together. Bert himself later said that night felt like stirring in a large pan with a thick wooden spoon, and the longer they played the thinner and lighter the contents became.

Together we had achieved what was intended. I asked Francis, the woman who had organised the evening in her centre, and she told me that her coffee ladies had been talking about that evening for many months thereafter. They had never experienced anything like it before; they were deeply impressed.

Something very special had happened that night, but I can't exactly say what that was. I only know I remember that night as very special, a precious memory of a warm and nice evening, and I heard the same from everyone, without exception.

That had been our intention exactly.

Scars of the Soul

The first thing I did after the funeral was visit my parents. They had not been invited for the funeral, which was a dubious decision of Linda's and mine. It was a very difficult time for my parents. But together with some friends they had connected with us in spirit and burned a candle during the time of the ceremony.

I wanted very much to restore the contact between us, and of course I wanted to know how they were doing, and also of course to tell them about our experiences. That first meeting, after more than half a year was a happy meeting. Of course there was much to talk about, and of course we all had been wounded by our own actions. Linda's extreme situation needed our total isolation, preventing this reunion from happening sooner. It was time to take care of that, and to heal. It was time to begin.

Almost from the start of Linda's illness I had felt I wanted to write down what was happening. So much had happened and so many things were so unique and special that it would be a pity if all that would be lost. I once put the idea to Linda, but it didn't sound like a great idea to her. She could think of a title though: "9000 hours of pain... a book that should never be written in the Netherlands."

Now was the right time, and I decided to keep a diary. I had talked to other people who had lost their love or a dear one; some said that writing helps to cope with such a loss. In my youth I had written stories, so I had some experience expressing my thoughts.

My great *vriendin* was gone. I was left behind with the care of two very sick kitties, which also had suffered greatly during the course of the battle. Kleine Push Charonna had developed severe diabetes, an illness that often is related to stress. And Liselle, Push Maika, suffered from increasingly frequent cramp attack and was barely able to walk anymore. These complaints too had started during the last year. Unbelievable as it sounds, at the exact moment of Linda's transition Liselle had had one such seizure, forcing me, immediately after Linda had died, to quickly hold her and bring her back to her senses till the seizure was over, which luckily only needed a few seconds.

That was not a coincidence of course; cats are very sensitive as they respond to the people they love. Moreover, what I learned much later was that it was very important that I had to leave the room immediately after Linda had died, and focus my mind on something totally different, even if it was only for seconds. Often during the process of dying those emotionally very connected to the one in the process of dying, in many cases, for some reason, had just left the room moments before, maybe to go get a cup of coffee, or go to the toilet, whatever. Their presence can complicate matters during the moment of dying, because the passing person needs to let go of the earthly life. The close presence of a loved one can make it just that little bit more difficult to let go and step into the new 'life'.

Linda had said she wanted to die in my arms, and so it happened, but immediately afterwards I was forced to leave the room. This allowed the astral helpers or angels to complete the process of releasing her body. My presence, because of our intense bond, would have made this more difficult. And in fact it *had* done because Linda's passing took minutes where in other cases it is 'nothing more' (forgive me the comparison) than one last breath. But in our case that was okay, I knew it was okay.

I decided that my diary would be a letter to Linda, and I intended not to restrict myself in any way in what I felt and thought. I wanted to write down *anything*, without any exception, and not be held back by shame or by fear. I had a reason for this and that was that I had always understood that in the... Other Side, the Astral World, Heaven, or the Spirit World... it is not possible to keep your thoughts secret. On Earth we can hide our thoughts from each other, because we are 'in the matter'. We can pretend to be different than we really are, we can presume, we can pretend, we can lie. That's okay, but when misused it is how we create misunderstandings, resulting in fights and even wars. But at the same time this makes Earth the ideal place to learn to deal with each other, with our own egos, our fears, our pain and sorrow. Because we feel as if we are cut off from each other, separated from each other, separated from the Divine Source, afraid to share our thoughts, our energy and our love. We think we aren't whole anymore, we aren't one, and that frightens us, being scared... scared to show who we are.

Earth has yet to become a better world? So I wanted to contribute my share to that by starting very small. In silence Linda and I always had difficulty expressing our deepest feelings towards each other. That's where I wanted to start. No more fears, no more secrets, which we didn't have anyway. If this is normal in *her* world now, then she was able to know all my thoughts, and as such secrets wouldn't be possible anyway! Besides, I would only fool myself by not writing things down that she knew about me all the time.

It was silent in the house. I was alone with my thoughts, thoughts that were always the same. I was so deeply touched by what had happened and the pain of loss was so intense that I could feel it even physically. My heart and the whole region around it hurt. Every second that I was awake I could only think of one thing: what had happened, how I felt, about Linda, about how the future would be, about my sorrow, and again about her, about all that had gone wrong, and again about her. Only one week ago... just two weeks ago... just one month ago.

I thought that people could see in me that I had lost my beloved. I thought it was so strongly present in my mind that it seemed to be written in big letters all over my body, but apparently not, because out on the streets no one paid any attention to me. There were times when I just didn't know how to put one foot in front of the other, but nobody saw it. Nobody felt what I felt. But maybe... it was just me; maybe I was so busy with myself that I didn't notice other people. Maybe it *was* really noticeable, and the other people were keeping a loving distance from me, allowing me to regain my breath without disturbing me.

I had heard once of people who had lost their partner, dreaming very vividly of them sometimes; so vivid that it wasn't a dream, but much more than that. This happened to me a few weeks after her death. I made note of this in my letter:

This morning at seven o'clock, I was daydreaming a little when I suddenly realized that we were sitting downstairs on the floor together. I think we had been sitting there for a while already doing something. It felt like we may have been making a new decoration for the school again, but that probably wasn't it. It was so nice. I just sat there looking at you and thought how nice it was that I could simply close my eyes and look at you again and you were not even gone. I noticed that you looked very well in your face again, but later I thought that you still looked very earthly, and I don't think fully recovered yet.

Because Linda and I were so intensely connected I thought a lot about where she was now. I tried to imagine it. Together we had read and heard a lot about spiritual affairs. Linda had grown up with this. Now she herself was on the 'other side'. I wondered what it was like there? What is she doing? Who is she meeting? What is our relationship with each other, apart from the eighteen years we have lived together? Is it possible to make contact? How do you communicate with your deceased love? In the bible, I had heard, it says, "Thou shalt not call the dead." Those thoughts kept me busy.

Given our background it was natural I would try to contact her, but I assumed that summoning spirits, typing letters on an Ouija board and stuff like that wasn't the right way to do so. I even thought that Linda would deliver me a huge kick if I even dared to try. That way of making contact felt unethical. That's not how you communicate with your love. Apart from that... it's asking for trouble. Tapping letters on an Ouija board... the idea alone! I could see it all before me:

"Hello, who's there?"

"L.. I.. N.. D.. A.."

"How are you?"

"F.. I.. N.. E.."

"Are you really Linda?"

"Y.. E..S"

Sure! No doubt in my mind!

But then how do you make contact? Is consulting a clairvoyant so much better than tapping letters on a board? I thought so, but was it really the case?

As well, for starters it seemed to me that after such an illness Linda would need time to recover. You can't simply shake off fourteen months of pain. She now had no physical body anymore, but the memory would be so fresh and so she likely wouldn't be 'cured' as easy as waving a magic wand. Today we have trauma teams to assist all affected after a serious car accident. That seemed like a nice comparison to me. Probably there would be some kind of trauma team on her side, maybe even convalescent homes to help people with their last illness, that killed them, but now that they were in spirit their mind still needed healing. Therefore, it seemed not in the best interest of her recovery to go crazy trying to make contact. Besides... *she* probably would indicate when the time was right. After all, I had seen her briefly, and hadn't I noticed somehow that she hadn't fully recovered. Finally I came to the conclusion that it wasn't up to me to control, as if I could control anything at all.

At the end of the winter there would be a small local psychic fair in a community centre at walking distance from our house. Together with Linda I had often visited that same fair, but with the thought already in my mind, I doubted if I should go. What should I do?

'Coincidentally', I had met Linda for the first time in that same centre, during folk dancing lessons in the same room where the stalls would now be. Now it would be the first contact with her in this same room. Was that a coincidence? I decided that this was a hint.

It was a nice event and I took plenty of time to look around, grab some flyers and speak with people behind the tables. Sometimes I sat down for a brief consultation with a psychic, but this didn't make me much wiser. The only similarity among them was that Linda was still very tired, but I had seen that myself during my dream, so nothing new there. Yet I had a feeling that Linda too was very motivated to make contact with me, but it looked like all the psychics there simply didn't have that special skill needed to pass on clear and convincing messages just like that. When one of them remarked that Linda suggested later making a holiday trip to Jupiter I started having second thoughts about being here.

Then to my surprise, I saw Marianne! She was there to promote her therapy, and I sat down next to her for a while. So now we could finally talk about what had happened, because the whole situation had a deep effect on Marianne too. She said that she was a therapist only very recently and that she was very uncertain, doubting her skills. And with Linda she had been confronted with something like a worst-case scenario to start with.

I told her that she was the only therapist who had been able to come this close to Linda, because she had accepted her for who she was. As critical and inaccessible as Linda was, that was a huge compliment! Even Igor had patted her on her shoulder, saying how well she did in his own language. That had made a big impression on us all and Marianne had tears in her eyes when Igor touched her. She had just been the only and right therapist!

In those days I was totally lost. My head was bursting with many questions and painful memories and I was searching for answers. In addition, I was confronted with what people said to me. For a few months you're allowed to grieve and to mourn and everyone sympathises with you. Then you realize that life goes on for everyone else, because conversations are not about that what fills your head all the time. Talking about death is very hard for most people.

There's a general consensus on how to deal with the deceased that boils down to this: 'let go', because 'life goes on'. Look forward, not backward. You must go on. Leave the dead alone.

I didn't understand that. Within two months I was confronted with those words, but what had happened had made a huge impact on me and I had come out of the battle wounded. Some wounds were so deep that they would be a part of me forever, visible like scars, scars of the soul. Crazy as it seems... I was proud of them. They had formed and made me who I am.

How could anyone speak to me about 'letting go'? Those words only hurt, because it felt that I wasn't even allowed to think of her.

And life indeed did go on, and how it did! My father had had a heart attack and to make things worse he was now diagnosed with a brain tumour, with only a few months to live. Our two cats too hadn't come unscathed from the battle. Liselle, Pusj Maika, showed symptoms of paralysis and incontinence. Kleine Pusj Charonna had diabetes. Life was at full speed indeed.

It can't be wrong to be sad? You can't just efface a relationship, a marriage, for some people almost a lifetime in just a few months, can you? Of course nobody means to simply forget what you had together. But where's the line?

I think these words are often uttered by people who themselves are struggling, projecting their thoughts on you. With this they suggest that they prefer talking about something else, because conversations about death evoke pain about other deceased love ones. Almost everyone has lost beloved friends, relatives or a partner, and talking to someone who has just experienced the same reactivates that pain, in which you feel forever separated from the ones you love, making you feel broken, not being whole again, not being one.

In the course of time I have heard many statements meant to cheer me, even from people who had experienced it themselves, but often they had the opposite effect:

"It will go away."

I wondered... what will go away? The sorrow? The pain? The love you feel? I assume that meant the grief, but I was glad to be able to feel sad, because the sadness showed me that I could *feel!* That was something I had had trouble with all my life. Crying felt like a relief!

"Time heals all wounds."

I don't agree. Time heals no wounds, only covers them. The so-called healing blanket of time can be removed any time and then the grief is right back again. Even after five hundred years after Igor's death I still felt the intense grief of Nasja.

"You get used to it."

Getting used to it? That didn't cheer me up either. It didn't sound like an improvement. It made me feel like it meant you can't deal with it, so you leave it like it is.

"Over time you can give it a place."

So you put your grief in a drawer in the archive, labelled: "Linda... grief... 2001"

"For her, the suffering is over, but her loss now is your suffering."

Crazy as it seems, this statement supported me because I felt understood. It gave recognition to my feelings. This note came from the bakery where I always bought the extra dark white bread for Linda:

"We love you."

On a card, with only this message, a line from Linda's parents, who had already lost a son, and now their only daughter.

This statement is the best I've ever heard.

A White Rose

During the weeks thereafter I tried a couple of times to gently contact her. For example, I sat at the computer, held my hands above the keyboard and said out load something like, "Well... if you want to say anything... then use my fingers."

Automatic writing via the computer, that shouldn't be so hard, especially as I knew Linda in her healthy years. She had a very strong willpower like no other. She was well capable of 'sending cars away'. Sometimes while driving your car you are being slowed down by a 'slug', like a truck from a far away country finding its way through unknown streets, or a grandma proudly driving safer than everyone else, much slower than the allowed speed. After tailing such a car for a while you get bored and wish that this car wasn't there. Linda had a fun solution to this problem and she mentally sent such a car away at the first possible exit to the left or the right. She was so adept at it that sometimes a whole row of cars, at the first opportunity, would turn onto a dirt road leading to nowhere but grasslands, a road we had never seen used by vehicles other than tractors. Of course she was chuckling triumphantly after such actions, justifying them with words like, "Everyone says that I'm a witch, but I'm never allowed to act like one. But occasionally I need practise, or I will unlearn my skills."

Mmm... is that so?

So controlling my fingers shouldn't be a problem for her. But that she should wish to contact me through automatic writing, I wasn't so sure.

Yet I tried a few times, and nothing happened, except that I always felt that it wasn't the right way to make contact. As always during such sessions, I arranged a candle, a stick of incense and soft soothing music, keeping my thoughts as positive as I could. That felt like a good preparation, but I hesitated, because if there came words like 'your guardian angel Amiris', or 'your love Linda'... how would I know if that was true? An evil entity could claim that. Honest and wise sounding words could easily be copied from the Bible. Once reliant on what is passed on, you're easy to manipulate and vulnerable. That can cause lots of trouble. Evil entities love to cause misery, but they are smart enough to use kind and loving words to win their victims first, so you start trusting the words you see on paper.

'Trust'... hadn't we heard that word before?

A few months later, it was at the end of the winter, I read a magazine, 'Paravisie', and my gaze was drawn to a particular article. It was about a clairvoyant woman, an extensive interview. At first I didn't understand why I was so strongly drawn to that article, but while reading it I felt a very strong urge that this was the one I need to speak to!

The clairvoyant woman in question was Loes van Loon, living north of Amsterdam. She couldn't be the same person whose business card we had lost somehow, could she? The article mentioned that Loes also had written a book, '*Bonded by the Light*'. That sounded... *felt*, like a must-read to me, so I decided to buy it right away.

After only a few pages I decided I would write her a letter. I longed for help, to talk to people who could understand me, but even people who had lost a partner themselves didn't seem to understand me. We had taken a lonely path, understood by no one, and now that Linda had died it seemed like we had made bad choices again and again. Everyone had been right and we had been wrong. *"We told you, but you wouldn't listen"*.

Personally, I felt we had done well, but thought no one could agree with me; I felt I was alone there. No one was able to give me answers on an equal level, because I felt they didn't have enough knowledge and wisdom to convince me. And I was looking for someone like that; someone who kind of stood 'above' me with a higher wisdom maybe, really knowing for sure. Only then I would be able to accept what they had to say. Otherwise I wouldn't accept it.

All that time I hadn't found such a person, and now... While reading Loes' book, I immediately felt that the information contained therein came from a different source. The title 'Bonded by the Light' suggested this already. And I discovered something interesting... In the book it was explained that Loes' real name was written differently: Lucia. That name contained a 'c', a 'u' and an 'a'! That was the name Linda and I had been looking for so long, but never found!

That same evening I sat behind the computer and started writing a letter, summarizing what had happened to us, the strange experiences we had encountered, like with Igor and Amà, how hard it had been, and why I was writing this letter. While writing, I had a special feeling, a feeling of 'concentration', satisfaction, or being 'full'. It felt like I was doing something that I really went for, passionately, because I enjoyed it, I really did. I said a lot about myself and I was pretty intimate, so it was a very personal letter. But above all, it 'felt' good.

Next to the computer monitor, on the wall behind it, I had hung a beautiful photograph of Linda. While I was writing, with my eyes concentrated on the monitor, I suddenly heard a loud tap, and from the corner of my eyes I saw that picture move, as if someone had tapped it using their thumb and forefinger. That picture hung on a place with no draughts, and could never be moved just by itself because it was tightly attached to the wall. But I had clearly noticed it moving and heard the sound!

It was no coincidence and I could barely believe what was happening. I had heard about the deceased seeking contact with those left behind, sometimes even through very physical events such as sounds. This seemed to be one such occasion, so I asked aloud, "Do you wish to tell me something?"

But if so... how was I to receive the answer? No accident of course that this happened during the time of day I sometimes gave to trying the automatic writing on the computer. Now that this was happening I could be sure that Linda was close by. So if now wasn't a good time to make it happen...

I opened a new blank document on the computer and waited with my fingers above the keys.

Now what? Wait? Okay... let's wait.

And... wait a little more.

But nothing happened; I heard nothing, the picture didn't move anymore and I felt, like every time before, that it wasn't the right thing to do. Apparently I didn't have the gift for it, or maybe it was the wrong way of making contact. Anyway, after a while I decided to go on with the letter to Loes, because that felt good. With that I was really on a roll. That wasn't unlike anything I was used to, and the words flew from my fingers as I found I was writing a very beautiful, be it personal, letter to Loes.

I couldn't finish it that same night, so the next day I continued writing, and the same thing happened again! I heard a loud tap and the picture of

Linda clearly moved! Until yesterday that picture had never moved by itself! This really couldn't be a coincidence, no way! So again I stopped writing and asked, "Do you wish to tell me something, Love?" And again I opened a blank document and waited with my hands above the keys.

How silly can you be?

Of course nothing happened! And with more clarity than ever before I felt, "Automatic writing is not your thing!"

I received no response from the keyboard of the computer, nothing happened. However I did have a strong feeling that what I had been doing was good; simply writing this letter to Loes, writing down what I was feeling, putting my feelings in words on paper, because I was being completely pure in that. Perhaps Loes was that clairvoyant that Linda and I had sought and Linda gave me a sign, confirming it by these taps on her picture.

An hour later the letter was finished. In a few pages I had written a summary of our story, almost a nano-version of this book, along with many questions and doubts that were troubling me. Reading back I found the letter remarkably well written. I used to write letters often, but it usually took great effort and I was never really satisfied with the final result, always thinking I could have expressed things better. Not so this time, I was satisfied! The letter felt so good. I kept reading it over and over again; strange to be so confident with your own writing. Finally, I put it in an envelope and mailed it in the post-box, with a stamp of course.

Since then I never again tried to make contact with the Spirit World through automatic writing. I really dislike it. What I did do however was write this book. And in case you don't realize it: Linda and I wrote this book together. Not by means of automatic writing, but by listening to my feelings, by being absolutely honest in everything, without judgement and without fear. That doesn't seem very paranormal so to speak, compared to fingers typing 'by themselves', but this process is fed from two sides at the same time; from the Spirit World and from myself. If I write something wrong, being not with complete integrity for example, or just trying to write from my rational mind... then I notice that I can't get any meaningful words on paper, they lack... Force. The sentences don't feel right, there's no flow in the words and it makes no sense, and at a later stage these texts will be deleted or replaced. Maybe Linda would have written several things differently if she would have been able to physically use the keyboard herself, using different words, adding a few here and there or omitting a couple, but there's no doubt in my mind that she agrees with the *essence* of every page of this book.

After all, I had asked her before she died to inspire me, and this was exactly what was happening now. The beauty in this is that when the Spirit World is allowed in Earthly matters, they succeed in fitting everything together so neatly. Linda now can tell from her perspective. It still strikes me every time how 'they' manage to get things done so precisely with so little use of energy, attaining multiple goals at the same time. So this book started as a letter from me to Linda, a form of grief counselling and training at the same time. Gradually it became a more conscious contact with the Spirit World and more and more messages are given between the lines. Now this book has become a story for other people, for you to read, with all our mistakes and our good moments, a learning process, in which you may recognize yourself. Hopefully you can learn something by reading it, and maybe it might make you very sad at times, but maybe by experiencing the sadness it may give you comfort. After all, aren't we all together as students in the school of Light? We belong together. Unity!

Now that I write this I remember something that I had done, but had already half forgotten - in the first three months after Linda's death I started to realize that my life had taken a completely different direction than I ever would have foreseen, I had spoken aloud something to 'Above'...

I realized that I certainly wasn't meant to be grieving for the rest of my life. Linda would rattle me briskly if I would do that. With that in mind, I came up with an idea that I spoke out loud the next night: "Ideally I want my life from this moment henceforth to be working in cooperation with the Spirit World."

How that would be developed was something I didn't give much thought to at that moment; it simply *felt* like the right thing to say, and I really felt like standing by it. I was prepared to bear the consequences of that statement, although I couldn't foresee them of course. It wasn't just a statement I made lightly, though later I often wondered if I really knew what I was getting myself into. It's just that it was beginning to take shape now, but I didn't realize it at the time. Linda had started to teach me, and one of the first things she taught me was that automatic writing wasn't my 'thing'. Because then I would just be a 'receiver of messages' without being able to tell where the messages were coming from. There was great danger in that, and we both had personally experienced all too well what consequences that could have. Never again!!

A few days later the phone rang, and on the other side of the line I heard a clear female voice with a very Amsterdam accent saying, "With Loes van Loon."

I was perplexed. I hadn't expected a reaction that fast, and certainly not over the phone; a letter maybe, with a phone number to make an appointment, but not this. I felt that Linda was leading my way step by step, to put me in contact with Loes, and through Loes, with herself. First that magazine, then the book, and the tapping on her picture when I was writing, and her help writing the letter, and now it seemed that Loes was precisely the woman we had sought. Finally found! But a bit late in my eyes, you know! However, that certainly wasn't without a very good reason.

Loes said she was deeply touched by my letter. She still had tears in her eyes when she picked up the phone to call me, she said, and she had the letter in front of her. She told me that someone was standing with her in the room, very eager to speak with me, someone very 'impatient' as she put it.

During the following telephone conversation that lasted about three quarters of an hour, I noted down keywords and phrases of the conversation like crazy, so when the conversation ended I was able to almost word for word recall most of what Loes had said. Some of that I will repeat here:

"She had pain," Loes said. "Left, on her left in her abdomen. Suffered from pain left in her head too. She was very nauseous. Her eyes can't see well. All is vague and she can't focus in the middle."

I had not told her those details in my letter. Of course she could have concluded from my letter that Linda must have had pain in her abdomen, but the poor vision due to the medications was really accurate.

"She has had a great sorrow, couldn't bear leaving you, wanted to persevere for you. Had a hard time on the other side, felt safe with you. On her left lower arm there are long scribbles."

That was true! That was a leftover of the big catfight in our garden years ago. Linda had jumped right in the middle of that fight to separate the fighting cats, but suffered badly from that, resulting in several long scars on both her arms.

"Well then," Loes said, "then now you know for sure that it really is Linda who is standing in front of me."

Next followed a very special conversation between Linda and me, with Loes as a translator. Or as she describes herself, "I'm just a fax machine."

"I'll be fine,' Loes relayed Linda's words.

"She hears you, also your thoughts."

She told me that Linda could always hear me, all that I'm thinking. It is a world of thoughts and just like us they have memories and can think; you don't need physical brains for that.

"He sends me so many candles that I don't know where to go with all the light," Linda said with a laugh.

"Her guide is male," Loes said. "He was once her father in a previous lifetime somewhere around 1500, and since then has ever been her guardian angel."

Immediately I wondered if he had been her father back then in Uzbekija, because Igor had died in 1532, so that could match perfectly, but I couldn't ask that question, because Loes was speaking so fast I didn't want to interrupt all the time.

"He is very funny and makes her laugh a lot, shows her a lot too. She's very conscious there, but she still needs to process her life, and that's something she doesn't want to think about yet. She had to learn to accept. That was something she couldn't do in other incarnations again and again."

"Amà isn't her guardian angel," Loes continued, "but she is a friend. Linda was allowed a peek into the Spirit World this way, as a gift, but also in preparation so she wouldn't need to be afraid, and also to know that there is help for her. That is quite special, when you're allowed to experience it in such a way. Usually people get to see things shortly before their transition, during the last hours, but she was allowed to experience this long in advance."

"Her hair is so beautiful! While she was ill it had become dull. Her hair is very important for her. But now it shines beautifully again."

"Your voice made/makes her calm. She feels/felt very safe with you."

"You should do something with your hands, Linda says. He has 'lightened' me."

She referred to all those endless treatments I had given her. I can magnetize with my hands and had helped her a lot. Healing, illnesses, is about karmic lessons and you can't change those. But lightening with your hands can be done anyway. "You know that," she said.

Hébenes, Loes' guardian angel, came into the exchange and said to me, "Dare to be who you are!"

He tried explaining that a little further, but he hardly got a chance because Loes suddenly said, "She's quite impatient!"

Loes had to laugh, recognizing herself in Linda, as I understood later. She too could be quite impatient at times. That's Linda, I thought, and obviously she hadn't lost that, because Hébenes could barely finish his sentence. It amazed me how 'human' things were on the 'other side'. Well, what did I expect anyway about how 'life' is over there? Apparently they aren't sitting on luminous clouds on the right hand side of God. During Linda's lifetime on Earth she used to make fun of that biblical view. Now it turned out she reacted just as I knew her. She said, "Now that I have a chance to say something, I want to say what I want to say." So Hébenes was allowed to explain something, but hurry up will you?

"Her belly was full of cancer, very extensive, darkened with cancer," Hébenes said. So it was! It could hardly be otherwise, but now it was confirmed.

I asked one question about Dottore. Loes had to consult with Hébenes, so she kept silent for a moment.

"He doesn't understand the karmic lessons," was the significant answer. No judgment, only this observation, which was the answer to many questions at once. For me that was enough and I didn't ask more about this, as not to waste valuable time on this subject.

"There's a little girl with her," Loes said. "She has dark brown curly hair and her hair is very long. She looks a bit like Shirley Temple. She's actually a small guardian angel, to show Linda around."

At a later date I learned from Loes that Linda needed a contact like this. In the first stage of being in the Hereafter people have to get accustomed, get used to everything again. It's not true that all your memories, both from before your birth date and your years on Earth, are always restored immediately, and that you know who you are as a soul. Our guardian angels decide about this, out of love for us in our own interest. They take it one step at a time. For the same reason this little girl was there, making Linda feel totally safe and very familiar. Loes described Linda sitting on one knee to rearrange the girl's hair. That sounded very nice. This girl knew all about the Spirit World and took Linda with her to show her everything, not as an adult person, but as a little girl. Later I learned that in fact this girl was indeed an adult person, who was active in what is called 'The Children's Realm', but to Linda she showed herself as a little girl. That's not a problem for them, because 'thought creates', and they aren't tied to a physical body. For Linda this was the perfect way after such a heavy period of time to familiarize with the Spirit World that now was her home again.

I suddenly thought of something and I asked, "Is she the same girl who asked us if she could be born through us?"

Loes now said that the girl was now enthusiastically clapping her hands, to confirm that I guessed right. This was indeed the girl that had come during one of the many visualisations with Amà. Linda then had said that this little girl was capable of breaking down her defences and convince her that she could want a child; quite an accomplishment, knowing Linda.

Linda was now speaking and Loes repeated word for word what she said:

"Don't think that we didn't do things right," she said. "I don't mind that you're sad. That's okay. You better be!"

"She's laughing," Loes added. Then she said, "But it really hurts me when you doubt. I trusted in you. We have done well! You can always reach me. I can hear you everywhere."

Suddenly a small dog comes to Linda. "Who's that?" asks Loes, being surprised about that. So Taksi had made his entrance now too!

"She's very grateful to you. Without you she wouldn't have succeeded."

Loes added that Linda was showing her a bunch of red roses. She asked me if I understood this. I said that recently I had bought two roses and put them beside Linda's picture on the glass table at home. "That's it!" she said. She took out one rose and that appeared to be a white one. She gave that one to me! That felt awesome.

"She thinks she has done very well, also because of you. It was about acceptance" Loes went on. So *finally* I had the confirmation I wanted that we had done very well, finally! Even the part when I had restrained her so long, because after that she said, "Don't give up."

"She wasn't allowed to give up either. She now has seen what its like when someone really gives up." Apparently she was very shocked by that.

"She has found the road that was good for her," Loes said.

And with that remark Linda's favourite song 'Somehow, I'll find my way home' got an even more special meaning.

"The help she gets from the other side, that's very special," said Loes. "So *much* help too. She gets many compliments. "Very clever! very well done! They're so proud of me!"

"You are very special," she told me. "And because you're so special I love you. I will always keep watching you. Keep the faith in God's plan."

"He's so sweet," she added to Loes. That sounded nice to me. When she was alive she used the same words to other people every now and then about me with me present, and with the exact same intonation.

"We got along very well together."

I added that I would love to be there, but Hébenes interrupted immediately, saying, "You have to hang in there for a while. What difference does thirty, forty years make?... it's just a needlepoint on the evolution. You too have said 'yes' to this life as it is."

Oops... okay, I thought.

"Don't forget your white rose!" repeated Linda. I almost forgot, because of all I had received during the phone conversation. Apparently she thought this rose to be very important.

Then she said something that really struck me; she said, "You can never lose me! You shouldn't think that. It hurts me when you doubt. I thought you knew me better."

It didn't sound like a serious accusation but more like a living admonition.

"Trust my love."

That was about what I could recall. We had spoken almost 40 minutes and I thanked Loes sincerely for the time she had set-aside just for us. Linda too thanked her. I was very impressed and had received a lot of answers to my questions. I had a lot of things to do that day, but just before shopping closing time I suddenly realised that I was about to forget one important thing. Quickly I got in the car and drove to the flower shop where Linda used to buy flowers for my birthdays, mostly roses. I bought a bunch of the most expensive red roses and selected one big white rose and had it added in the middle of the red ones. At home I put those next to Linda's picture and I was deeply touched by the sight of these roses, and by what they meant to be.

What I really liked was that I wasn't told to 'let go' or such bullshit. Of course I knew perfectly well that I had to continue my life and not keep mourning, sticking to a love that was no longer on Earth. That would keep both Linda and me imprisoned in a cage of sad thoughts. In that respect, yes, one really should learn to 'let go', or in other words... resume your life. But I didn't need to hide my grief; I was allowed to be sad. That felt very good. That gave me freedom to be who I was. And that was what I needed so badly, and with the reassurance that I would never be alone. All my thoughts... they were no secret. Maybe something to get used to, but at the same time it was a very safe feeling.

By the way... I have to add some special detail to this. Years later, when I had given Loes this now published book, she told me that she had never been to any psychic fairs in Apeldoorn, and so she could not be the one who we had been looking for, the person whose business card we were searching for, with an Amsterdam accent and a name in which a 'u', a 'c' and an 'a' were present, something like 'Judesca' or so. Loes said, "This Judesca you write about is a very good psychic friend of mine. In fact her name isn't 'Judesca', but 'Judoca', and indeed she does have an Amsterdam accent, just like me. Plus, my daily name may be 'Loes, but actually it is 'Lucia'".

The white rose stood on the glass table beside Linda's picture for two weeks, blooming so gorgeous amid the red roses. Every time I looked at them it brought tears to my eyes, good tears, so beautiful! And as I pondered they're meaning... a white rose! That's a very special flower. Not something you give without a good reason. People may have thoughts about your intentions such as... *Oh yeah? What are you saying here: not something you give without a good reason...*

No, of course not. I always knew what roses stand for. Roses stand for love; everyone knows that! But since then I had a nagging feeling like '*go check it out*'. What is so special about the *white* rose? I had never really checked that meaning out. I knew it all too well: roses stand for love. So why should I check it out any further?

Finally, after about one and a half months, I *did* check out the meaning of a white rose. I had reason to because two days later I was to visit Loes together with Linda's parents, for a proper consultation. And I had planned to give Linda a white rose too, from me for her. But before doing that I had to check out the meaning of a white rose so I could be sure I knew what I was actually saying. So I browsed the Internet, finally! It wasn't hard to find and several times over I found the same text:

The white rose has four different meanings:

Innocence and purity, humility, I am worthy of you, You're heavenly, and secrecy and silence.

Besides this I found something else, and that is that red and white roses together have a special meaning: oneness, forever together.

Now what was it again that I had said at her funeral: to be one?

Slowly it dawned on me that she wanted to tell me much more than 'only' love or I love you, what roses symbolise anyway. What especially caught my attention was that one sentence: I'm worthy of you.

That touched me because it said so many things at once. If I put the emphasis on 'you', then it says 'I am worthy of *you*'. I had just been given a huge compliment!

Then I wondered, "Can I, with this meaning in mind, now give *her* a white rose?" Would I dare to say that I'm worthy of *her*?

The consultation with Loes was very special and I will quote a few things that were said...

Flowers can be offered to loves and relatives in Spirit World through a psychic during flower séances. They then accept them and at that moment an astral copy of the flower is created in spirit, and what's more... the love with which they are given can be seen in those flowers. Also, because the earthly flowers haven't disappeared they then get a second function; through the psychic they can be given to other people on demand of the spirits. This is what makes a flower séance a very special meeting. With Loes we didn't organise a flower séance but the action was the same.

I had indeed bought a white rose that was wrapped in transparent plastic. During the conversation I picked it up and offered it to Linda. Linda grabbed the opportunity to first give her parents this rose, telling them how much she loves them and how grateful she was to them for their support all her life. Then she turned to me.

"She says," Loes, said, "I take it with me. And here it remains forever. So I will keep it eternally... until you are here. And then you shall see it."

Loes continued, "She is saying, word for word... If I could express in flowers what you have given me, I would hire the Keukenhof [8] At this point she gets emotional, so I get emotional too because I pick up her feelings. She is thrilled. And she hints at... gosh how awful that you had to do this... and gosh... how good that you did it! A touch of sympathy for you."

Loes quoted Linda again, 'If you think that you have not done well you are *so* far from the truth. That's the only thing you can say that would make me grieve, because you have done extremely well; and to express that in flowers like I just did, I would surely give all the flowers of the Keukenhof to you, all of them, piece by piece, and I would even water them too.'

Loes replied to Linda, "Child! Do you know what you're saying? You'd take care of the entire Keukenhof without a sinner to help you?"

"One day I might remind you of that," I said with a smile.

Linda came back with, "I was already afraid you might say that." And she laughed.

Loes described Linda taking the rose with her. "And immediately she rips of the damned plastic," she added with her Amsterdam humour.

---

[8] *The Keukenhof is the biggest yearly Spring flower show in the Netherlands*

One Ring... To Be One

At that time I was thinking a lot about life after death, as you could expect. Because of that I became increasingly aware of the influences from the Spirit World exercised on our lives that most people find hard to recognize. I had no doubt anymore that Linda was still 'somewhere'. She had no earthly body anymore, but I got the impression that she was doing everything to let me know that our love had not stopped with the border between life and death; I began to recognize that more and more, and I developed an alertness in picking up those signals.

In this book you can find dozens of passages showing the influence of the Spirit World. Usually these influences are inconspicuous events that are easily ignored, but sometimes things happen that are so remarkable they are best described as small miracles than ungratefully described as 'coincidences'. Sometimes you are unexpectedly alerted to them. Something might 'strike' you, said by a person on the television screen just after you've switched it on. Or you walk passed the table in the kitchen while briefly noticing a headline of the newspaper giving you the answer to a question that was pickling your brains for days already. On the radio a touching song might start to play, perfectly reflecting your feelings of that moment, supporting you. Previously I wouldn't have paid any attention to how and when these signals came to me, but now that I did I discovered how remarkable the synchronicity and the number of the signals, influencing our lives to a great deal.

For example, I was working on this book daily in the early morning hours for more than half a year when finally I came to the moment of Linda's transition. I hadn't planned this ahead, but I found it very special that that day was Ascension Day.

Another example. In February, several months after her death, a certain song kept playing in my head all day long, an old tune by Kate Bush named 'Wuthering Heights'. I remembered bits of the video clip: a transparent figure of a deceased young woman outside the windows with flowing hair. Linda was a fan of Kate Bush and had several of her LPs. So I played the one with Wuthering Heights and while listening I read the back cover with the lyrics of the song. It brought tears to my eyes, especially when thinking of Nasja and Igor:

Bad dreams in the night
They told me I was going to lose the fight
Leave behind my Wuthering, Wuthering, Wuthering heights
Too long I roamed in the night.
I'm coming back to his side, to put it right.
I'm coming home to Wuthering, Wuthering, Wuthering heights
Heathcliff, it's me, Cathy, I've come home

So I made a digital copy of this song in my computer, as I had done with many other songs so I could listen to background music while working behind the screen. I played those songs randomly and there were so many now that I could listen for hours without songs being repeated.

Now, years later while writing this book, writing about signals from the Spirit World guiding our lives on Earth, I wanted to use this incident to illustrate the presence of our loved ones, but I couldn't find the lyrics, which I had stored somewhere in the many folders. It took me a while to find the document and when I finally did and started reading the first lines I suddenly was shocked when I realized that these words were just then being sung aloud. 'The computer' had selected this song to play so I could listen right along... timed to the exact words I was reading.

Sometimes our guardian angels can be very surprising...

One day I got into the car on the parking lot of the supermarket. It was one of those days when all seemed to work against me. I was angry and was in a bad mood. Now I needed to pull myself together, because I felt like wanting to fight against anything that would come my way. Impatiently I started the engine, but then I realized I had to be careful because driving a car in such a mood is asking for trouble.

I was parked in a corner of the park and diagonally behind me was a car parked perpendicular to me. I had not seen anyone getting into that car, but in fact I hadn't noticed anything at all because of my bad temper. I started to reverse speaking out loud to 'above': "Please help me, else I may cause an accident!"

As I spoke I looked over my shoulder to look back through the rear view window, and my elbow 'accidentally' touched the horn on the steering wheel. In a reflex action I stepped on the brakes. I looked back again and saw to my horror that there was this other car almost touching mine. By the look of the shocked face of the driver he hadn't seen me either, but he too was alarmed by my honking, just in time.

So I was reminded that our spirit guides are always aware of our actions and even our thoughts. I realized that when you have a problem or question all you need to do is ask, and help will be given, although probably slightly different than you expect. Don't reason this away thinking of it as 'coincidence', because then you skip some precious moments in your life, and actually it is ungrateful.

Coincidences are mainly indications that we are surrounded by our friends in the Spirit World, supporting us with all their love, letting us know they are there, sometimes pushing us, sometimes slowing us down, sometimes consoling us with beautiful music at the precise moment or, like I discovered, by arousing us harshly if necessary. Anyway... two cars were saved, my bad temper was gone and a fun story to tell in this book! Clever guy my spirit guide!

And Linda is a clever one too...

Because of her illness and all the pain I had witnessed I too had in fact experienced a kind of trauma. Of course her death had quite some impact, but that's 'normal'. In addition, I consciously and unconsciously recalled images of Linda who moaned in pain walking up and down the nightly room. Or again I saw the blood on the bed. Or I heard her saying again that she wanted to put an end to her life. I had great difficulty remembering nice things, of which there were very many, but I couldn't connect to those memories, because the pain was on top of all the beauty.

One night I dreamed of her, in which I thought she had been entertaining me all night long with fun and humorous things she had ever done or said. She always loved to make fun out of me if she could find a way.

When the dream faded I woke up hearing a very strange sound in the bedroom. It sounded like the croak of a frog. This alarmed me immediately because I knew Linda had a strong phobia of frogs. She would have easily jumped through the window of an apartment building if she was chased by a mad guy with a frog. So the first thing I thought of was to get that frog outside quickly before she would wake up and hear this croaking nightmare. I was like that for a few more seconds before I realized that she wasn't lying beside me, and while I listened I couldn't locate the origin of the sound. For minutes I kept on listening, turning my head to pinpoint the direction. Could it be my own stomach? No, my stomach was very quiet as always. The sound came from further away. My brain started to wake up more and more and I began wondering how on earth a frog could have gotten into the bedroom; firstly getting inside the house and climbing a staircase, and then finding its way onto yet another staircase, an open one! That must have been a really determined frog! Absurd!

Then what was it? This wasn't a dream! The sound was very realistic. Finally I noticed that the sound indeed originated from my own stomach. Why wasn't I able to hear that before? Ridiculous, as my stomach never makes sounds in the morning. Then, while remembering my dream again, I realized that Linda had played another trick on me. Apparently she was even able to manipulate my belly! Could I hear someone laughing out loud somewhere, or what? Anyway... her action had effect, because since then I think a lot easier about her as the cheerful Linda with her funny and clever humour.

Now these are all 'small' incidents that might not convince you, but I'm now going to describe something that can hardly be dismissed anymore as 'coincidence'. In fact I would say that this entire book and every event herein is absolutely no coincidence, and certainly no 'bad luck' as the hospital had wanted us to believe, but part of a much bigger plan. Let me start by telling you what happened to me about half a year after Linda's death.

Besides Loes, who came on my path in such a special way, I had been in contact with Vera, a clairvoyant woman whom Linda and I had visited more often. Now don't think we were consulting every psychic in the Netherlands, because Loes and Vera were the only ones I made appointments with.

Luckily Vera lived in Apeldoorn too. When I went to see her she described Linda as she stood in the room. She was wearing a beautiful dress in a light greenish colour with thousands of tiny crystals. A moment later she had changed all this and her dress looked very different. Vera laughed when she described it, because Linda was entertaining us, playing with the heavenly opportunities she had, creating with her thoughts.

At one point Vera said that Linda wanted to tell me something. I had to look for something for her, because somewhere in the house she still had a ring that she had worn a lot. I was bemused. A ring she had worn a lot? She never wore rings. Only when I had known her for a short while, nearly twenty years ago, she had a ring from Israel, but when that one broke she was not even sorry about that. "Then I suppose I don't need it anymore," she had said simply.

When I mentioned this to Vera she said that I had to get that ring repaired and that I should wear it. This surprised me, because Linda and I had never given rings to each other. Marry? Engage? We didn't do that! Give each other a ring? We thought it to be nonsense; we needed no ring to show the world that we loved each other. Still, it kept my mind busy. Indeed, there was always a desire in both of us to have more... unity, but because of our fear of showing our deepest feelings and desires, we rarely talked about it. I had seen Linda looking often through the window of a jeweller, to see if there were special pieces of jewellery, but she was very critical and there was never anything that matched her special taste. Sometimes I asked her if she wanted a ring from me, but she never responded really enthusiastically. Maybe it was not smart of me to ask that question, and instead simply do it. But I couldn't really tell. It was never our plan to marry, and we'd never exchanged rings... and now this?

Then suddenly it dawned on me: She's offering me a ring!!

That impressed me and I was very happy with this proposal, but when I started to think about it I wondered... Rings of Love are worn by two people. What about her?

But I thought, "When Linda offers me a ring... wouldn't I be able to do the same and offer her a ring too?"

That night I wrote in my diary/letter to Linda the following lines of text:

What I'm doing now, and of course that's secret (but what is a secret when you can hear my thoughts?), is designing a ring for you. I want it to be something really special. But now I wonder: when is something special?

When you've put a lot of time in it? Or is it the idea that counts? And when you realize this idea in just a little time? Or is it more than anything else that you do it from your heart?

That's what I think.

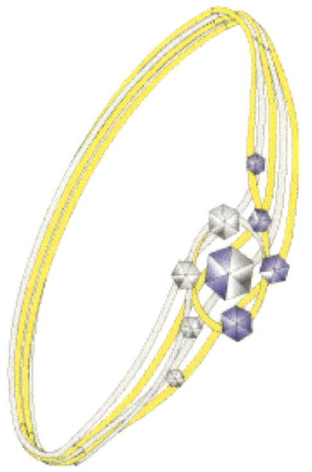

Taking care of Linda so intensively, followed by a mourning process had taken a heavy toll on my health, so I had made several appointments with Marianne as a therapist. These sessions were not only conducive to my health, but they were also very pleasant. Just the day after I had been with Vera I had a scheduled appointment with Marianne, and when I told her about the ring that had been discussed with Vera, she pulled out her bio-sensor, a special kind of pendulum. That way she could ask questions. She was very skilled with it, because Linda had asked her many questions about her illness. Fortunately, Marianne never attempted to answer questions such as: "Will I get better?" I could tell without the pendulum that such information shouldn't be given, and I admired the fact that Marianne stood her ground.

Marianne's biosensor confirmed that Linda had indeed offered me a ring and that I should wear it, but not as a memory ring on a chain around my neck. Marianne thought it brilliant that I wanted to design the ring myself. According to her the white rose was just the beginning.

Beginning of what?

But she couldn't tell me and the biosensor didn't move either.

Designing a ring is one thing. I was no goldsmith, so which jeweller or goldsmith would I need to contact to make this ring? Marianne and I worked through a whole list of options: the one in the Brinklaan in the centre of Apeldoorn? No... wrong one. That other one then in the Main Street? Again no good. There's another on the other side of the centre, with beautiful jewellery and art in the window. Of course! That should be the one. But no, wrong again. Then I remembered Linda and I going to Borculo one time, to a goldsmith with lots of beautiful stones. Before I had finished my sentence the pendulum started to move like crazy as if Linda was pushing it! I wrote to her:

At first I didn't understand the importance of the right jeweller. But then, for starters it was about adapting your old ring for my finger. Do you need a special goldsmith for that? But now I understand it's not only your ring you want give me, but that you know, knowing me, that I want to give you a ring too! And of course not the ring you see in the display window of the jeweller around the corner. What you get from further afield...

Now that I was sure of being on the right track, other ideas started playing in my mind. How does it work with exchanging rings between living and passed loved ones? Can you offer a ring to a deceased person? Do 'they' still have something with rings? Aren't rings earth-bound? Love is something universal, isn't it? So imagine Linda wearing a ring in the Spirit World, wouldn't that mean that she's still Earth-bound? Shouldn't she too 'let go'? That is so important isn't it? This didn't look like that. So what's going on here? And err.... something like 'Living Apart Together' is taken to a whole new level this way. What's the right thought on that?

Questions...

Of course I know perfectly well that marrying is senseless in the Spirit World. But it isn't that... bonding... but it's more. I can't really tell. There's still something more to it I think.

I asked Amhirez, my guardian angel, to make sure I am not doing something strange, to protect me from too weird ideas coming into my mind, because I now wonder what I can do, what is allowed, what it is you have in mind with this. And how far can I go, without making a fool of myself?

But I'm very happy with your proposal. I had never expected that.

It took a few days before I knew how the ring I had in mind had to look like. That was new to me. In the past, when I wanted to make a painting, I would ponder about it for a long time, not knowing what to do, where to start, what to make at all. Eventually, I always got an idea and knew how to complete it, but beginnings were always especially difficult. "That's the way things are", I thought.

And now... I had a certain feeling about this ring. What I did was nothing other than search for the shape that matched the feeling I had and express it precisely, and for some reason I managed to do that very easily. I didn't need to ponder it. The number five was important, don't ask me why. Just like gold and silver, because they express a Yin-Yang principle. It had to be a cosmic ring and I got the idea to symbolize the stars using crystals in the shape of the galaxy. The entire ring would be like a spiral, without beginning or ending. Experimenting with iron wires, and using the computer to assist me, I tried to see if this idea could be realised, and to my surprise, I found solutions for every problem. Faster than expected the design was finished. Now what?

So yesterday I did what you did, only in another way. I made you a proposal.

I know you can hear my thoughts, so then... sit down on the couch here. So I at least I know you are there and I can face you when I talk to you. So I asked you if you would like to... if you would like to bond with me.

To marry is of the Earth. In that way you swear allegiance to each other, that you'll stay together, commit no adultery, will provide for each in good times and bad, that you will dot dot dot to be your lawful wife or husband, etc etc.

We didn't need this, for several reasons. We didn't want children for starters. The whole fuss around marriage didn't appeal to us. We didn't need a white wedding dress for you. Some women find it wonderful, for that reason alone, to marry. A fairy tale wedding! But I really can't imagine you in a white wedding dress. Well... I can, but... it doesn't fit. It's almost a contradiction.

Would you secretly have wanted it a little bit? Sometimes I wonder. But I think not.

But last night I really made you a proposal, on my knees, indeed, and not to ask you to marry me.

But I did ask you if you would like to bond with me in total freedom... something like that. I don't even know how it should be called.

And... now that I think of it, I didn't plan it to do it yesterday. I thought of it yesterday and I did it right away. No careful planning ahead, no thinking over what I was going to say, no feeling nervous before. Can I do that? Isn't it disrespectful?

So there I was, on my knees, by the looks of it for an empty couch...

After having made the proposal I would have been very glad to have had an answer. But how long was I going to wait for it? The ground was very hard. The longer I sat upright, the more my back was starting to hurt. I closed my eyes for a while, but that only worked for a few minutes. I stared at the wall... it could use new wallpaper, I saw, and... jeez, where did all the dust come from on that table under the plant? That wasn't there yesterday! No way.

I tried imagining Linda in front of me on the couch. In fact I was pretty sure she was sat there, silently grinning or laughing about her beloved boyfriend doing silly things. Was I making a fool of myself? People would consider me gone mental if they knew I made a proposal to a dead person. The idea alone! My knees started aching. This was getting me nowhere. It would be stupid to sit here all night waiting for the cows to come home.

All in all, I felt it was okay to pursue my plans and get the ring forged, or to be exact: it didn't feel wrong. So I took the sketches I made and went to the goldsmith in Borculo. We had a nice conversation and he was really enthusiastic about the design. It was something special and he saw a challenge. It could take him many hours, but in this case money was not an issue. He took the assignment and would start working on it.

Two nights later I had a dream. In the middle of the night (it was three thirty) I wrote down what had happened:

Are you celebrating something now? Because that's how it feels. Something very, very special has happened this night. I dreamt of you, or better, I was with you. Or even better: you were with me!

You know the feeling when you go somewhere where your loved one resides e.g. jail, a madhouse, a holiday camp, something where the person stays for a long time (because these are quite some comparisons) and there is an open house and the family can come for a visit and see how things are going.

But... now who is where? Are you here with me... or am there with you?

Actually you are visiting me. I'm in jail... though it seems not, voluntary maybe, but grudgingly. And prison is not the right word, but sometimes it comes darn close. But that's what you can call it.

There were others around us, relatives, but on the other hand not... I don't know, but you were certainly there. The atmosphere was good, togetherness, something like it, not very clear.

I was with you, but felt that I still had to bridge a distance between us. You were Linda... but then again not only Linda... you were more... but then again not so much more; it was about that distance. You weren't detached from my love, I could feel that was so, however, it also felt as if you were not mine only anymore.

It resembles what Loes said: I see two women. (She meant Linda and her grandmother)

That too gave me the same feeling of distance. She didn't say: I now see your vriendinnetje. That's a good comparison.

And comparisons, that's what's all about. Because we did talk... communicate, that's the right word. But what was notable was... not that you went away from me... or I from you... but while I was in that... jail, I woke... became more human... and then you want to express this in words... and that is so... limiting.

So I've now experienced true communication... without being able to say it in words... In any case I felt what a limitation it is by trying to make use of words. I knew it... now I have experienced it. I can't recall it, but I will remember!

The 'dream' I had that night was indeed, very special. Never before in my life had I had such a vivid experience of something that, according to Western standards, can't exist. But then maybe it wasn't a dream, but an out of body experience, or a combination of both? Immediately after I woke up it was early in the morning and it started to dawn on me. I had a very strong memory of what I had just encountered. I had experienced a true communication! The word 'telepathy' is far too limited to describe that. Telepathy is individual. That is from your mind trying to communicate with the mind of someone else. This was much more than that! This was not from thoughts, but from something much deeper. I could sense what Linda tried to tell me, and vice versa. There was absolutely no question of misunderstanding, because it felt like we were one - connectedness from oneness!

Years later I learned that this kind of communication is called universal communication.

When you want to tell someone something you search for words to express what you mean, and unconsciously you add gestures and facial expressions. By how the other reacts to you, you can tell whether or not you're understood. Often you realize that the other misinterprets the essence of your message. Or maybe you only think it is, because you misinterpret their reactions with the way *you* are thinking. Everyone knows this problem. That's how misunderstandings are born... with different ways of thinking, but our heart is never mistaken. Our brains think... and doubt, but our heart *knows*!

What I sometimes do when I'm not sure if the other understands me correctly, is to use other words to say the same thing; silly of course, like trying to cram in an oversized Saturday newspaper into an already overfilled mailbox, when on the other side a whole week of newspapers are sliding out. There's no point in doing that.

Universal communication means that you understand each other, without any effort, without any doubt, without loss of time... timeless, and complete with all emotions and feelings that belong to it. In fact there's not even a distinction between question and answer, because the communication is direct, derived from a connectedness.

I could transfer the entire contents of a book, of a complete Encyclopaedia Britannica, if necessary, of a complete lifetime at once, in the knowing that Linda would understand me immediately and totally, without a single misunderstanding. Conversely, I could experience something from her in one indivisible moment and then kind of need the rest of my life to write it down in words.

In fact... this book is an attempt to do just that: to write down what I experienced that night. The experience is like a very strong knowing deeply engraved in my soul, but it's impossible to express it in words, if I could I would be a poet then. Moreover, what I'm describing here is only the last part of that experience, when I was back inside my body again, back in the matter and 'returned to time', because that last part is just about mentally comprehendible for me; that part alone made a huge impression on me. Yet another experience that forever changed my life. It would probably have been no good if I could have brought back more memories of the experience. My energy pathways might have burned out, with me ending up in a madhouse, not being able to, or willing to live anymore.

As always since her death, I had pen and paper beside me so if I 'experienced' something I could write it down straight away, just like in this next instance. But while I was writing something strange happened...

11 July 2002, 04.30 o'clock

Had a runny nose yesterday (kind of allergy that wrecks me in the evening), felt pathetic, and sometimes it might cause 'something' to happen.

This was very special. And again, I can only recall just a little bit, and even then only the last, more human part. Compare it with a family visit to a compulsory... well 'mental institution' is the wrong word, because that's not the case here. A jailhouse, but, no one has done something wrong, but the feeling of isolation is just like that. And then, you (with your family) sometimes are allowed to visit her, or vice verse, she you!

Well, the latter. It seems as if she's in that 'prison', but as I write this I feel it's the other way round. I'm in there, although it seems... feels different. So... now who's isolated?

In any case... in the middle of this programmed event, you get the chance to talk to each other. Even while you're still together you can't talk aloud. She has explained to me lots of things, and I her.

It strikes me (now) that she... looked different... Linda, yes... and yet... not so... but more. But not changed and thus grown apart, no! Can't explain it precisely - I would need to find a comparison, but... for now... very earth-like, as if she had chosen something special for the occasion to make it easier for me.

I have been able to 'exchange' a lot, ... and that's logical... at last it disappears, I'm becoming more earth like... asking more earthly questions... and those I can memorize easily, but hardly contain any information, and it's already hard to write that down, so much information is in there.

E.g. I asked the question if she could reach me well with her thoughts, her 'mind', and then I see something like 'fingers' drumming on my skull... something alike... and she says: takes a lot of energy, it's pretty difficult, and vice versa... the same. What I should do is simply... think very strongly of her.

Again: thinking very strongly of her! Focus your thoughts... Because that's very easy, you do it daily... but do it more conscious... and don't be afraid.

You see: these answers I can... you can... give now, because you have a... new memory module installed, and therein are answers. You only need to verbalise them.

What struck me is the big distance between us still in a personal and physical sense. We don't grow apart, but the distance will grow bigger... especially by what I'm going to experience. Yet it doesn't have to be like that. I do it myself. So... I can reverse it myself too. E.g. if I would have another relationship... the distance would become bigger. But it doesn't have to. She too feels that like... pity... doesn't have to be. But will move on.

That piece creates distance... like 'indifference' is distance. And yet it isn't indifference, but a logical act. After all, you can't do anything else with it.

I understand a little what communication really is: simultaneously transferring lots of information. Silly to use words when you can do it that way.

One moment I said to her: now come, sit close by me. And then I feel immediately... yes that's us.

It's no reluctance... only distance... she's so much more, bigger... without being big... remember that feeling.

Again a general idea: it's for her just as difficult. The reverse is also true: distance... I'm different... but not grown apart. But yet: think about Loes saying I see two women standing here - that distance. Not: here's Linda, your love.

Give us time... and we will come to each other.

She has told me lots of things, explained, showed, but all will probably come slowly to my consciousness.

I believe: most importantly, I've come one step <u>closer</u>. I have <u>again</u> learned <u>more</u>. That feeling of distance was shown to me. I needed to feel that, that it isn't pleasant, that it's not even necessary. Work on it, try to understand.

You see, I'm... now translating in stupid simple words. Between the words you sense the true meaning of what I'm saying... ?

Find a way in yourself to remember that feeling, because you can do that!

She tries to help me. But this, what I'm doing now feels like such a limitation... using words. And I need so very many words... useless time. That's why.

We will be able to communicate with each other... work on that! Try materializing feelings. See, now it looks as if I'm writing (Linda). It seems just like automatic writing, but you know, you now know that you do it yourself. The translation-step was made already. You already have the message. So your body is still in-between. That needs to disappear. You now still make use of that memory module and that's from where the answers originate. It's as if I'm communicating with you, but I'm already back, on the 'other' side. So you use a clone of me. But that's okay... for now. You are going to do it directly... believe that. You still doubt. You know that you can now do this too? You're now halfway to automatic writing/direct communication with me.

That distance needs to go away. That can! You're working on that for a long time. That will happen. That's okay! See, you trust your hand(s) more and more. You first see the words and then write them down. So much easier than you thought, isn't it? But don't forget... you first needed the... message... that memory module... that's what I give you. If that doesn't happen first... then you only have your imagination. Just believe me.

I'm far away that's true, but I've let you feel that distance, that counts for me as well... for us and with 'us' I also mean 'you', you and me, we two. We have a lot more together than you think, than you know. You're still so afraid... so afraid to have lost me. That's not the case. That's not true... Believe me... vriendje, I love you, kisses.

Your vriendinnetje

The rest you must do yourself.

Come and get me. I'm waiting for you. You can...

You see... I'm a lot closer that you think and then we are really sitting in the grass together... only you and me. That too is what we have...

I know you! That's what I want you to feel, my vriendje... who can indeed be so big. If you doubt like this you're really very small... but I understand... I would be too... it's never bad... I love you... I <u>know</u> you... don't be afraid... don't doubt my love. You see... now you can receive the message Loes gave yourself. I'm with you... that distance I meant to make you feel. That... feeling counts in both directions. YOU can change that... with you. That I will teach you, and you can, be certain of that. I love you and I won't let you go. Love me. You're learning right now. You see, you think of a memory module; that's recorded information from the past, even if it's only fifteen minutes ago.

This is more... I'm with you. Call it a translation machine... I'll keep watching you. We are/come/stay closer that you think... watching you... evermore closer and closer... till you get hot... literally (hee hee). You will experience something yet... don't doubt, because then you are writing yourself... I'm here... and with you... Now I'm with you... go on... I love you; that I can't tell you enough; that you need so much.

You think I'm making that up, but I'm on the line. I'm here... that translation machine is still there, but you can nearly skip that thing.

Yes you can, writing not easy to keep up go talk to me.

The communication had sped up so fast at that moment, that my hand couldn't keep up writing anymore, so from that moment on I started talking aloud to her. What exactly we exchanged I don't know anymore, but I've written a few important words down to summarize

(Linda) say to Marianne...

(Linda) You like her, aye

(me) yes.

(Linda) You wish to tell her this

(me) yes. She's like a special friend to me

(Linda) yeah, she's our vriendinnetje

And I've talked about the ring and about my proposal and her answer was YES (with many many underlines). And with lots of joy, understanding, smiles and especially love for her vriendje.

This is more or less how it felt that night.

Well...

That was her answer to my proposal. The answer I had been waiting for. Somewhat different than I had expected, but... what more can you wish for? There's no doubt at all anymore. So that's how it feels! As if she communicated with me from inside myself. What began as the notes of my out-of-body-experience, turned out to be an exchange of minds in which I could hardly distinguish who was who. While writing the communication went on and my hands were chronically miles behind the actual communication, which, compared to the dream-experience moments before, was still very earthly and slow, because that experience felt much, much faster, if you can speak of speed at all, because it was timeless. That wasn't about speed anymore. That was about: to be! Being there! 'Speed' means you're still bound to the rules of time.

Even while writing that special feeling had not entirely gone. At first I felt very clear who was who, because I was conscious of my body and bodies are by definition separate units. Only during very intimate moments, as bodies find each other, when feeling takes over the mind and brakes don't exist anymore, you sometimes can feel that unity for a brief moment. On the other hand, in a spiritual way of speaking, I really couldn't make out where her consciousness began and mine ended. I sometimes wrote 'I', but in fact I couldn't tell if it was Linda of 'I' saying that. I had to discover that while writing. As if there was no difference anymore, as if we were one being. When we are one... then I Am.

'To be one'... "

Err... . what had I said during my speech ? Here it is: It is my desire still, to go with you very often, and find together what we are both looking for. To be one.

At that moment I felt great joy in this special gift. Much later I realized that that night had changed me. Maybe it was the intensity of the grief that I could let go of, the despair that I had left behind, the despair of not knowing, of the dependency of what a psychic tells you, or what the priest or pastor says about the afterlife. You have to assume that they know, hoping it will be the truth.

The contact with Loes obviously was a huge boost, but now I had experienced from inside what it meant to be in contact with her. That she was still there... somewhere. That she loved me and would always continue to do so, whatever I would do, even if I would do everything wrong by manner of speaking.

It's about Love and true Love is unconditional, without judgement; and is timeless.

Changes

Believe it or not... a few days after this particular incident I was thinking about a new love, a new relationship! Although there was no plan in my mind and there was no one I could think of who might qualify, yet this thought haunted me. I simply *knew* that I would soon meet someone. For one reason or another, the ring I had exchanged with Linda was causing this. As if, now that we had expressed our deepest feelings to each other we had given each other the freedom to enter into another relationship. Very weird!

Even when Linda was alive, long before she got ill, I had had this premonition, a sense of a future in which I would 'have' someone else. It was even foretold by a psychic. I always blocked that premonition because it made me very sad, implicating that we first had to separate, to divorce, not being able to live together anymore. Either one of us would fall in love with another, or we would start quarrelling. That thought hurt me a lot.

Because I had ignored here own words, it never occurred to me at moments like that that she would die instead. When she finally got ill, I remembered the premonition, but I had pushed it away quickly. I didn't want to think about it. And now that she was deceased, it appeared indeed that the road was free to enter a new relationship.

Marianne?

Linda had called her *our vriendinnetje*...

But Marianne was a married woman, slightly older than Linda who already was six years older than me, and she had three children. The very idea! Impossible!

Whatever: I had changed profoundly by what I had experienced. And the extent of that became clear a couple of days later...

When I had met Marianne at the psychic fair, I had asked her if I could make a painting for her, because she had done so much for Linda and for me. She had really helped us. At that moment she didn't know what to say to that, but later, when I came to her practise for a couple of treatments, she told me she would appreciate it very much if I could make a logo for her practise with the name 'Marisun'.

Before Linda's illness I sometimes got 'stuck' in the process of painting. I had specialized in the airbrush technique. That's a way of painting with air flowing through a small pen, being mixed with a tiny amount of liquid paint and sprayed on board or canvas, a technique that can be used even for photorealistic paintings. You see the same technique, but with special paints, on customized cars, especially in the USA. Linda herself had introduced that technique to me, just after we had met many years ago.

Now, more than eighteen years and hundreds of paintings later, I had mastered that technique pretty well, though lately of course, I hadn't had the time for it. Apart from that I got frustrated a little, because, despite my technical skills, I usually couldn't express the specific feeling that I had before starting a painting. I made beautiful paintings, judging by the compliments, but often they lacked 'something', something unique, something special, something of beauty and perfection... that I didn't find in the end result.

Precisely that had changed. When I designed the ring for Linda I surprised myself that I could so easily express something that was in total harmony with what I had in mind, with my feelings. What I felt and what I designed matched, even when it was still only a sketch for a ring. And never before in my life I had done something with jewellery. I already had experienced that same thing while writing the speech for Linda's funeral, and later while writing the letter to Loes. Even while writing in my letter/diary to Linda I sometimes noticed that I was capable of expressing an indefinable feeling, materializing it somehow, making it conscious, looking at it from different sides, to suddenly discover that I had written it down already!

To achieve this, so I discovered, one should not be stopped by fear. Don't be afraid to express what it is that keeps your mind busy, because fear is the prison of your mind.

Now that Marianne had asked me to make her a logo, I wondered what I should make, because making a promise is one thing...

At a certain moment I *knew* that it wouldn't be just some silly company logo, but a round painting. I also *knew* that the name Marisun would be surrounded by five stars. It just felt like that. Again the number five!

One day I had all the time in the world to paint. I spent that morning airbrushing to build up and deepen the colours. Unlike ever before, I spent a lot of time doing so... taking the time to only 'deepen the colours'. Somehow 'taking the time' sped things up which was a strange contradiction. I was amazed by the depth of colour that developed in the painting. For the location of the stars I had already made a tiny sketch, but I didn't know if the locations were correct. So I put the sketch away, thinking it was 'just a sketch', grabbed a school chalk and jokingly said to the spirits, assuming someone were around me: "Well... tell me. Where shall I put them? Lead my hand."

After all I had asked Linda to inspire me and *now* it felt like a neat moment to start with that (me silly, no way :-)). I felt that the location of the stars was important, but how to proceed? I couldn't calculate them, because who was I to know the locations when I didn't even know the constellation, if any at all. So instead of calculating I had to... let it happen. I squeezed my eyes almost shut, hovered my hand above the painting almost nonchalant and placed a dot here and there, something like: "Well, this looks nice. Put one there, and why not one there too?"

Oddly enough, the stars ended up in the same locations I had drawn on the tiny sketch... I simply couldn't place them elsewhere. But one had been placed in the centre of the painting, almost in the sun I had painted. That was ridiculous, I thought. In real life you can't see stars next to the sun; impossible. I painted that star at first, but I removed it later, doubting my eligibility for Linda's inspiration, and I restored the sun's halo at that spot.

The final result had become a remarkable round, deep blue painting. In the middle I had written the name 'Marisun' in strange symbols, edgy pyramid like runes on the left side and smooth curves on the right side, with a staircase of colour-grades being the central 'I'. I was impressed myself with the result, because this painting was in total harmony with the feeling I had before starting the painting. I only doubted the locations of the stars. But... if it would prove to be an existing constellation it would be more convincing.

On the shelves Linda had an old constellation booklet and that night I took it, studying it, quickly turning pages from beginning to end. I was surprised by the large number of constellations and saw all kinds of them I had never heard of before. But I found no match. I was tired, and, slightly disappointed, I went to bed. Yet the thought of it haunted me and early the next morning I picked up the book again.

Now I went ahead more deliberately. First I disposed of all constellations with more than four stars. But wait... maybe I had to include all constellations with five stars too, just to be sure.

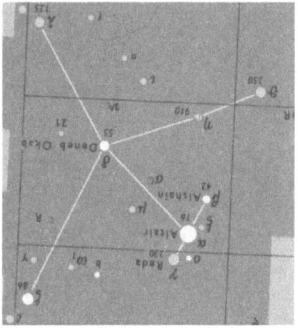

That worked, because now there were only five constellations to focus on. I studied them one by one, but didn't 'see' it. Then I thought that maybe, just maybe, I had to turn the book 'upside down'. After all, in space there's no up, or down. I studied them again and suddenly I saw it! There! The constellation Aquilla... Eagle, isn't that a close match? But... then that fifth star near the Sun had to be in place!!!

When I compared both constellations, the painted one and the 'official' one in the book, I discovered that the match wasn't only 'more or less accurate', but awfully exact! There was only one difference and that was the presence of two tiny stars near the biggest star 'Altair'. Well, no problem. I added those to the painting just to complete the picture.

Inspiration, to be inspired, it pretty much began to look like that! When I did a search on the Internet for the symbolic meaning of the star constellation Aquilla, I was surprised yet another time.

In the ancient Mesopotamia the Aquilla constellation was associated with the legend of Etána, flying to the heavens on the back of the Eagle god Shamash, to find a painkilling drug for his pregnant wife... And I thought:

"That's me! We too had tried to move Heaven and Earth to relieve Linda's pain, flying even on the back of a visualised cosmic bird!!!

Elsewhere on the Internet I discovered more...

A Chinese legend speaks about the brightest star of this constellation, Altair, depicting a beautiful lady, She-niu, being separated from her love on the other side of the Galaxy, the star Vega in the constellation Lyre. Again I saw the comparison with Linda and me, separated by a cosmic veil.

For the Indians, the native people of North America, the Eagle is one of the noblest of birds. The feathers of the Eagle are used by the holy men to give more power, because Eagle medicine is the power of Great Spirit. Over the phone I had spoken to Marianne, saying that her logo/painting had to do something with constellation Eagle, nothing more.

When we met a couple of days later, bringing the painting, she showed me a booklet that described how she had felt her entire life: a shaman. Maybe once in another incarnation she had been one. She felt related to the Indians. And a shaman she still is, with a modern device maybe, but doing the same thing more or less.

The Eagle, the Power of Healing, in a modern contemporary twist. She loved her painting!

That's an awful lot of coincidences simultaneously!

I also told Marianne about my nocturnal encounter with Linda and I told her the whole story surrounding that night. I showed her the image of the ring and when I looked at her she looked strange. But she didn't say anything. Only much later, she told me what had happened that night. She found it rather embarrassing to say at the time, so she hadn't said anything about it, but what she had experienced was that she had felt clearly that this ring was pushed around her finger. That shocked her severely. "Isn't this *their* ring!" she had thought.

She said something else that night that was memorable. I had read to her from my diary of that night with the 'dream' and after I finished speaking the first thing she said was, "This is the beginning of a book."

Were Marianne and I meant to start a relationship with each other? It didn't make sense, because she was married and I had just lost my soul mate; not the best conditions for a love relationship. But I had to admit that I really felt something for Marianne, and that we could talk effortlessly about anything.

That I could feel something for someone... it was hard to accept, but Linda meant that it was possible and that confused me profusely. Because Linda was my love, right? Was that love diminishing? Did I need her physical presence to be able to love her? But it didn't feel like that at all. It seemed rather that our love was far greater than ever before. Our gigantic struggle had brought us very close to each other, and we were very intense even before that. We did everything together. How then could I feel something for another woman? Marianne made me aware of these thoughts. I couldn't push them away and that caused considerable confusion in my head.

Now that I had made a painting and also designed a ring, it was as if the floodgates were opened. At the oddest moments of the day there were ideas in my head for new paintings, something I wasn't used to. But I was happy with that and at a suitable time I made sketches of what 'I had thought of'.

The painting I started next was one I intended for Loes, because she had spent a lot of time to help us, without looking for anything in return. Those contacts were invaluable for us! That's why I wanted to make something for her. The idea that popped up in my mind was a Holy Grail, from which rays of Light radiate, and flowers streaming over the rim.

The feeling I also had, but against which I rebelled greatly, was that somehow or somewhere in the painting there would have to be a cross. But I hated crosses! Throughout history the cross was so abused that in my eyes it had come to represent everything that had gone wrong. With the bible in the hand, waving a large cross, weapons were blessed, wars had been started by the 'will of God', and millions of women were sentenced to death, because they were possibly clairvoyant, knowing more about Love than those quoting the Bible. In the name of God, the Indians were killed because they were pagans, blacks of Africa and indigenous from the entire Pacific were kidnapped and abused as 'savages', and those who survived were 'converted' and robbed of their identity, their lands ripe for exploitation by those who followed. And now it was expected of me to make a painting with a cross!

I didn't think so!! But the feeling remained...

And so remained my resistance.

Eventually I began to understand that the cross is a symbol that was abused itself. I accepted that the cross is not a symbol of death, destruction and suffering, and also isn't a logo for a church or whatever religion, but that it's a symbol of Love. Of someone sacrificing himself to be an example for humanity, showing that, if you can accept suffering, and even death, you can overcome death...

The cross stands for Love! To understand that you don't need the intervention of pastors, priests, reverends, imams or whomever. That feeling comes from within. It grows inside as a result of you finding your way through all learning processes and sufferings. If you've experienced the valleys, you can appreciate the beauty of the mountaintops.

I discovered that when I didn't paint the cross as a neat straight lined cross with a suffering Jesus figure, but as an energy flow in the background of the painting, I could be at peace with it. The cross as an energy emerges from the veiled purple background, being composed of the Holy Grail as the cup of plenty, overflowing with flowers. In a way it even resembled an angel spreading its wings. In top, barely visible, a white rose hovered above its contents. Linda's rose, saying "I'm worthy of you".

The result was a painting that seems to radiate light itself, as if it warms you. That was exactly what several people were telling me... as if you can warm yourself to the painting. I called it 'Lucia', which means Light, and which was Loes' real name.

When I later gave it to her she said that this painting represents the victory over suffering. If the pain and suffering are understood, the suffering falls away (the purple veils) and the cross that symbolizes Love, triumphant upwards. She told me also that my guardian angel, once a painter himself, had inspired me to make this, helped by Linda, who had presented certain details like the white streamers coming through the bowl. I hadn't been aware of this, but I had been very driven and felt really well while painting.

Loes said something more: "This painting is not for me. This is what you show to the people. It's for everyone. Just give me a nice reproduction."

During the summer period I went a couple of times to the goldsmith in Borculo, because I was very impatient to get this special ring. Each time he reported that he had had no time to work on it, because of various problems that had to be solved first, like the crystals that were difficult to get. Finally I kept quiet for several weeks, but when I didn't hear anything for two months my patience ran out and I went to Borculo with the self-assured attitude of someone who wants clarification. When I walked into his shop he was busy with someone, but right through the conversation he called at me, "And I also can't help you!"

Great way to enter the scene! I waited impatiently until he was finished with his customers. When he finally came to me he told me what I was afraid of: he didn't want to continue this assignment of making the ring. He was short, did not answer any of my questions and disappeared as quickly as possible to the rear of the shop. His girlfriend came into the shop and then I was told what had been going on there that summer. Every time I had turned up he had felt bad, because this ring had kept him from sleeping. The design kept him busy all the time and the story behind it confronted him too much. He was a very sensitive man and felt all too well the sadness behind our story. He had experienced a few things himself and simply couldn't take anymore. He had done his best, but whatever he tried... he made no progress at all. Now he was finished with it, so that's why he now gave back all the sketches.

So there I was. Two months had passed and no progress made. I was angry and didn't understand. After waiting so long it wasn't so strange that I wanted to see some results, was it? Surely there would be a very good reason for all this, but right now I was unable to see that. I sat in the car driving home and spoke aloud my displeasure to Linda. Now that I knew that she could hear me at all times I started kicking butt. This man was the assigned one? Together with Marianne we had figured that out beyond any doubt. So what's wrong here? What is going on? Was it not the intention, should something be changed? Was the whole idea for this ring too far fetched? Was I out of line, thinking about rings being exchanged between the Hereafter and the earthly life? Was it not allowed to be? Was I blocked this way, by batting above my weight?

Maybe I should search for another goldsmith, but we had rejected everyone in the entire region and now the only remaining person quit the job. This wasn't right and it frustrated me immensely. By the time I arrived in the outskirts of Apeldoorn I was so angry that I loudly exclaimed, "I don't care by whom, but that ring will be made! Or else... I will make it myself!"

When I heard myself say this it was like something clicked with me and I thought, "Oh dear. That can't be true, eh?"

At home I went through the phonebook in search for someone I thought might give courses on precious metal craftsmanship. As a creative arts teacher, Linda had the responsibility for the inventory of all the materials of her profession and she bought most of the stuff from Jan, a gentle old man with whom she had a good understanding. Because I often went with her when she was ordering materials, I knew the man and remembered him saying he gave lessons.

I found his number, made an appointment, and a few days later I went to see him, taking a look in his classroom at his home. And indeed, 'coincidentally' it was just before the start of the new season and 'coincidentally' he still had one open place for one new student. He remembered Linda all too well and when I told him the story and showed him the sketches he said, "So then this will be our mission!" That were the words I wanted to hear.

So that's how they work! Voluntarily you are pointed which way you have to go. You do have choice, but you simply have to go that way. And yet there's nothing else that pleases you more. Did I hear someone up there laughing out loud, or what?

So two weeks later I started the course of precious metal craftsmanship with Jan who proved to be an excellent teacher. In eighteen months I worked through all the subsequent courses and what I never had expected before was I loved it! It was so much fun that I decided to use Linda's legacy to purchase all the tools and materials a goldsmith needs around, and I converted one of the sleeping rooms in the house into an artist's studio.

Within the group of students I soon got a 'name', because every project that I made during the course in order to master the techniques had to do with spirals, vortices and cosmic energies, just like all the paintings I also made. People started to recognize my works and I often heard laughing comments like, "That has to have been made by Wim for sure!"

Meanwhile I made another painting. Again I didn't need to do anything else but enjoy what I did, just follow my imagination and let it happen.

This painting was round again, and around it I made a secondary ring that could rotate freely relative to the central painting.

When finished with the painting part, I had the feeling that the central part needed something more, a big symbol.
I found that quite risky, because the painting seemed really fine as it was. Why then take the risk of spoiling it with a symbol? That could turn out very wrong. But if I had to put a symbol on it, what symbol would it be?
ecause my mind was busy with vortices and spirals in those days I focused on that. Vortices can be found in the water running through the outlet of a bathtub. You can find a spiral in the old-fashioned telephone coil cord between the base device and the earpiece. That wire can rotate clockwise or counter clockwise as I had noticed during endless conversations, while playing with the coil with one hand, as surely most people used to do

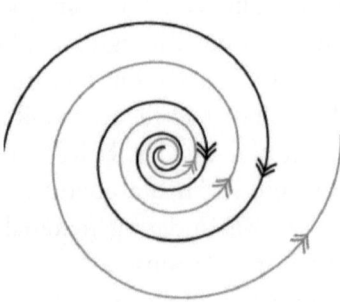

Spiral with U-turn

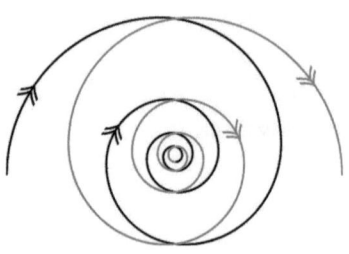

Spiral with crossing lines

during long calls. I had been intrigued by some weird 'problem': how can it be that for some reason such a coil can be made to rotate the other direction somehow? Often you see both directions in the same coil: the clockwise spiral *and* the counter clockwise spiral! Between the two directions there are always a few strange curves. Even as a small boy I had been trying to undo the 'wrong' spiral, not always succeeding to my satisfaction, and even if I managed to restore the coil, I found that the problem would return within weeks.
You might wonder why I even bothered to worry about this, but that's me. Everyone has his or her idiosyncrasies, shall we say. In any case... this old dilemma surfaced again in my mind and I focused my attention yet again on this in an attempt to find the solution for once and for all: how can a

clockwise rotating spiral be made to rotate in the other direction in a gentle way?

I found an unused coil of Linda's thin silvery wires for the school, somewhere, and started playing with it. I tried several possibilities and wanted to prevent crossing wires. Also making a U-turn in a wire was not an option. Suddenly I discovered a solution so simple, so insignificant that you normally would pay no attention to it. But when I went on with it, perfecting the shape I had found I 'felt' that this was it somehow. It matched my gut feeling I had had before searching for the solution, as if something fell perfectly into place. I had found a shape that I conveniently called reversal symbol: it reverses the direction of rotation.

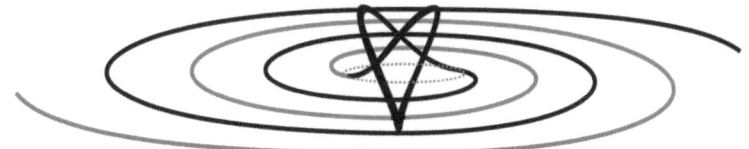

For this to happen I had had to leave the two-dimensional plane, because only in the three-dimensional plane the solution could be found... a 'flatlander' discovering the Z-axis.

I fashioned the corny ball that I had in my hands until it looked more or less round and held it against the light and with my free hand took up a pencil and drew the lines on a piece of paper. That symbol served as the basis for the symbol that I later applied on the painting in gold leaf.

During one of my visits to Loes I showed her this painting and the first thing she said was, "That painting is an aura healer!"

It's what?

I didn't understand what she meant, let alone how a painting could be capable of healing auras, so Loes explained that when people look at this painting they will take in the colours and the energy of the painting. Auras consist of harmonious changing energy compositions, a radiant field of energy that is the result of all body cells' internal reactions, organs, exchanges of electricity in between and also the souls' expression in that body. Sometimes people get out of balance and their energy field will reflect this as an imbalance in the colour spectrum of their aura. When certain colours are lacking or are abundantly present then this painting helps those people to restore the balance. Because the outer ring can rotate freely, the energy of the painting can be tuned personally to the observer. All they have to do, Loes said, is to put it somewhere in the room, and take a look at it every time one walks by. Maybe after a couple of days the position of the outer ring needs some adjustment and that's it. That way it heals the aura.

I still struggled to comprehend it all, not believing that apparently I was capable of making something like this, but it felt right and from that moment on this painting had its name: Aura Healer.

Akaija

I did not believe because I could not see
Though you came to me in the night
When the dawn seemed forever lost
You showed me your love in the light of the stars
Cast your eyes on the ocean
Cast your soul to the sea
When the dark night seems endless
Please remember me

from "Dante's Prayer"
words and music by Loreena McKennit

Blood is thicker than water...

It had seemed unlikely that Marianne and I would start a relationship but I had already expected that the cosmos moves in incomprehensible ways, and one day it struck a spark in us. That moment marked the beginning of a profound change, not just for me. Not an easy change, but ultimately very rewarding for everyone.

Marianne brought, and brings, much happiness to my life, but my grief at the loss of Linda was far from over. In one way I was confronted with that grief at an accelerated pace. Marianne didn't want to take Linda's place, just as I didn't want her to. She also didn't want me to deny or push away my grief. No pretence. She knew full well that she had come into my life a bit soon after Linda.

I could laugh, have fun, and enjoy beautiful things, music, everything that we did together, but I also noticed that I experienced periods of sadness. Sometimes it was not even clear where exactly the sadness came from, what started it. Obviously it had to do with Linda, but I couldn't always pinpoint why I suddenly felt that way.

There were many things that, consciously or unconsciously, evoked memories. For example, I could walk down the street and suddenly realize that I had been standing in front of a certain shop. Now I was there with Marianne. Every time I did something with Marianne that I had ever shared with Linda, it was as if that memory with Linda was affected. I usually said as much and was glad that Marianne declared that it didn't bother her at all; she had no problem with that.

Linda had already announced she would look for another woman for me and apparently she was successful, because Marianne is one of... many thousands. It's not easy to have a relationship with a partner whose former love is deceased. I never had to conceal what was going on inside me, and undergo those many moments of mourning alone. After all... a memory doesn't have to be overshadowed... I would almost say 'taken' by the new partner. I've heard from partners who are jealous of the deceased, because they are elusive and seemingly always standing in the way. Whatever they do, there's always, somewhere in a corner of the heart of their loved one, another one, against whom they can't fight, because that one isn't physically there anymore. Consciously or not, they often try to outdo the other, just like a dog sniffing the terrain, marking it with a few drops of urine as if to say, "This is mine".

They forget that they simply can't ever win such a battle, and that they... by not starting that fight, never have to lose either.

I noticed that even before Marianne came into my life, I was reluctant to go somewhere where I formerly had been with Linda. Happy memories that I didn't want to spoil by pathetically sitting there with a new partner. But now I discovered that, by doing so openly and talking about it, new memories are created, and so the old memories were honoured. They became a part of all three of us. Marianne had such a great heart that she could leave me entirely free, so that I could heal at my own pace.

That perhaps was the most beautiful, but in a way, also the hardest thing for me to learn: to be happy with Marianne and discover that I didn't lose Linda by doing so, and also, to keep loving Linda without compromising Marianne. A luxury problem you could call it. I'm just a very lucky duck with two women loving me very much, one on Earth, and one in the Spirit World. What more can you want? And at one point Marianne and I were confronted with that thought in a very special way...

We were in bed, tired from the day and happy with each other. We had talked a lot and now were pleasantly quiet within. We were very aware that our luck hadn't just come out of nowhere; there were lots of precedents. Suddenly I became aware of the typical faint beep in my ear that I had learned to recognize as a sign from Linda. I mentioned this to Marianne and spoke in the space around us, "What is it girl? What do you wish to say?"

Almost immediately I had a thought of the song that had made such an impression on Linda and she had wanted me to play during her funeral more than once: "Somehow I'll find my way home." Firstly, that line and the melody popped up in my mind, and then I thought of a sentence somewhere in the middle of the song. But I could not remember the exact words of the sentence. Was it "My friend is close by your side?" Or was it "My friend is close by my side?" Or was it "Your friend is close by your side?" It could even be "Your friend is close by my side". I couldn't remember and I said so to Marianne, and as I said it, I suddenly realized it was that what Linda tried to tell us. Exactly that! It doesn't matter how you put the words, because each version is correct. And we both started crying with emotion.

Because Marianne was the therapist who had treated Linda, she brought the therapy device with her and so I came in contact with a totally new world of people: therapists. With Linda I had consulted many of them, but now I got a different point of view. I now could watch over Marianne's shoulder, attend therapists' meetings, and meet her fellow colleagues.

Linda had long been looking for another job, but her qualifications as a teacher made her unfit for any other work except teaching, and in despair she wondered if she was doomed to spent the rest of her life in the classroom. In fact that actually had happened.

Because of her chronic fatigue, and later because of her illness, we had experience with many therapies, some very weird and some scientifically well-supported. What particularly got our attention was Roberto's therapy, and the device he used: electro-acupuncture. Linda had already indicated more than once, that as soon as she would be better, she wanted to go deeper into that matter. She wanted to become a therapist, helping people in need.

Even during one of the visits to Loes she had indicated this, because she had shown Loes' books, as if to say that she was doing some kind of study in the Spirit World dealing with herbal medication and related knowledge. I wondered whether they were still using books, as that seems so earth-like to me, but maybe this was meant symbolically to make us understand in just one image. 'Accidentally' I now was involved with a new love that did exactly the same thing as Linda had planned to do, because Marianne's device was exactly that: a kind of electro-acupuncture!

For years Linda and I had sought the cause of her chronic fatigue, but no one was ever able to tell us exactly what was going on, let alone provide a solution. The chronic fatigue was a heavy burden for Linda, robbing her of her energy and the joy in life. The little energy she had left was used to do her job well, but even that had recently become almost too much of a burden for her, and she was only in her forties. At that age one should be at his or her best: years of experience combined with a life's energy, but not so for her. Moreover, she had become increasingly sensitive, or rather 'over sensitive'. During her illness this sensitivity had become more like hyper sensitivity and that was the reason we had been so isolated all those months, because she could endure almost nothing.

No television, because it made too much noise and the images were too busy. Even listening to music was too much to handle, else it could have been so healing. Flowers, though lovely as they are and she loving them so much... they were too colourful, too capricious, and sometimes the fragrance was more than she could handle. But worst of all, she could hardly endure a visit, and that had hurt many people, like her brothers, who felt helpless. They could do nothing and it had frustrated me that I couldn't explain to them why that was the case.

Marianne knew the answer, because the maker of her device, Health Angel, which she worked with, had researched this and had found a solution. He had called it 'electron-spin-inversion', a term I had never heard of.

Marianne said that this was often the case with people who are very weak, because of severe illness for one thing. From a scientific medical viewpoint the symptoms that go with this are usually explained as a logical consequence of the illness. Hospitals mind those patients, for example by refusing the presence of flowers, which many patients can't stand. But Marianne said that this weakness often is the result of something else.

She explained that an electron-spin-inversion is caused by a combination of two factors: a weakened energy system and an electromagnetic field that is strong enough to overpower that energy system. All matter, bodies included, consist of atoms, and around the core of the atom there are electrons. In such a situation, she explained, it is possible that the electrons, which rotate around the nucleus, but also around their own axis, start rotating in the other direction. "Compare it with the Earth, rotating around its own axis," she said. "If this would happen to the Earth then after an inversion the Sun would rise in the West and set in the East." The direction of rotation, or 'spin', is reversed, hence the name 'spin-inversion', or reversed rotation.

"As a result", she added, "the aura or energy field that surrounds every living being isn't energized enough anymore and thus gets thinner. The aura is the energy field that protects us against the outside world, filtering whatever comes our way, and when it's weakened it can't do its job properly. Compare this too with the Earth's magnetic field protecting us against the solar wind. Then all impressions, such as sounds, smells, images, but also energies and even thoughts of other people, and of course electromagnetic fields of computers and other devices, enter our system with full force, and that can make people extremely tired. They can't handle it. Chronic fatigue can be the result, and because of the on-going influences this situation maintains itself, so these people are pulled downward into a spiral that is very difficult to come out of.

Suddenly I realized that a lightning bolt had hit Linda in her car during a severe thunderstorm way back in 1985. That lightning strike was so powerful that it had knocked out the power grid of a large part of Apeldoorn. At that time her energy system was in good condition, but even the healthiest people can't withstand the electromagnetic field of such a lightning strike. She had always maintained that that was the moment her chronic fatigue had begun. Dozens of visits to doctors and therapists and thousands of dollars in consultation fees had not paid of, because her fatigue had grown worse over the years.

Now I had made a curious painting that Loes had called 'Aura Healer'. This term was significant, but at that moment no bells were ringing for me. I placed the painting in the living room and for a few years it stayed there.

Marianne's youngest daughter, Lianne, who in 2005 was in the middle of a professional musical dance course, came almost weekly to visit us for treatment with Marianne's Health Angel device against an electron-spin-inversion. Every week she was very tired, could hardly concentrate and was very sensitive, which, given her age, was totally inappropriate. Supposedly the spin-inversion she had was caused by lots and lots of tough physical training time between stage lighting and sound equipment in the centre of Amsterdam, already full of electrical power lines. For the treatment of the spin-inversion Marianne needed a drop of blood from Lianne, on a cotton ball. That was placed in the treatment circuit of the device and then a special program called 'spin-inversion-treatment' was activated. Within minutes the treatment was finished.

But Lianne was sick of having her fingers pricked for a drop of blood every week. So one day when I was sitting next to them just for fun, I had a hunch. I picked up the tiny iron-wire symbol and thought: this is an inversion-symbol and the treatment Marianne repeated every week was called 'spin-inversion-treatment'. Could it be... ? Well, what harm could it do? So instead of using a drop of blood on a cotton ball, Marianne placed the inversion-symbol in the circuit of the device. To her amazement she didn't measure a spin-inversion afterwards on Lianne.

"This can't be!" she remarked. "I don't believe it!"

But whatever she tried, she couldn't measure it. Lianne didn't mind at all and said laughing, "Well, I better put that metal thingy in my schoolbag and keep it with me all the time! Then I won't even need this treatment at all!"

Marianne looked surprised and she expressed my thoughts at the same time. After all I was doing courses to become a goldsmith and what do these people do? Exactly... make jewellery. Such a thin wire thing would be far too fragile in her schoolbag, but when I would design the same thing as a small silver pendant then she could hang it around her neck...

The following week, Lianne came back. As usual, she had felt fine the first few days, but then her fatigue came back and according to the expectations she had another spin-inversion. Meanwhile I had finished a small version of the inversion symbol in silver. First Marianne used the symbol to treat her and after doing so she put it on a necklace and gave it to Lianne. Suppose this would work!

The next week Lianne came again, but immediately she cried that she had felt fine all week long. She was certain that she didn't have a spin-inversion anymore and Marianne's measurements confirmed it.

Wow! We were silent. We could hardly believe this, thinking it was some kind of coincidence, or maybe we were just wanting too much for this to be true. Was this indeed Linda's inspiration? If so, then Marianne knew a few of her patients who would be helped a lot by this pendant.

So she asked me to make a few more, and I did. In the following weeks I made several inversion symbols. Most didn't really look like a professionally made pendant, but this didn't matter; the thing was they worked, but we had to wait a few weeks to find out. Patience...

When each of Marianne's patients returned for their next session all of them felt better, and the spin-inversion had stayed away. That was when we cautiously began to feel that we may have stumbled upon something important. Whatever was at work here, and no matter if it bypassed every scientific explanation... the measurements clearly showed the difference, but more important: the patients felt better! I was getting busier with making new inversion symbols; good practice for a brand new goldsmith.

We spoke to several of Marianne's colleagues working with the same equipment and asked them to try out this design on their patients with spin-inversion. They were interested, because it meant that they didn't have to prick their patients for a droplet of blood. Especially with children that would be great. Within weeks the responses came in, along with the questions from the patient where they could order such a pendant. That convinced us to bring this deceptively simple jewel out in the open in a more professional manner.

We were fortunate that at that time we had another appointment with Loes, and when we showed her this object she was thrilled. "This is powerful, man!" she said over and over again. "This is going to cure a lot of people!"

I asked if it would be wise to apply for patenting, which is very expensive. Her answer was revealing, "Yes! And with the proceeds of the first six hundred you can afford it."

The first six hundred!! At the moment we counted in stock two inversion symbols, and one of those was in her hands! If I worked all day long I might be happy to be able to finish three such symbols in one day. We would be happy to produce and sell one hundred, well... maybe two hundred in, let's assume, the next five years? And she talked as if six hundred was peanuts. What had I got myself into!?

Of course now we needed a name for it. 'Inversion symbol' didn't really sound great. Obviously Marianne and I tried to search for a suitable name in the languages of old cultures, like the Indian languages.

'Canada! Marianne suddenly exclaimed. She sometimes had those moments in which we felt she was connected to other realms, not just imagining it. We surfed the Internet and discovered that in Canada there still lived descendants of the Cree Indians. That sounded interesting, but how do you search for a name in a language that you don't understand a single word from?

Linda's mother too was interested and she suggested that she could ask her 'guys', because she sometimes practised 'automatic writing'. I wasn't convinced of her skills, thinking her unconscious mind was fooling her, but I didn't say so and at the same time I thought it would be great if she were to be a part of the inversion-symbol-project. After all... Linda and she had been talking about such topics all her life.

Two weeks later we met her again, and she said that she had asked the Spirit World for a name, but the 'only' thing that she had noticed was that one day she suddenly heard a very loud voice in her head nearly shouting only one word: akaija. Obviously she had expected a long automatic written text as an answer. She shrugged her shoulders as if to say, "Beats me... I don't know either. But maybe you can use it."

I looked at the paper on which she had written the word 'akaija', tried to speak it and had to admit that it sounded okay, more than okay in fact. It was short, powerful and somewhat mysterious. At home Marianne immediately started searching on the Internet. She typed two words: 'Cree Indians' and 'akaija'.

This returned a few hits pointing to a linguistic work of a researcher that had studied the morphology of ancient languages. He had discovered that on a remote island in the Pacific Ocean the indigenous people made use of six different words for 'we'. When we in Europe speak of 'we together' they use the word 'akaijau'. But when they are with three people in the same room, they use 'aijumtaj'. But when three people are addressing one or more other people, they have yet another word.

'Akaija' in their language refers to the biggest concept: We all.

That impressed us and we needed to look no further. We immediately were convinced: this is it, and from then on the inversion symbol had its name: Akaija.

We placed a few advertisements in Dutch magazines and in the following months we even succeeded in selling Akaija's. Right from the first sales we began to receive reviews from people who were wearing the Akaija, or only touching it. And the reviews were often more than we could have hoped for. Several people said that the Akaija made strange sensations in their hands and arms, like tingling or prickling. In some hands the Akaija felt awfully hot, and in others the contrary happened: it felt very cold. Some people were free of life-long headaches within one day! Other people were less lucky and were confronted with old complaints showing up, only for one or two days, but they had thought those complaints were history and the Akaija showed them that this was not the case. But after a few weeks they said that somehow their whole body felt differently and that they now finally felt better than they had felt for years! Some reviews were nothing less than small miracles. Like a man who couldn't sweat, feeling short of breath as soon as the weather got warm. From the moment he had his Akaija his shirts were soaking wet; or a few women who had suffered all their lives from headaches and abdominal and back pains every time they had their period. For the first time ever they were relieved of those extra pains.

The latter I found especially interesting, as I knew that Linda had taken the pill all her life, without ever skipping one week as prescribed. She had taken it continuously, because if she didn't and she would have her period, she would be plagued for four days by such extreme pains feeling like she was being torn apart by four horses, as she said. When she discovered that she could prevent this by swallowing the pill continuously she had made her mind up: never again this pain.

Now it seemed that she had, by inspiring me to make the Akaija, given her fellow sufferers something that could be a final solution to some or many such cases! How many qualities can you combine in one tiny object like this? This was unheard of!

In any case... there were more surprises waiting for us. I already had discovered that from a certain point of view I could see certain symbols in the Akaija. For one thing there's a circle, and also a Yin-Yang-symbol, the symbol of duality. More remarkable is that there's also a five-pointed star or pentagram. Again, that number, five!

During one of our visits to a spiritual fair we attended, Loes unexpectedly came by. When she saw the jewellery box on which I had had the Akaija imprinted in gold leaf, she pointed to it and said: "Linda wants to show something to you, that you haven't seen."

She laughed when she saw my reaction. "You don't see it! It's a heart! It's protected by a circle, meaning... your heart is protected!"

I looked again and then I saw it! She was right. It is a heart!

Can you imagine how silly I felt, because I had spent hours and hours to get this shape right for printing on the box. I had done well, striving to get it right, but without seeing what was clearly staring in my face. A heart!

There was another surprise when a woman who had bought an Akaija told us that she had done calculations on the word 'akaija' using numerology. She had discovered something really strange. In numerology a number can replace every character of the alphabet. So A=1, B=2, C=3 and so on. Doing so with the word 'akaija' then the first character is A, which is 1 and K=11. 11, 22 and 33, she said, are master numbers. You leave those intact.

Then another A=1. Then she said that there are I and J. In printed text these are two characters, but only in the Dutch language it used to be one character 'ij', which was the 25th character of the alphabet, an 'y' with dots. Nowadays with printed texts things have changed, and it is the y without dots. But because of this it is feasible to treat those characters as one, adding the numbers. You then get I + J, which is 9 + 10 = 19. 19 is 1+9=10. And 10=1+0, which is 1! And finally another A=1. All in all you now see six times the number 1: 111111.

Five characters result in six numbers. The 5 becomes a 6. The fifth day transits into the sixth day. We go to the Light!

The design of the Akaija does the same as the characters. Within the Akaija there is a circle, horizontally. When you start on the circle, following it to the right, starting with the A, there is a splitting up in two lines, which is the K splitting up in two numbers. The symbol K even shows it. Following those lines you'll see that they meet again, fusing into the circle again, which is the Y, or I and J fusing into one number 1. Fission and fusion!

The sum of all characters is 1+11+1+9+10+1=33, also a master number, which is left as is. Or, when you combine I+J or 9+10 you get 1+11+1+1+1=15 and 1+5=6. Or counting the ones: 6.

Number 6 stands for harmony and love. 33 is called a master number, because Jesus was 33 when he showed humanity that death isn't the end. I certainly don't want to compare Linda to Jesus, but in her own way she shows us the same: I'm still there! ☺

By the way, Linda was 47 when she died. 4+7=11…

But there was still another message, which I didn't see then. I needed several weeks before I realized that Linda was still having fun. She loved solving cryptograms, and she was good at it. Again I felt a bit silly when I combined both messages: Akaija=We, and Akaija=111111. There's a clear unmistakable message there…

Exactly! We are One!!

And what again were my words again during her funeral?

It is my desire still to go with you very often and find together what we are both looking for.
To be one.

You'll Never Lose Me

In the process of writing this book there were times when I temporarily couldn't continue to write. At those times I just didn't know how to proceed, and when I did try to write something I couldn't produce anything that made sense, so I left it as it was, trusting things would change.

So it went on for a few months without making progress. In fact I got stuck at the moment were Marianne came into my life and that touched something in me, which complicated the flow of words. A new love in your life, when the first love of your life has died, physically, but has never left your heart. In my case Linda, partly because of my question to inspire me, still played an important role in my life. It was a strange situation that I couldn't deal with very well. This had an effect on writing this book, but it also had its influence on Marianne, who tried to be there for me in every way imaginable, taking care not to hurt my feelings, supporting me when I felt bad. It is great to have someone like her around who understood me, seeing I needed help at times when I didn't even realize it myself. However, because Marianne came into my life so soon: only one year after Linda's transition, it had some consequences like this that had to be dealt with.

She had brought almost nothing from her former home, and so it was difficult for her to ground in her new home with me. Knowing that Linda's passing was a great loss to me Marianne gave me all the space I needed to deal with it in my own time, and didn't rush to make any changes in the house. That's a very special gift, because not many people will be able to act like that; but there are limits, otherwise it undermines your own being. In many ways she completely obliterated herself and that wasn't a good thing. She too had made some kind of transition, leaving her partner. Of course she had her good reasons to do so, but still this was an important change in her life and she had to deal with that, in a time that I could hardly support her the way she supported me.

As I said: it was a *great* gift!

Of course situations like these are difficult to deal with. I have met several people who had lost their partner, and what strikes me is that everyone in a grieving process wants to 'do it right'. Clinging to a deceased loved one isn't good, but desperately trying to forget the loved one, thinking that death is the end of all things, isn't good either. What way is best?

Then it is great that sometimes you get a poke from friends or family, to take action, making you realize once again that you shouldn't keep them from your love for them. That process of learning is called 'letting go', a term that so often is misused after a death, but that is so hard to deal with 'the right way'.

Letting go doesn't mean that the love between you and your deceased love disappears, on the contrary! In fact it means that your love is so great that you can even start a new relationship in assurance that you never lose each other, but the earthly bond of love is history, and there comes a day that you should act accordingly. I didn't like the thought of that but then I remembered Linda's words, which she had spoken more than once, "Shall I help to find you another wife?" Even shortly before her passing she had asked me that. She didn't want me to be alone adding, "I might not like it very much, but I want you to be happy."

Of course I knew how right she was. I understood how important it was that 'let go' counted for me as well. However, knowing this, and being capable of doing so, living it from the heart so to speak, can't be done by just pulling a switch saying, "now I'm doing it". Once again this is a matter of 'trust', and trust can't be bought. It's a learning process, trying to find your way. Such a period of intense grief is a kind of the 'dark' Road in life no one ever wants to go, but nearly everyone has to deal with this sooner or later. Below, I'd like to give you a few tips to help you. Maybe you are going through something similar, or it may help you to better understand others in the same situation. These are my thoughts on this... perhaps someone else will see it differently. I don't have all the answers and can only speak from my point of view.

Don't avoid talking about death

Imagine having a birthday party and nearly everyone has fun, except that one person who recently had lost his or her loved one. It must have taken a lot of courage to even be present at the celebration, to be confronted with people enjoying themselves. Then suddenly the deceased is mentioned and the conversation falls silent. Well... now what? Everyone realizes that this must be very painful and the good mood suddenly is 'tainted' by an apparently wrong remark. But you know what really hurts... if people keep their mouths shut! Because then the deceased one is truly silenced forever.

This is the moment to pay attention to... mentioning the pain by its name. Speak the name of the deceased, talk about him or her, acknowledge the sadness, even if it seems long ago, because what seems a long time for you may feel like days, or even like hours ago for the surviving partner. And often the pain isn't limited to just one person. Nearly everyone knows how it feels having lost a loved one. Then the conversation can be healing for many people at once.

Listen to music that touches your heart.
Many of the best songs are composed not long after the artist him or herself had lost a beloved sister, father, mother, child, or friend. These songs reflect your own grief and are so recognizable. The music forces you to face your pain, paying attention to it. That's good. Accepting your pain is the only way to deal with it.[9]

Write a letter to your loved one.
Yes, to answer your question... this book started like that. That was the reason; little did I know what would come out of it.

Why is that so important? During writing in such cases you connect with your own soul. The only condition is that you are honest in what you write or at least that you *try* to be honest. Maybe you regret something that you have done or said. Maybe there's a reproach to someone that you've never mentioned. Maybe there was a quarrel. Maybe you're going to do something now that your love would never agree to during life. Maybe you're just afraid what the other will think if...

---

[9] *On www.akaija.com, Lady of the Rings section, fragments of songs and music that helped me a lot can be found.*

You'll notice that in those moments when you start touching on 'difficult' topics, you get stuck and have trouble in carrying on writing; there's a blockade. Such things you'd rather not think about, let alone that you write them down. Imagine if... ?

But think about it: your love isn't alive anymore, but he or she definitely is somewhere, maybe even looking over your shoulder. Or maybe not, who knows, but realize that your thoughts in that world are no secret. They are bright and clearly visible. Why would you fool yourself by not writing the things that your love already knows about? Maybe he or she inspired you to start writing in the first place!

This may be a scary thought, but when you start thinking about it you'll discover that it's also very comforting, because... you're not alone in your grief! So write on... and you will discover that your letter or your text, becomes a kind of communication between two worlds.

When I wanted to write something that I struggled with, not being able to simply write it down, I first tried to avoid mentioning it, but I found that I had to mention it somehow. After all... often that problem was the precise reason I started writing that night, seeking for answers or solutions. I then fumbled my way around the hot topic at first. Then I tried looking at the situation from another viewpoint, i.e. from Linda's point of view. I tried looking at it from a 'high' point of view, as if looking down from a balloon, when things get so relative. All becomes smaller. The strange thing is that, while writing I often suddenly discovered that the load somehow had been lifting. It's like clearing a blockade, and after a while I noticed that I had already written down exactly what I was avoiding. And I thought... was *that* so hard to face?! What was I worried about?

It was there at first. It needed attention, acknowledgement.

Avoid using tranquilizers, sedatives and anti-depressants

GPs are usually present the very same day someone dies. In my country it seems common practise to prescribe a sedative or sleeping pill to 'deal with it', to sleep better etc. It seems very thoughtful and it seems so wise, but may I give you some advice?

Don't do it!

Of course... you probably will have a much better sleep that night, but what are you going to do the next night? Will you take another pill? And when you keep thinking about what has happened, grieving all day long... will you take a tranquilizer?

Yes, I understand... you should of course organize the funeral. Or maybe next month you need to go to your work again, which of course is very important. Of course you don't want to meet your children with a sad face. Maybe your family arranged a short holiday, especially for you, and you don't want to spoil the fun. However, if you don't allow yourself, not even during *this incredibly special period* in your life, to take the time for yourself, ask the attention for yourself... then when will you do it instead?

Everyone will understand. So why don't you?

So you take a sedative... because it hurts so much...

What I did, immediately after Linda's passing, is this: This pain I *want* to feel! This grief is letting me know that I can feel! That I'm alive! No one takes that away from me! I'm proud of the scars I wear. They show me that I'm a human being; that I'm living and have lived. Look at me!

Marianne, who is my love on Earth now, is a therapist and sometimes, because of my experiences, I'm called to assist with certain patients, to tune in, to talk; to say words that Marianne has trouble with saying in such a situation. Often I notice or hear about the after effects of the use of tranquilizers and sedatives. They can be functional (very temporary!), but what really is happening is that you are putting your pain away in a drawer. Believe me: "Opting for Freedom of Choice" also exemplifies what tucked away grief can cause. Grief can never be stored away forever. Time heals no wounds; that's a myth! The facing of it, the accepting of it, even the undergoing of your grief is what heals. The love of other people is healing. The love for yourself is healing, but time alone never heals. Your pain will surface sooner or later... somewhere in time, if necessary, hundreds of years later, as you've read in this book. And it has lost nothing of its intensity. It may even have increased, because now you realize that you've lost so many years that could have been much happier for you and those around you. That too is like an extra heavy burden on your shoulders. Eventually, you cannot even determine your grief, tucked away as it is under many layers of pain, frustration, guilt, grief, shame and regret. You're sick, and you don't even remember where it all began. Only... your body does remember! It has stored and memorized everything... and finally it becomes ill, in an ultimate effort to make you aware.

Your pain asks for recognition! Many serious diseases such as cancer are a result (among others) of tucked away sorrow, hidden frustrations, buried pain, and old traumas. The world is full of people who suppress their grief by artificial means. Only the pharmacy flourishes happily with that!

The funny thing is... it seems like an insurmountable mountain that you're facing; but know this... every time you climb a piece of the slope... the mountain in front of you gets lower. Facing the pain is nothing more than that: opening your eyes to the pain! By this I don't want to trivialize it, don't get me wrong.

Let me give you an example of tucked away sorrow...

Someone's mother has died and the daughter, in her forties already, still can't deal with it. It happened many years ago and she's using all kinds of medications: tranquilizers, sedatives, sleeping pills and some more. Maybe you recognize her. Maybe you have been there, experienced something similar.

Have you ever said goodbye to her? Or do you not want to do so, thinking that if you do that she will be gone forever? So this way you keep her 'alive'. It sounds hard when I say this, but what you're doing is keeping your mother captured in a glass cage of sad thoughts. It doesn't help you and it hurts your mother, because she's in the Spirit World wanting only the very best for you! She wants you to be happy. She wants that you resume your life. It may even block her from moving on. That's not the way to show your love.

What you can do is to say goodbye to her, even now. It's never too late to do that. One evening when you're alone and have all the time to yourself, you close the curtains, put a picture of your mother on the table, light a candle for her and if you wish an incense stick. Add a beautiful crystal, a flower your mother loves. Whatever! Maybe you write as in a diary, it doesn't matter; you know best. Some music might help, music you and your mother have shared memories of during her deathbed.

Think of her, imagine her face. That's how you connect to her. Ask your guardian angels to support you. Pray to God. Nothing is a must, anything is okay. What does matter is that you do it consciously, with feeling, from your heart; that you open up to the love of your mother (or whomever you're thinking of).

And when you're ready (even if not tonight, then do it a next time) say aloud, or at least whispered, that you take leave of her, that you let her go free, whishing her all the love and happiness, that from now on you will carry on with your life, that you will do your best to be happy, and... that you love her!

Can you do that? It's important that you not only think those words, but *speak* them, at least softly, as if your mother is sitting in front of you, hearing what you're saying. That can be very difficult, it may seem impossible maybe, and if so then you'll know that there's a block. Maybe you have to do this more than once before you're capable of speaking the words.

Now... let's say you've done so... have you *lost* your mother now?

Think about it.

You change something. It's hard to describe, but you're doing something that makes a difference. You free yourself. You face the facts, and you act accordingly. You take responsibility. Your grief is still there and you still have a long way ahead of you, but you've taken a step in the right direction. That takes courage, but you've set the first step. That's important. Life isn't about arriving at the goal, but walking the path towards it... . walking the Two Roads.

You can do this more often, when you face important decisions. Normally you would have discussed things with your mother but... well, she's not alive anymore. Yet you can connect to her, you always can! Talking it out helps to make your mind clear, and it also adds weight to your intentions. You reveal your heart, clearly visible to the Spirit World. Of course it was clear to them all the time, but now *you too* actually take part as a conscious and responsible being, as a human, in the movement of the Cosmos.

Getting back to all those medications; be aware that if you do take some you're on a slippery slope, since when the drug wears off the pain returns. You still have more of it, so what will you do? Take another one, because that's what is easy? And when you still can't sleep at three in the morning? Well... you *have* to sleep don't you? So after lying awake half the night you take another pill. Other people take some alcohol, a cigarette, a soft drug... or all at once.

It doesn't help, does it? Then the following night it's the same song. Don't let 'them' fool you into believing that those medications aren't addictive; they are, if not physically, then mentally. The longer you run, the harder your fight will be to get done with it.

Don't get me wrong... I am not accusing you of being a fool when you can't do it yet. On the contrary, it's all very understandable. But know what you're getting yourself into, and get loving help when you face your pain. Love is always the best medication.

At the end of this book I would like to say something, because the road Linda and I opted for during her illness is not really the advice I would like to give to you. But would we rather have done it differently?

On the first page of this book I wrote: "Linda was a woman who didn't like to speak in the past tense about someone who is deceased."

The time period described in this book has changed us, and not just a little bit, because how she was is not how she is now. That was her goal on Earth, and that's the goal we all have in life: to grow in Love. I really wouldn't dare predict what I would do in a similar situation. I think that at all times you should listen to your Heart, what your heart tells you. Then one person may walk an alternative route, like we did. Another one will opt for an allopathic route, maybe supported by alternative therapy. Yet another person might choose to seemingly do nothing, and now it's still possible to enjoy life like never before, with a bucket list maybe, or being together with family and friends. Even that can be the exact right therapy! You're free to choose, to opt for freedom of choice! Follow your heart!

Linda told me several times, even shortly before her transition, that, despite how difficult things were for her during her illness, she had absolutely no regrets about the choices we had made. Apparently that was almost impossible to reconcile, given the extreme pains she suffered from for so long, but they were our choices, obviously influenced by many factors, but the choices were made in freedom. Also I do not regret the road we had taken. On the contrary, the road we took was a deliberate one, the one we wanted to go. How bizarre that may seem for many people! But I am delighted and feel honoured that I was allowed to stand by Linda's side so intensely.

During the several conversations with Loes in the years thereafter, we of course also mentioned that I was writing this book, and I have asked Linda if she agreed with it. She immediately saw right through me, saying, "Can you for once ask me a question to which you *don't* know the answer?"

Then, there were several comments from Linda, passed on by Loes, which Linda wanted very much that I record and emphasize. So I would like to give *her* the last word, in *her* book.

Loes said: her guardian angels had indicated that Linda had followed the road she knew from her heart. "And according to earthly standards that was almost nonsensical. But now I'm exactly where I wanna be!"

She thinks it important that people understand *why* she made these choices. "Let everyone be who they are in their own right", she said.

"That she thinks, is very important", Loes added.

"Yeah," Linda said, "and what I especially want to give to everyone, and please emphasize this most certainly... *is that they dare to have faith, even when it's hard.*"

In her name... she wants that to be said.

I said to Loes, "Well, she had to learn that for sure."

"Yesss," Loes replied, "but once she mastered it, it helped her, an awful lot. From what she now knows, she says she now sees the other side, how these things work, how they do it, what time and what attention and Love is put in from all the guardian angels around us... for which she has an incredible respect... That's what she wants us all to know. From her side, when you see what's happening here... she would not... but then she *says*: I want to say to all humanity, trust them, because they really know what they are doing. So sensible... sensible! She says."

"Faith means to her... so she says, that she wants this to be written down as well, because she considers it important... Having faith, trusting, to her, means to surrender to what is on your path, but at the same time always take responsibly and keep thinking!"

"And she says: One thing is for sure: we all are guided. That she now sees very clearly on the other side. *Then*... she *wanted* to believe it, *wanted* to trust it was true, and that took a lot out of her.

And that she wants to make very clear to mankind."
Marianne brought my attention to my own words which Linda had passed on to me much earlier, and that now made much more sense. Words that represent my feelings too...

"I gave you my trust
You Can Never Lose Me"
We are One!

Wim & Linda

Thank you very much...

All those wonderful people on Earth and in Spirit who supported us, in thought and with candles, with help, with words, with Love, wringing their hands maybe... but your Love helped us through.
Amhirez, my guardian angel, always present somewhere in the background.
And Linda's guardian angel too!
Amà, Taksi and Zebra, thank you for your love and company. You enlightened us!
My parents and my sister Mieke, Mary and Wim, Rob and Martha, Marco... Wow... what a family!
All therapists, especially Rob Grit, Lobsang Tsultrim, Jacob Duursma, Cor Tijssen, Linda Krug, Eef Ufkes, Michel de Sonnaville and Hans Hoogeveen.
All allopathic nurses, general practitioners, doctors and specialists, you too have showed us a good road, though we hardly ever listened.
Dottore, Cor and Fiona... despite all that happened, your role was important in the process to make Linda and I accept.
Adri, Els, Bert, Peter, your help made a difference.
Sattia, your patience was incredible.
Loekie Einthoven, so special!
Francis Ruesink-van Oers, how good that it was possible this way.
Bert Smits and your band, Bravo!
Marco and Josée, what a dance!
Ton, did Linda give you a hard time?
Jan van de Hout... our mission.
Loes van Loon and Hebenes.. thank you!
Yvonne Baank, your lessons were important.
Vera Fischerova, the story of the ring... started with you.
Eliza White Buffalo... thank you too!
Liselle and Charonna... what would we have done without you two?
*And Marianne... without **you** this book would never have been written!*
And the Akaija project would be a mission impossible. I, we... love you ☺.

The Sequel... Finding Nasja

When this book was first published in the Dutch language in the Netherlands in 2009 we already had been given the Akaija as a symbol of Oneness from the Spirit World. This happened in 2005, though I made Aura Healer with the unnamed inversion symbol already in 2002.

After a few years I thought we more or less understood what it was about. Because the message was made clear to us, the working as a healing instrument, though not *fully* understood, was pretty obvious given the many testimonials from people. There was one thing however that kept bugging me.

I always had had the feeling that the Akaija has some kind of relation with the Earth, and sometimes I imagined that a huge Akaija could surround the Earth. Some people even had hinted in that direction, unconsciously knowing something maybe. But no one could explain it to me, as they didn't consciously understand it themselves.

So I tried to imagine how the Akaija could be related to the Earth.

 How can such a shape as the Akaija be connected to the Earth then, I wondered? Maybe the Earth could fit inside a huge world circumference Akaija, so I imagined.

But the horizontal ring inside the Akaija then wouldn't align to the Equator, because that ring isn't a *great circle*, which is a math term for a line or circle that divides a sphere in two equal hemispheres. That ring could at best align to Tropic of Capricorn or the Tropic of Cancer as it's not exactly in the middle of the Akaija.

So this thought didn't cause a typical feeling of 'Yes!' when things suddenly fall into place. Instead the feeling remained that I should look better, that I should figure this out somehow, so this kept me busy. Every now and then I pondered on it, but always I dismissed it again after a while. I hoped someday I would see the answer.

Obviously I overlooked something important...

It wasn't until a few years later, after long experimenting with plastic balls and coloured cotton threads, that I figured out how the Akaija could be combined with its mirror image. This resulted in a big silver object that was clearly showing a 5-pointed star pentagram. The only problem was that this shape was so difficult to make as a small pendant that I finally consulted a 3D-software specialized company to produce the first wax shape for making a mould to cast pendants from it.

For the time being we called this the double Akaija, but then it got a name from Linda's mother: Akaija-Iloa, in which 'Iloa' means 'I Am'. This made perfect sense, because one can say: "When WE truly know that WE are ONE, then it is: I AM."
In fact *we... we all together* are God: I Am that I Am.
Or: אֶהְיֶה אֲשֶׁר אֶהְיֶה, ehyeh ašer 'ehyeh, or sometimes called Yahweh.

Although to be honest... I have big trouble accepting this myself. Yet I can't take anything else from it. The message is unmistakably clear!

Then I discovered something strange, because we had received a few critical remarks from German people. They were somewhat scared of the Akaija, because they saw a pentagram symbol in it. Although the

Akaija, as a pendant, is pointing upwards with one of its points, on our images of it we present the Akaija with one point downwards, and that made it a 'bad' symbol in their eyes, as some satanic cults use this symbol that way.
I had put a lot of thought into depicting the logo on the jewellery box as I did, clearly with one point downwards, and now these remarks made me wonder: was that really a smart idea? Was I inspired to make it *that* way?

Then I remembered Loes had mentioned that I had not seen something very important. When you look at the Akaija-silhouette with one point facing down, and then you tilt the Akaija slightly backwards, the horizontal circle that's created by 2 points of the 5-pointed star becomes visible and... the remaining 3 points together make a... Heart! Loes told me what Linda had tried to show me: "Your heart is protected".

It's the circle of We, protecting the Heart! We are One. One for all and all for one.
And think of it... we *all* are one!
We all? So... err... who's included?
And who's not included?
Of course... all the good people are included. No doubt about that!
But what about the rest of us... err... we?
Yeah, them too! The black people and the white people. The red and the yellow then too and for sure there are some more races. But... even a murderer is part of we, isn't it!
And what about you? Your positive side is included, that's easy enough. But how about your negative side? Can *you* accept *all of you*? All your... shades of grey?
God, the Great Spirit does.
We do!

This is what the Akaija is about... Both versions of the pentagram are part of the Akaija. Both! Pointing upwards and pointing downwards. It's the same symbol, it's just a matter of how you look at it. What do you want to see? What do you not want to see?

The single left-handed and its mirror image, the right-handed (speaking about duality) Akaija consist of 1 complete circle or ring, from where a weird bending line orbits this ring to return to it in opposite direction. The Akaija-Iloa however consists of 5 perfect rings or circles. In Dutch there's a say for this: The Circle is Round Again, meaning so much as: Things have taken a way of their own for a long time, but now something has happened that completes the series of events, we connected the ends, and all makes sense now. Five circles, 5 rings were complete now.

But I had totally forgotten about the one ring, the invisible one, the secret ring, connecting all the other rings through their centres, the sixth ring... the one ring that in Love *unites* them all...

My next book will be called 'Finding Nasja'. It will describe how the Akaija is connected to a forgotten *ring* of ancient megalithic sites around the world, linking the Great Pyramid, the temples of Angkor in Cambodia, the Nazca tracks, Easter Island, the Dogon in Mali, Ur, Persepolis, Mohenjo Daro, Cuzco and many more important sites all laying on one straight line that sometimes is called 'Great Circle', or as it is also called 'Tipped Equator'. One location on this circle however is particularly interesting: the island **Aneityum**, where the name Akaija originates from, meaning: we all. It's almost unbelievable, but this island is one the 5 key locations!

We have made it our goal to visit all 5 key- or anchor-locations. Meanwhile we have visited this island and spoken to the holy man and storyteller of the native people! And he gave us some pretty interesting information!

And while we prepared this book *The Lady of the Rings* for publishing we were preparing our trip to Angkor Wat, the next key location.

Secondly this book will tell you about a new symbol that also is totally dedicated to oneness: the Two Roads symbol. 'The Two Roads' is a project of Eliza White Buffalo from Northern Ireland and it connects to the Two Roads vision of Nicolas Black Elk, once a holy man of the Lakota Sioux tribes of North America.

Linda guided us step by step on the way to this by first having me make a strange object called 'Faith', way back in 2004 already! It combines the Holy Grail with the Christian and the Celtic Cross and with the... native American Medicine Wheel! Then Linda gave me an 'assignment' to make her a painting of a Rose.

Then Eliza connected to Linda, and to... Igor!

Thus a new chain of events started that keeps to be in full swing. It simply keeps us swinging all the time ☺. And guess what: Eliza is the one who corrected the English translation of 'The Lady of the Rings - Opting for Freedom of Choice', making it possible that you could read this book.

The latest development is that we - Marianne and I did this together - created a symbol that is based on the number 6! Connected to this symbol is an adventure that brought us to Russia a couple of times. First we visited the ancient site Arkaim and then we went to Altai in South Siberia. This new symbol is called 'Chram' and it appears to be connected to the Kremlins of Russia. And there's a connection to the Jogrom-archives, a nearly forgotten cosmic knowledge territory. Put the words Akaija and Chram in sequence, just like the number 5 (Akaija) and then the number 6 (Chram). Akaija is about saying 'yes' to Oneness, and Chram is about Creation and Life. Translated in cosmic origin sound language Akaija Chram means: *I say YES to the Power of the Great Spirit and the Light to create new Life.*

The title of this book will be *Finding Nasja*.
It describes the search for finding you, your Self, your higher Self. Or shall I say... *our* higher Self, because from our Heart we all are connected, in our Heart we are one!

We all... hope you'll love it.

Wim & Marianne
and... Linda ☺

Linda

Marianne

Wim

Kleine Pusj

Pusj Maika